The Sparrow's Dreams

Volume 5

~

Heaven III Series

By

Erin Aleshire

© Copyright 2015 - Erin Aleshire

ISBN-13: 978-1517218751

ISBN-10: 1517218756

[The 5th Stone]

DEDICATION

~

This book is dedicated to:

God, My Father

Jesus, My Lord and Savior, Husband and Best Friend

My Beautiful Children

~

And to my Sparrow Family and Friends

ACKNOWLEDGEMENTS

I would like to give special thanks to those whom God sent to help during these dreams, and to their supportive families:

Jim Horn: Editor and Publisher, for his tireless efforts to continually and without hesitation work behind the scenes to house the dreams, the forum and facilitate the production of the books. You are a wonderful servant of God and a dear brother in Christ.

Melanie, Lucy, Rachael, Julie Ann, and Joi Blessed: For your support typing and proofing my dreams. You have been a God sent and blessing to me in so many ways. Thank you.

To my Sparrow family and friends: There are so many from all over the world, who have continuously prayed for me and my children. I can never thank all of you enough for your kindness and support. I pray that one day soon, in Heaven, I will be able to meet all of you. You are my dear Friends in Christ. May God continue to work in your lives and bless you!!

Notices:

This book is available in paperback and eBook formats.

All Scripture references are from either the King James Version or the One New Man Bible.

Copyrighted © 2015 by Erin Aleshire

TABLE OF CONTENTS

Introduction and Foreword	6
Chapter 1 – God's Timing	11
Chapter 2 – Drinking Deep	25
Chapter 3 – Cake, China & Changing God's Clock	32
Chapter 4 – Fresh Oil	44
Chapter 5 – Healing Rain and No.9	56
Chapter 6 – Oceans and Almond Branch	66
Chapter 7 – God's Numbers	81
Chapter 8 – Breakfast with Jesus	95
Chapter 9 – God's Clock & the Olive Grove	103
Chapter 10 – The Cave, Uriel, and the Snow Storm	116
Chapter 11 – Faith Training	127
Chapter 12 – The Alpine Meadow & the Tevah	137
Chapter 13 – Faith and the Ocean	142
Chapter 14 – Four Dreams	157
Chapter 15 – Training - War Assignment	161
Chapter 16 – Training - Harvesting	171
Chapter 17 – Faith Training and Psalm 23	183
Chapter 18 – God's Garden for Children	194
Chapter 19 – Paradise - Tropical Beach	204

Chapter 20 – God's Garden for Teens	217
Chapter 21 – The Lion	231
Chapter 22 - Faith and the Fig	241
Chapter 23 – Jesus & the Storm	240
Chapter 24 – Word from God & Dream of War	255
Chapter 25 – Faith vs. Fear	258
Chapter 26 – David vs. Goliath	268
Chapter 27 – God's Quiver & Harvest	275
Chapter 28 – Angel Army and the Lion's Roar	278
Chapter 29 – Seasons	282
Chapter 30 – God's Mountain and the Key	288
Chapter 31 – Jesus' Promises	293
Chapter 32 – Golden Wheat & Rainbows	299
Prayer of Salvation	301

Introduction and Foreword

The Dreams: A background Bio from the Author

On November 21st of 2004, I went to the hospital for a routine procedure. I opted to be fully awake for this procedure as my body had historically rejected anesthesia and most pain medications. During the procedure I was able to talk with the staff while they worked on me. I experienced great pain, followed by sweats and I began to lose consciousness. The last thing I heard was, "Erin, hang in there just a couple more....we're losing her."

During this first episode (NDE) in the hospital, God took me to the base of a mountain and told me that I was going to go through one of the darkest seasons in my life. As always, the Lord was correct, and I began a journey with Him through the darkest of valleys for a seemingly endless seven years. My heart condition began to worsen during this time period. This initial event began the first of a series of Near Death Experiences, or NDEs for short, as a result of an unusual arrhythmia which actually caused my heart to stop. It is called Sudden Brady Response. During these SBR's I would experience these NDEs, many of which were classified as "non-registered events," I would have visits to parts of Heaven and God's Golden City, the Home of His Throne. I kept these visits confined to my journals as I didn't want to appear to be, "not of sound mind" medically speaking. These visits foretold of the dreams that were to come later.

On Good Friday 2008, my heart stopped during a presentation at work in front of witnesses: an architect, a builder, and several of my co-workers. In this NDE, classified as a "registered event," an Angel of the Lord told me that I mattered to God. Even as I type this, the memory is still so vivid. Shortly after this NDE, I finally received a formal diagnosis from the doctors. Facing the very real possibility of death, I agreed to have a pacemaker implanted.

After the pacemaker surgery, my visits to Heaven were temporarily suspended. I went through a desert period, a dry spell, wherein I didn't hear from the Lord for two years. In many ways, this period of aloneness was unbearable. I made some choices in my weakness during this time in which my enemies sought opportunities to attack and gain ground.

While under attack, I sought God with reckless abandonment and with my whole heart I chased after HIM. I was concerned that my time of Miracles had ended with the pacemaker. I petitioned Him on my knees every day, sometimes for hours at a time. In my persistence cries for God, my long desert period came to a close. God began to work supernaturally in my life!

In October 2012, I began to experience an amazing string of prophetic dreams and visions which have continued to this very day. After about a year, my friends and I prayerfully made the decision to gather these dreams and publish them. In terms of how this all began, and as further background, here is a brief outline of how the Lord grants me these dreams: I have the dream at night. When I wake up, I take communion and pray. When I sit to write the dream in my journal, Jesus gives me an open vision of the dream. The vision is so clear that I can even turn 360 degrees and look wherever He leads me to look. Then, as I relive the dream, I write. Somehow this all happens with me not even looking at the journal that I am writing in, as I am in the vision. Amazingly, my writing flows from the Holy Spirit, and I am able to write in ink without any need for correction. These hand-written pages are then sent to my friends for typing.

Interestingly, if not humorously, if I ever try to write something different from exactly what the Holy Spirit is requesting, my vision of the dream shuts down immediately so that I stop writing. My memory temporarily goes blank. However, once I stop and pray, the Lord allows the download to begin again. Thus, I am merely a reporter, nothing more! What is so wonderful about this is that I am given a threefold check to everything I write, wherein the details contained are so incredible and God-inspired!!

(1) I have the Dream.

(2) I relive the dream in a detailed Vision.

(3) The Holy Spirit helps me write what I have witnessed.

As I experience these dreams (and subsequent visions), I actually learn from the Lord as I go, all in 3-D and live! The downside of these dreams is that I also experience the dark events in 3-D and live! This can be quite horrific at times, especially with all of the accompanying sounds and smells that are often hard to describe adequately. On a side note, my pacemaker records my heart events, averaging about thirty per day.

Every few months, I get an actual printout of these heart events, which register like a seismograph. It is entirely possible that the events I am experiencing in Heaven are registered in my pacemaker event log! I am not a prophet, or even a self-proclaimed prophet. I am merely a seer and a scribe. In reality, I am just a reporter. Ironically, I don't even enjoy writing. For whatever reason – only the Lord knows – He, quite humorously, chose me to write more often than I would ever have desired. I am certainly not a scholar, nor am I so special that I deserve this gift. (However, Jesus specializes in giving generously to undeserving people!) Within the dreams, I am merely being used as an example ... an illustration, really.

During these tragedies and losses, I gained a love relationship with Jesus, which forever changed me from the ordinary. I have seen the beauty of Heaven, but only a minute portion of what is waiting for those who love God! He is so much more than we have been taught! The Bible has become a Divine Love Story written on the Tablets of our Hearts through its pages, and very few will discover the layers and layers of the Love God has given us through HIS words. Heaven is a Divine Mystery!! There is no lack, yet it is perfectly Holy. It is a place of perfection, as there is no death or decay of any kind. It is a place of Beauty, Precision, and Craftsmanship unlike anything on Earth and it is also a place with state of the art technology, which cannot be fathomed or matched by anything man can create. Heaven is logical and in contrast, intricately mysterious! It is infinitely Grand yet, intensely personal too!!

Through these powerful dreams, and with the help of the Holy Spirit, I strongly believe that you will come to know your Lord and Savior more intimately than you ever dreamed possible. Remember, Jesus is always the Grand Subject. Now, He is making Himself – and the

Home in Heaven that He has planned for us – known to people all over the world. By no means are the dreams a substitute for Scriptures in the Bible!! However, the dreams beautifully illustrate scriptural truths. Remember in 1 Corinthians 2:9, "But as it is written, Eye hath not seen, nor ear heard, neither have entered into the heart of man, the things which God hath prepared for them that love HIM!!"

And if, as you are reading through these dreams, you are asking yourself why Jesus would choose her for these dreams & visions, I asked the Lord the very same question. His answer was simple "Why not you?"…

All my blessings…

Erin Aleshire - Author

Chapter 1 – God's Timing

Communion

Dear Father, Thank You for Another day! Thank You for my children. Thank You for my new family and friends. Thank You for allowing me deep rest during my illness. Thank You for making it so I am too sick to go out and be busy and labor but not so sick that I cannot come to You in praise, worship and offering. Thank You Lord that You continue to speak. Thank You for meeting me here.

Jesus: "Erin Come up!"

Immediately I am on the Lord's doorstep. His door is completely open to me. To my right was a very large angel.

Me: "Oh, Hello!"

Angel: "Hello Erin, He is waiting inside for you today. I am here to assist you and remove your guess work today."

Me: I was giggling. "What the Lord did not want me to wander around His front door today? – To knock or not to knock! To wait or not to wait! … I was laughing.

Angel: "Yes He knew even with the open door that you might need some assistance just walking through. I am here to help you do this." He smiled.

Me: "The Lord is so wise!'

Angel: "Even with the door wide open, He knew you would second guess so He has sent me. Please Erin take my hand the Lord has something special for you today." The angel reached out his hand and I took it, I was still laughing at this. The angel walked ahead of me slightly, and then opened the door further. He put his hand on my shoulder with his other hand and moved me through the door. I took my sandals off so my bare feet could feel the floor.

Me: "Does the Lord have even more homes and just how big is this one?"

Angel: "Yes, He has a home in the city as well, this you have seen. He is near to yours and by the Throne of course."

This angel was so huge; muscular, tall, and very much a warrior – yet he was so handsome with a very kind voice. The angels were/are not feminine. These are the angels who guard, guide and protect as we are going through or about to go into battle – they also guard God and Heavenly interest. I have seen female angels. They are very beautiful. I notice they minister and comfort. I saw a female angel once and she dialogued with me with witnesses present. I wonder if the females are scarce because of what the enemy has done to sexualize them on Earth. The male angels have a beautiful rugged handsome look, most have longer hair, and beautiful eyes. They are not wimps and are not gaunt or scrawny. Those who have seen angels as a-sexual or neither male nor female are incorrect! There are many angels who care for the children here also – these appear as feminine. They are fully robed and modest.

Me: "Well, I know that the Lord sent you! Who am I to argue with one of the angels of the Lord? Since He has called you to help me then clearly He knew I would hesitate." I giggled while saying this. I lifted the hem of my robe as I hopped onto these beautiful large Jerusalem stones. "I have clients who would love these!"

Angel: "So you do not like these for yourself?" He smiled as he said this.

Me: "Oh I would love these I just could never afford such a luxury."

Angel: "Well you are blessed then, you are the daughter of the King and He has enough to purchase some for you!"

Me: I was laughing so hard. "You are right! Thank you for reminding me!"

He led me back down the entry. I could see we walked easily 100 steps or feet passed these large columns and beautiful fiber optic damask curtains. I followed just behind him. I was too busy studying my surroundings. I saw above the capitals of these columns were a type of crown. This crown was illuminated and directed my eyes to the ceiling. The ceiling was hand painted. It had to be my Michael Angelo himself. As I walked toward the open doors to the courtyard the story stopped but it was not over. I realized because I never looked up, I missed one of the most amazing features.

Me: "Hold just a moment angel, I'll be right back."

The angel turned to see where I was going.

Me: "Don't worry the Lord will understand."

I ran back to the front door, the closed front door. Thank goodness it was closed with me here! I giggled to myself then I turned to look down the entry. The angel was standing at the courtyard entrance. I started at the front door. I saw an image of God's hand and a finger extended. The ceiling was a large Barrel Vault. I began from there and I saw the story of Genesis; the beginning recorded in the painting. As I walked I was amazed at how intricate this oil painting was. Not only was it incredibly detailed and perfect, it was made of modern materials. The pigment was perfect. The bonding agents were flawless – there were no cracks in the plaster. As I walked, the paintings moved and appeared in motion. As I walked forward, Kadima came to my mind, I giggled. The paint was illuminated and seemed to have the breath of life upon the canvas of that ceiling. The ceiling was God Breathed. Wow! I was fascinated! I looked up and tried to run to see if the painting would move faster – it didn't. I had to stop and walk steadily for this to work. At one point I tried to step backwards thinking I could make it reverse. I was giggling. While I was still looking up at the ceiling I heard the Lord.

Jesus: He was laughing. He said to the angel, "Well at least you got her to walk in through the open door!"

Angel: "Yes Lord, she became distracted when she looked up. There is much to see and she is easily amused!" They were laughing at me.

Me: "Oh forgive me Lord, and angel. (I still remained walking and looking up.) Lord, this is the first Seven days of Creation on Your ceiling and it moves!" He was laughing.

Jesus: "Okay, Erin what is God doing here on the seventh day?" He looks up!

Me: I was laughing. "Well He appears to be resting as He is not lifting a finger! It is beautiful Lord. It must have taken many years for this artist to paint this. What an honor. Who did this?"

Jesus: "Erin there is much for you to learn but this was painted by a child."

Me: "Impossible!" I stopped myself immediately. "Of course all things are possible here! Lord, why when I walked faster did the motion not move at my pace?"

Jesus: "Oh, you were expecting the story of Creation to move at your pace? You wanted God to even reverse this when you walk backwards. Interesting… He and the angel were laughing, I heard angels in the courtyard laughing too.

Me: "Oh this is a parable! Okay Lord You got me again. I guess I thought since this was a story I could flip pages faster or even go back a few pages. But, Lord in Your infinite wisdom; in order for me to read what is on the wall, the ceiling I must go back to the front door, the beginning and start from there. I cannot move ahead, but I must walk at a steady pace allowing the events to unfold before me. I also cannot go backwards. This is a parable of time also!"

Jesus: "Very good Erin. See how much you learn here. There is wisdom beyond the open door. There is even more when you look up!" He was smiling.

Me: "Lord, I looked <u>only at things my</u> feet touched and items at eye level mostly. My eyes looked for things I could understand and describe. Why would I need to look up in Your house when all I need to do is look right in front of me to find You?" He was laughing and nodding His head in agreement.

Jesus: "Very good Erin. Come with Me or would you like to dine in today?" He was laughing.

Me: "Lord I will eat where You would take me. I am a guest here!"

Jesus: "Yes and no Erin. You are much more than a guest."

He reached out His hand and I took it so gladly! Every time He put His hand out, I felt so welcomed and protected! I was also humbled as I knew that His hand could be withheld just as easily. As I took His hand the Orchestra began to play. I heard a chorus of Angels. It was so beautiful. He led me out to the courtyard. There I saw the amazing pool and clock above it. I saw the 4 angels guarding it. There were fountains there. The sound of water was wonderful. The air was fragrant, and today I smelled jasmine and white ginger. I smelled roses also although I noticed that Heavenly roses don't have that hint of musty scent. It was perfect. He guided me up the stairs into this architectural gazebo with the gold capped dome. There was the beautiful table set for dining the King. There were some beautiful cakes set out along with other confections. I was a bit surprised as I had never noticed these before. There was fresh bread – smiles – both leavened and unleavened. The angels were pouring water into our cups. The table was set beautifully! I couldn't believe the craftsmanship in absolutely everything before me. The linens, the chairs, the plates, utensils; everything was like things on Earth yet advanced in execution beyond Earth yet similar in relationship.

Jesus: "Erin, your thoughts!" He said this as He motioned the angel to seat me and He sat next to me at the table.

Before us was the courtyard with the clock, fountains, flowering vines, and beautiful garden elements. Beyond that we faced the orchestra and choir. But even further in front of us, you could see an incredible view of the Valley. A very large building that was the size of Niagara Falls, only it was like a giant God–Made Falls and aquaduct. Let me back up. There was a giant pool to the right, and seven spouts in which water poured out over the side of this massive building. There was so much force that the water formed a mist and the rainbows created from the sun were so intense, well...like nothing I have ever seen. Off to the right and in the distance, I could see the City of Gold. The sun shone upon it and the rainbow effect from this was incredible. It was more fascinating as there were more colors in the spectrum but I couldn't tell how many.

Jesus: "Erin, your thoughts."

Me: "Lord, You just read all of them. This is the most beautiful sight in all of creation. I can't find my breath. Everything God designs is

perfect. All things even created by man's hands originate somehow from here, if this is possible."

Jesus: He was smiling. "Here Erin, have some bread." He hands me a piece of both and I laughed. As He ate it, I ate too. The bread was amazing too!

Me: "Lord, take this bread. It is wonderful. I have never tasted anything like this on earth. It melts in your mouth. It needs nothing to spread on it – It is perfect just like it is with no embellishments, no condiments."

Jesus: "Well, this is good too. Things meant to enhance sometimes distract from the true flavor of the Bread, right? Sometimes just enjoying the plain bread and what it stands for is far greater than that which we dress it up with!"

Me: "Okay Lord, this too is a parable. Your Word stands on its' own and needs no embellishments."

Jesus: "What? Wouldn't you like some honey on your bread? Wouldn't this make it more palatable?" He was laughing.

Me: "No, Lord just spending time with You. You are the Bread of Life, Lord. You are perfect on Your own."

Jesus: "But Erin, I have honey here, there is herbed oil, sea salt and even butter, is this not also good?" He was smiling.

Me: "Lord, those make earthly bread so I will want to become a glutton, this is not good. It is far better that I get my fill just on the Bread You have to offer. The only condiment I will take with my Bread will be wine, water, and some of this beautiful fruit from the Tree of Knowledge!"

Jesus: "Good Erin, then also take this wine and remember Me. I will then hand you some fruit and giving you some Living Water as well. Very good!"

Me: "Lord, all things here are good. This table is a King's table and You have even brought dessert." I pointed to the cakes – small like petit fours.

Jesus: "Now you have questions today. You had another dream, tell me about this."

Just as He said this, that small sparrow flew right on the table to the right of my plate. She sat there and appeared more interested in hearing what we had to say rather than eating crumbs. I began to laugh and broke off some of my bread for the sparrow. She ate a little crumb then flew away to one of the balconies where I saw 3 baby birds in a nest. She put the bread forward and each of the birds took a piece of the bread. It made me tear-up as I saw myself there in Psalm 84.

Me: "Lord, Your Courtyard is the Living Word– live! Your House is a living tabernacle Lord!"

Jesus: "Erin, how could you know this? You haven't even seen the entire place – just the entry and courtyard. You have only seen a portion of the East end. What do you see before you?"

Me: "I see before me 20 columns. So is this the North side or the South side?"

Jesus: "How many columns did you see in the entry?"

Me: "Six on one side, six on another...12 in all. Oh I see 20 columns but if I double this there are 40 columns. Lord, this is double the size of Your tabernacle. Earth has a smaller replica by half? So we are looking south and I come into Your front door from the North. I see the City off to the West and I am looking directly at the East Gates of the City, is this right?"

Jesus: He was laughing. "I guess from an earthly compass, you could view things that way. Here however, there are two compass points. The Throne of God and wherever I walk this is where the pointer goes! This is funny Erin, you make me smile. How you speak of architecture. You are gathering relationship to Earthly things, let's change your perspective. Remember the Age of Heaven; God's House was established before Earth. So what you are experiencing here will have the opposite on Earth usually. What you view as having or seeing there has one common problem, do you know what this is?"

Me: "Yes Lord, since the fall of man, death right?"

Jesus: "This is correct Erin! There is life here. It is okay to reference Heaven based on Earthly standards because this is a common practice, but now that you have seen this perhaps you will understand that things on Earth were once based on Heavenly principals and all for God's Glory by design. Now the counterfeiter resides there."

Me: "Lord, is this why I had this strange dream? I was deeply disturbed by it."

Jesus: "Give me an overview."

Me: "Well a man, a very wealthy attractive man was luring people to his estate. It was massive. It was more a lure to children as there were amusement parks, candy, sweets, and fattening foods. There was a recording studio and a stage for large public productions. There were virtual computer gaming rooms and I knew if my children would see this place they would turn away from me and possibly choose this man."

Jesus: "Interesting, tell me a bit more."

Me: "Well, his estate had shops and earthly things. He had automobiles, planes, and a safe with jewelry. All kinds of lures! He was trying to tell me that he could take care of me and my children. He tried to seduce me with this estate, but when he took me to his courtyard; it was overgrown with briars and weeds. The smell was a stench like manure and there were dry wells. The pool in the center was dry. The clock was destroyed and I saw something like an LED clock with batteries powering another type of clock. The gazebo was standing and the golden dome was the only thing left. The man told me he was renovating the courtyard to be a church. I felt sick to my stomach!"

Jesus: "So why do you think this dream came?"

Me: "First, the enemy knows about Your beautiful Home. He knows that in Heaven You have prepared a place for us. He has tried to keep Heaven hidden from us. He has sent counterfeits to twist Heaven. He is luring us with things of the world to cloak us from You and the Truth!"

Jesus: "Very good Erin. You said that he had a replica of different things from My Courtyard. Interesting!"

Me: "Lord, did Your Gazebo come before the Dome of the Rock in Jerusalem?"

Jesus: "Of course. Erin the enemy uses the Earth to mock God and Heaven. What was the stench in his courtyard? Keep this in mind and remember when he lures many to his house, no matter what he tries to do, he will fail at his attempts to replicate Paradise. His job is to embellish truth."

Me: "Lord, he is the spread that embellishes and enhance the bread."

Jesus: He was laughing. "Yes, this causes many to become gluttons of bread of lies. Not the Bread of Life! This is dangerous."

Me: "Lord, they have recreated Your Gazebo in Jerusalem too."

Jesus: He was laughing. "Erin it is only My Gazebo, it could be worse, we have spoken about this before. Now, notice their clock. It even had batteries. What happens to batteries?"

Me: "The batteries die!"

Jesus: "Yes they do. So they cannot replicate this clock because they are missing the key element. Here, take my hand."
Immediately we were on the balcony down over the Courtyard. It was so beautiful! I saw the pool with the clock. The Lord waved His arm. The sky became dark. The moon was full, and there were several constellations. Then the impression stayed on the left side of the clock. Then He waved His hand again and the sun and some faint stars were etched in the water on the right. Then we looked at the clock. It was beautiful and like everything else here, highly advanced!

Jesus: "Now remember, they do not have the key. They do not have the power over God's ring. Remember only God has this." As we stood there, another event illuminated then disappeared.

Me: "Lord, there are still many events left."

Jesus: "It looks discouraging from your view, but let me download what this clock looked like when you saw it only seven days ago." Just then I saw it. Then He removed this visual instantly and I saw the current clock.

Me: "Lord, there were three things which came and passed – 3 events. What were these?"

Jesus: "Erin one of the lost tribes are coming back. Remember as far as the East."

Me: "So Lord, is our gauge based on the Prophecies? Wow."

Jesus: "Erin, my Word is such that you can dig deeply and find treasure there."

Me: "Or you can simply see it hidden right on the surface of the page too! Lord You are amazing, what other events occurred?"

Jesus: "Well, there are seven but 3 in which God marked. Now remember your gauge is Israel. The enemy wants all evidence that the Jews occupied Jerusalem gone. Even the city's name bears witness to its origins. This is obvious and in plain sight. Jerusalem – look up the origins of this, but Erin - 'God will see' - and Shem greeted Abraham with Bread and wine there. Who was Shem Erin? Noah's son! So – dissect this word to find the roots of Jerusalem. This land is God's. This land was given to God's children."

Me: "Lord, forgive me as I have been sick and under attack this week, did more division occur?"

Jesus: "The Lord is unearthing evidence of the origin. See Erin, you must understand. God will not punish on here-say. His judgment will come after physical evidence is brought forth. Then after evidence is uncovered, then the Lord God will expect a Just Verdict based on physical evidence. This is fair. Now here is the problem. Earthly Courts are not just. Erin you know this, you have lived with results of an unjust system. I have told you that very soon, you will be vindicated as justice is God's, vengeance is His. Now, this is a matter of a land deal. This angers God. Erin, do you remember walking in the Entry? You just walking backwards couldn't undo history, in as much as running faster couldn't bring the course of history quicker?"

Me: "Yes, I realize my place as there is nothing I can do, only God can. There are so many scriptures about this!"

Jesus: "Very good. So now the enemy is trying to erase history, even destroying the evidence. He uses the lure of the world and even deposes and employs Kings to execute his agenda. Remember the length of a contract of the enemy? He cannot even keep a contract for 9 months. So there cannot be a covenant of peace, this is false. After 9 months there will be an attempted extermination. Erin you saw this."

Me: "Lord when will this be?"

Jesus: "It is coming. Remember history repeats; there are patterns. There is nothing new under the sun (on Earth) – Heaven all things are new!"

Me: "Lord, I'm scared."

Jesus: "Why, take comfort that God My Father is in control – No man or even the enemy of God will be able to speed up this clock."

Me: "Lord, please send more signs! Lord – make them so remarkable that there is no mistaken place of origin. Lord, come for us before the time of trouble!"

Jesus: "Look at the other rings Erin. They remain steady – these were set in place by Enoch. This was appointed by God. None of us know the timing Erin."

Me: "Lord, thank You for this clarification! Thank You. Could You show me what we are looking for? I cannot read the script on God's clock. What does that mean?"

Jesus: "Erin, this is Heavenly in origin. You cannot understand that which is written."

Me: "Lord, it looks like there are hundreds of events yet. How can this be? This is discouraging."

Jesus: "Hmmm... Interesting! So let's just say there are 500 events left on God's clock – in seven days, three registered events came and went. Now, look at weeks and years. Erin, do you really know? Do I? How do we know God will have seven events a day, 52 weeks from now? We do not know. So this, too, is good."

Me: "Lord, then why do the angels guard it? The enemy cannot calculate what I'm seeing, if You cannot."

Jesus: "Erin, I can read the clock, and so can the enemy."

Me: "Oh, because he originated here. Of course! But he can't control God's order, as God uses no gears on His clock."

Jesus: "Erin, you are gaining wisdom. The angels guard this, to bring you comfort. This, too, is good."

Me: "Lord, after this last dream, I was under attack. I need Your help."

Jesus: "Erin, you were not. What signs did you have as warning?"

Me: "None."

Jesus: "Correct. Now, what happened?"

Me: "I had extreme attacks on Tuesday. It was relentless. All was in minutes of the last blow. It was in every area. I thought I had opened the enemy's doors. I was hammered in such a short, compact time – all within 36 hours."

Jesus: "Okay, then what?"

Me: "Then three days of blessings free and clear – so much supernatural it was hard to believe."

Jesus: "Then why are you sick?"

Me: "Lord, good question. Why am I sick?"

Jesus: He was smiling. "Erin, you are healed. This was allowed because you needed the rest. Was this bad?"

Me: "No, it was a good time. I was too sick to do anything other than rest and sleep, but not so sick that I needed to have hospitalization."

Jesus: "Erin, remember – as these dreams become more involved, you must recognize one day of rest for your body. Just as you give to God what is His, you must also give one day over to God for your rest and renewal. By doing this, you honor Him! Remember – in the Entry ceiling, what did God do on the Seventh Day? Did He lift a finger?" He was laughing.

Me: "No, Lord, He rested."

Jesus: "Begin at the Beginning. There is much today. The Laws were good, meant to bring Life through the Word of God. These were God-Breathed. Now, Commandments are still good today. They are commands. Erin, when I came, the enemy decided it was a good time to change direction – off of the Word of Truth. Therefore, many Christians will claim that they are no longer even subject to the Commandments – what they are really meaning is Rabbinical Laws. They have put the two as one. They are not reading the Bible, but siding with opinions. Don't entertain fools who choose not to read the Word! This is not healthy. Erin, choose Life. "

Me: "Lord, have I not obeyed?"

Jesus: "You must rest one day, Erin – Work Six, Rest One!"

Me: "Forgive me, Lord. I have done this."

Jesus: "It's okay, Erin. This is meant for your benefit. As I gave you a period of extreme trials, I also gave you a double portion of blessings."

Me: "Lord, You are wise and clever. Even the columns in Your home are a double portion!"

Jesus: (He was laughing so hard.) "Erin, you delight me. Yes, you are right! Now, as to God's clock, it is powered by God – take comfort. The enemy's clock runs on Triple-A Batteries! He who mocks God will be portioned out also – remember Haman. The enemy will appear to be winning; then they will run in fear after their short-lived victory."

Me: "So, Lord, there is more hidden here. Is the Peace Treaty to last nine months once signed? Will You then come for us? I thought it was right upon signing?

Jesus: "Erin, go to scripture now, with new eyes. Think of this clock. Look at the Old Testament prophets. What is left? Then formulate. Just know that God regulates timing. I do not know when He will send Me for you! I do know that you will be removed out of the desert to the Land of Trees. You will be in a safe place until the day of My coming."

Me: "Lord, will You invite me back here? This seems so final today."

Jesus: "Oh, did I say such a thing?" (He was smiling.) "I don't believe this to be true. Would you like to learn more or see more?"

Me: "Oh, yes! Please, Lord!" (I leaped) He laughed.

Jesus: "Well, very good then, we will spend some more time, as God allows. You didn't eat your cake!"

Dream over….

Blessings...

Chapter 2 – Drinking Deep

Communion…

I received texts from my 14 year old son that my 12 year old daughter was not on the bus. I had become frustrated so I phoned the school. They had not seen her. The school referred me to the Bus Barn. I texted my daughter – No response! I phoned the bus Barn – they did a bus search in case she had gotten on another bus. They phoned her bus and the driver said that she had not boarded the bus. I phoned the school again, 20 minutes had passed and I was beginning to panic. The school put a page out to her but received no response. All of her teachers were paged. I told them at work I would need to leave.

My daughter never would board the bus, without letting someone know. She wouldn't go home with a friend without asking. Her brother has done things like this but never her. I phoned the school again 30 minutes had passed. Everyone was searching the school grounds. Teachers, the principal and other employees were looking for her. I was panicking. I asked the school when and who calls 911 when this happens. They told me to come to the school and stop at the local market as sometimes kids go there to get snacks after school. I said she didn't have money. They began to infer that maybe I didn't know her. I said, "Look, you know my son, he is in your office quite often, with him I wouldn't be surprised, with her no way!" She agreed and laughed a bit.

Forty minutes had gone by – I was in my car as school buses passed me on the road. I had put two calls in to the kid's dad. When I blurted out "My daughter is missing, no one can find her", he too decided to come to the school. By then I was in all out panic! I phoned the school again. She had vanished somewhere between 6th period and the bus – on a beautiful calm sunny winter's day! My heart was pounding! I was driving faster than normal. I thought about her and I thought about what could've happened. I know that bad men trolled school parking lots. I realized I knew none of her friends at the new school. I quickly phoned and texted her again, nothing. I panicked. I said to the Lord, "Lord please, please don't let this be your will? Please Lord!"

Just then, the phone rang. I heard her voice, "Mom, it's me. I was on the bus the whole time. I'm home and safe!" I broke down in tears. I kept it together up to that point, but then I lost it. I had pulled off into the parking lot of a nursery and became a blubbering mess. I asked her what happened. She said nothing. Then we laughed – I had straightened her curly hair that morning. Everyone had remarked that she looked like a different girl. She even fooled the bus driver and her brother from a distance. I was so relieved.

I got off the phone and proceeded to phone her dad, the school, and the Bus Barn. The Bus Barn dispatcher and driver felt the worst. I comforted everyone and apologized for not staying cool at the 40 minute marker. After I made all of my phone calls, I wept. Today could've been very bad. I was so relieved. I cried all the way back to work. I had no more appointments for the day, so I didn't need to worry about my red eyes, smeared make-up, and puffy face.

When I got back to my office, only one hour had passed from the first phone call. I'm usually the one who remains calm and level-headed at the scene of an accident with broken bones and gaping wounds. I rush to aid without missing a beat. I can keep people calm in a disaster too! I had that ability even when I was little. Today however, I learned something new about myself. For 45 minutes, I put God on the shelf. Even though there would've been very little I could do as a parent with a missing child, I still reacted as if I could control things I couldn't see or understand. God knew where my daughter was. He always does. She is His too, not just mine, but also His. I became very humble after this experience. The last few days this took a great toll on me. I have been exhausted.

Dear Father,

Thank You that my children are here and accounted for. Thank You for the quick response of the school, the bus driver, and the Barn. Thank You for keeping my children safe Lord. Thank You for all You have done for me. Lord it has been a difficult week. It has been a week of harsh contrasts; extreme attacks then extreme blessings! My spirit has been heavy and I'm trying to understand it.

My dreams have been odd too. Last night I dreamed I was in a large Earthly estate. It was in England. I was invited to dine as an honorary guest. I was invited early so they could take me for a tour of the estate. Compared to Heavenly Mansions, this was pale in comparison. It had an old feel and was in slight disarray. I suddenly realized that I was not invited for social reasons, but for professional reasons. I laughed as I realized they wanted free interior design advice. The dinner was scheduled for 3:00 pm although the invitation said noon. I thought I was there as a guest, but instead I was a worker. They took me to the kitchen. There I saw before me a room of the finest china in all of the Earth. There were stacks of Staffordshire, Belleek, Wedgewood, Danica, Pickard, Aynsley, Royal Copenhagen, Spode, some interesting Calico, etc. I was in complete awe. There must have been a million dollars' worth of fine porcelain china before me. The owner of the home and I guess my new client by default said, "Erin, there will be a delay with the dinner this afternoon."

I laughed and said, "Yes I think there is no room to cook?" He said "No, look up." On the ceiling there was a massive hand-carved wooden chandelier about 9 feet in diameter.

It was French in origin – odd in an English country estate, but I wouldn't expect to see Danish or Irish china there either. Then as if blending into the chandelier, there was a woman sitting on the chandelier. The woman was wearing prep-school clothing. She looked crazed. The chandelier was beginning to pull out of the ceiling. The lathe and plaster ceiling was about to collapse under the weight. In his British accent, he said calmly, "I have served dignitaries from all over the world on the finest china. The ones she is holding up on the chandelier are $1800 each, your American dollars."

I looked up and I saw a stack of plates that were absolutely breathtaking.

I said to the woman, "Miss, when the chandelier falls you will surely die and all of this china will be destroyed, but your only legacy will be as a mad woman who broke plates. No one will remember you. The plates will be mourned, but your value will be of no consequence.

Please come down so you can be redeemed in the eyes of the estate owner." The estate owner said, "This is my daughter whom I love more than all the china in the world. Please help us!"

"Sir, call help now and pray. We need a ladder and a miracle!"

Dream over….

Erin: "Lord, this dream was extremely significant. I need your help! Lord I miss You!"

Jesus: "Erin Come Up!"

This time I was inside the front entry. The door was closed behind me. I was relieved I heard music from the Courtyard. I saw the doors to the courtyard open. There was a breeze and the fabric panels with beautiful damask lights woven into the pattern were moving with waves. I went to go open the front door to look out to see if the angel was outside. I opened the door about 3" but didn't see the angel. The wind blew through the crack in the door causing things to move around. It was a beautiful day in the Valley out front, and there was a mist and quite a breeze. I laughed and quickly shut the door. I took off my sandals and felt the warm stones under my feet. I was so glad to be there. Today I ran down the hallway to the courtyard.

I glanced up briefly to look at the amazing ceiling, but I knew I was running to fast to have the story unfold. I ran out into the courtyard. It was so beautiful and lush. Seriously, this was the ultimate inter courtyard of an estate; The wonderful blossoming flowers and vines, the sound of the fountains, the music from the orchestra just ran through the House of God from all the open windows and doors – it was far beyond any earthly estate. Far beyond anything ever conceived by man there! It was beautiful, tears streamed down my cheeks. I turned to see the 4 angels guarding God's Calendar and Clock. I turned to my right and there was the Lord! I ran to Him. He was just walking to the Garden door and the entry area where I had come running.

Jesus: He had his arms out to receive me. "Erin, I was expecting to greet you at the door today. You came running why?"

Me: I was laughing and crying both. "Lord, I wanted to be with You!"

Jesus: "Oh, I am honored." He was smiling. He is so handsome and calm. "What is the matter?"

Me: "Lord there is much to talk about."

Jesus: "Calm down, do not worry! You are thirsty, come!" He walks me over to a small spring bubbling out of His Courtyard. The water was blue green and cool. He dipped a cup into it and handed me the cup. "Erin, you will love this." I took a drink and it was the most amazing water I had ever had. I was crying. "Drink deep, you are very thirsty!"

I began to gulp this amazing water. It was so refreshing. I had only had water once like this. I was drinking from a small stream of glaciated water north of Banff in Alberta Canada. It was so cold that my hands became numb but it was amazing! As I drank from this small well-spring in the courtyard of God's Home, I began to cry even more. My tears mixed with the water. As the water went into me I felt a warmth and tingle as the water mixed with my blood. I felt color going into my skin. My skin glowed like a golden pearl. A shimmer coat enveloped my outer skin and I felt restoration.

Me: "Lord, I had no idea how thirsty I was. Please forgive my gluttony!" I continued to drink.

Jesus: "Erin, you are free to drink as much as you like. You are parched and tired. You even ran to me today! You didn't wait for me to come to you. You came boldly in. As I always want you to come to me when you have a need! The angels thought I would need to retrieve you or send them!" He was laughing and I saw the angels laughing about that too.

Me: "Yes, Lord they are right. I can't wait to see more of your home whether You show me here or You wait until I live here in Heaven soon. Today though, I wasn't distracted by the sights, only by the front door.

Jesus: He was laughing. "I thought I would just by pass the door today and bring you right inside My Home."

Me: "I was surprised. I usually have to walk through something." I was smiling.

Jesus: "Oh do you now prefer to be outside the door or inside?" He was laughing. "Maybe I will need to mix this up a bit to keep you guessing!" The angels were laughing.

Me: "Lord, You already keep us guessing, I don't think You need to mix things up! I have no clue what You will do from one day to the next. When I look back over the course of my life's events then it makes perfect sense. I see You weaving the tapestry of my life together. But, I look forward to the Divine Peace of Heaven. Things are more predictable here because You work this all together and You reside here.

Jesus: "Erin, are you saying that Heaven is predictable – this sounds as if you will become bored," He was laughing. "What do you think angels in Heaven, boring?"

All of them laughed, I heard almost in unison 7 angels in the courtyard say, "Oh, no My Lord!" I thought this was such a cool thing.

Me: "Lord, forgive my expression. What I meant is, I love feeling safe and secure here with You. I love the stability and the life giving atmosphere of Heaven. It is Divine not dead."

Jesus: "I knew what you were speaking of Erin. When you opened the front door what were you looking for? Why look back when you knew I was here?" He was smiling.

Me: "I guess it is a habit, I saw a door, I wanted to see what was on the other side."

Jesus: "Yes, you do have a habit of looking back, but this was closed door – why open it?" He seemed more serious.

Me: "Lord forgive me, I knew I was already in Your House. I didn't have fear opening the door to look outside as this is Your front door not mine. You have the beautiful Valley in front. Why would I be afraid to open Your door? Did I do something wrong? Again there is much meaning behind one door."

Jesus: "When you are here you are safe, this is true. Just remember this on Earth. Don't open doors behind you and tread old battlefields. Old battlefields contain hidden dangers like minefields. Your steps are weighed and feet can trigger trouble. Erin, continue to look ahead and move forward. You were told this ten years ago. 'Don't look back!' Remember Kadima. Now this is a compact lesson today. You will leave with questions. I will discuss this more with you tomorrow. Tonight rest. You drank from the well-spring of life. You are renewed. Rejoice! I will see you again."

Me: "But Lord this is short. Did I do something wrong?"

Jesus: "No, Erin – you are perfectly 'Erin'! You bring me joy and all of us laughter. You make me smile. I would like you to release your story, your dream and your visit with your friends. I have given a few of them the interpretation! This is good. Then I will meet you again to discuss what happened to you with your daughter. Now drink – you are loved Erin!"

Dream over…

Chapter 3 - Cake, China & Changing God's Clock

Communion

Dear Father,

Thank You for all that we have. Lord, You have blessed me and my children! You have given me dreams from Heaven – miraculous dreams and visions! I am blessed by Your awesome works! Lord, You are coming soon, please bless my friends whom I love with Your voice, Your Divine Presence, Dreams, Vision, Miracles & Open Heaven too! It would be so amazing for all of us to operate together. Lord, I could use healing. I could use some miracles too. Please Lord, find a blessing or two that You could give all of us as a sign that You are here with all of us!

I am still heavy about what happened with my daughter on Thursday. There was such great panic, sorrow, and joy that my Earthly heart would've failed if not for this pacemaker! Thank You Lord; I have slept a lot these past few days forsaking my household duties. I have never been so relieved to hear "Mom I'm okay!" Thank You for this! I know there were so many layers to this even and live parable. It reminded me also of the joy when the landowner saw his prodigal son come home. The Father in Luke 15:24 must have been so happy to see his lost son. Here and now we have so much technology, we are very blessed. That father in Luke had no technology to locate his son. There will be a time when this could happen – well, actually You have shown me this Lord.

I need Your help again Father. My dream last night was disturbing. My children were tucked away in a safe spot but I needed to visit my parents. They were living near Portland, Oregon – even though they actually live in Idaho. I visited them on my way to another place. I had a small piece of luggage, a laptop, phone, and tablet. I had my car and enough money to travel. There was some event that occurred at night. It forced all of us to go south and east. It was a mass exodus. My parents seemed to turn it into a social event. We happened upon a small town almost deserted when I realized I had left my things back in Portland – up north. We were car caravanning and with several others. So I said goodbye to my Mom & Dad and their friends, and turned around and went north. I estimated I would lose six hours and would barely make it to my final destination. My mother was concerned about me traveling at night. I asked her if I could have a key. She said, "Yes, keep this, we won't be needing this!" I dreaded the back-tracking, but I needed the things I had.

When I got back in record time, it was dark – the traffic was going south in north-bound lanes also, so I had to drive back up using the area between the highway and guard rail. When I got back up to their house, I grabbed my things and proceeded back to my car. There were massive parties of people staying behind and celebrating those who left. There were fireworks and drunken people who seemed happy about the event. Several people came up to me and told me to hang out with them to watch the stars. I had put everything in my car and as I was getting into it, people were saying "Look-look up!"

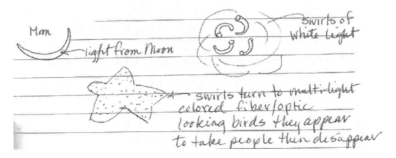

Up in the sky I saw several stars. I saw a moon crescent-shaped like a smile and several light swirls coming for us. These swirls turned to large types of lighted birds and appeared to take people away then disappear again. I could see past this and I knew these were false. They were mocking the rapture – these were demons.

Dream over...

Lord, You are giving me these very odd clear dreams, please help!

Erin Come Up!

Today I arrived right on the Lord's Threshold into His Home. The door was wide open. I was literally right between the jam of the door, neither in nor out. I went inside. I was laughing and shaking my head. Our God has such wisdom. I went to grab the handle to step in. I decided to close the door behind me. I faced this beautiful valley. It was sunset. The entire landscape was pink, gold, purple, fuchsias and some blue. I notice that sunset and sunrise in Heaven are long. They last awhile so we can enjoy the colors. I love it. I smiled and closed the door. I took off my sandals. I was dressed beautifully. I was always dressed like royalty. It wasn't a matter of vanity but of worth. I no longer viewed myself of little worth. I was an heir to the Heavenly land. My gown was pale pink with pearls and diamonds. There were woven strands of gold and silver. It was silk. My skin was perfect; there were no creases or wrinkles. I felt so healthy! In Heaven I am an Earthly size 4, maybe 2? On Earth I am a 6/8 depending on the time of year – smiles. Here in Heaven I am not skin and bones, but lean. I am not muscular like an athlete, but I am very much like I was when I was a (ballerina) dancer. The difference was here in Heaven, I can enjoy food and live. I don't need to worry about my weight or fat.

Now let me rewind a bit. I still remain about 5'2" in Heaven. I don't mind being smaller and I never have. I have noticed there are many heights on people in Heaven. Not every woman is a size 4; they are all perfectly proportioned, but healthy. The men are strong; some are more muscular than others, which must be by personal choice. Most men appear about the height of Jesus. He is about a foot higher than I am. I have seen some taller men and I have seen some slightly shorter. We are all recognizable, but glorified and perfected. The essence and personality of each person is seen and recognized. Some appear more serious. Some appear laughing and joking. Some seem quiet and demure. There is one thing in common with everyone! Peace! Each one glows with God's Glory. Each one is welling up with Joy and Peace. There is comfort and safety. People serve and are kind. We are all so thankful to be there, kindness is a form of Christ's love – It is His love in action!

Today, I walked down the Hall Entry looking up to the ceiling. I walked at a pace of one minute for each day of Creation unfolding in this beautiful painting. I had the biggest grin. It took me seven minutes to walk down this Grand Entry. Jesus met me at the doors to the courtyard. He was smiling and laughing.

Jesus: "I knew You would appreciate it! Come; let's look at the calendar today!"

He walked me over to a stepped area with a small platform. I could see God's ring of events from there. As the ring turned, 2 more events disappeared. I became sad.

Jesus: "Why so sad Erin, 7 more events occurred just last week? Rejoice."

Me: "Lord, there are still hundreds left before You come."

Jesus: "Erin, you didn't see this clock 20 years ago. You would not believe how much has happened. Now this week there were important proclamations which occurred. This was ground work laid into the next series of events about to unfold."

Me: "Lord the two events today that I saw – One was very large, what was this?"

Jesus: "Erin, you will see it, the news will be your source here."

Me: "Lord, I have been watching all of the events unfold in the news, it is hard to know which ones are the events of God!"

Jesus: He was laughing. "Erin, God sees all things, what events do you believe are noticeable?"

Me: "Ones with destruction, ones with World leaders – Unions' maybe? Perhaps small ones though, I can't get inside God's head, I am one small human woman."

Jesus: "You are somewhat correct. There are always wars, bombs and destruction. Sometimes this is a marker, sometimes not. Look to the Prophecies for your guidelines. Also, like I mentioned to you before, things are being unearthed as evidence right now. Look also at land deals and contracts. Israel again is your gauge. Now let's have some dinner, are you hungry?" He was smiling.

Me: "Yes, Lord, I was thirsty yesterday, today I am hungry!" He was laughing as He walked me over to His beautiful Gazebo with the golden dome. There were two Angels serving us and holding our chairs. The Lord was in a beautiful white fine linen tunic, comfortable with His sleeves rolled up. His tunic had a beautiful purple and blue sash with royal blue tasseled ends. The tassels were woven with silver. He was wearing linen white pants and His beautiful woven sandals. Immediately I began to notice the incredible china on His table.

Jesus: "I thought you might like this." He was laughing.

Me: "Lord, this was like my dream except this china before me is at least 1000 times the quality! Do You mind if I look at this?" It was delicate but stout – it had a motif of birds on the plate, there were strands of gold wheat braided on the outer edges of the plate. There were 3 strands of wheat. There were different birds on the plates. Mine had a replica of the sparrow with silver and gold. I saw a platter nearby with an eagle, and another small dish with a beautiful gray dove. I looked over to the Lord's plate. I giggled as He had several different birds on His plate. No one in particular, His was clearly special. Each of these pieces reminded me of the Royal Flora Danica plates only Heavenly. I saw interesting dishes with tree motifs also. They were the most exquisite china I had ever seen. I could see through them as they had depth and were clearly like nothing on Earth – these were fired in Heavenly kilns from the finest craftsman!

Jesus: "Okay, you are fascinated with these; tell me your thoughts Erin."

Me: "First, Lord these are amazing and clearly divine in origin." I picked up one of the plates to see if there was a mark (hallmark) under it. There was, I began to laugh! "Lord, You are so clever! I see Your Signet Mark in the center surrounded by several different marks. What are these?"

Jesus: "What, aren't you hungry? Okay, yes, I knew you would enjoy this. These are craftsmen here; they have come from periods of time long forgotten. Very little is known of these craftsmen, but their work is remembered. This is a collaboration of all of them working together here. This too is a craft."

Me: "Lord, they put together such fine tableware for You. Each one of these tells a story and clearly these are priceless."

Jesus: "Yes, they honor me with their gifts. This brings me such joy."

Me: "Lord, there is love here in these. There is no pretense. This is a casual dinner but formal plates. Fit for a King!"

Jesus: "Erin, you understand that I do not require such things."

Me: "Lord, I know this. It reminds me of Exodus and the Israelites giving all they had to build the tabernacle. This is like that." I looked around.

Jesus: "Somewhat, Erin this is My courtyard. There are some relationships, but the magnified Holy of Holies Structure is in the Golden City. This is different."

Me: "Lord, wherever You are there is the Holy of Holies."

Jesus: He was laughing, "Okay, where my Father's Throne is; this is the Holy of Holies." Jesus was laughing.

Me: "Okay, Your Throne is there too Lord."

Jesus: He was smiling and nodding. "Okay, we are both correct here. You will understand more when you dwell permanently here. Then you will see everything together. It will all make sense then, what God has prepared. Are you finally hungry?"

Me: "Yes, Lord, I will eat what You are serving." Jesus waved and the Angels brought food, water, and wine. Jesus took a sip of the wine first, and then waved to the Angel to pour some into my cup. He then served me both breads; flat bread and leavened bread. I was smiling. "Lord a question: Why the dream with all the China?"

Jesus: "I sent interpreters on this for you Erin. Your friends have wisdom. Not all have responded, but soon they will. Let's wait on this until all is stated. You can be patient, right?"

Me: "Lord, as You know, I am not very good at patience. I am too excited!"

Jesus: "There was an observation you did leave out, can you tell me what that is?"

Me: (I was just responding with a "No" when all of a sudden the down-load came – I got a big smile) "Oh yes, in the kitchen there was more china on the outer counters, away from the valuable china."

Jesus: "Hmm, interesting, tell me about this."

Me: "I was thinking about this last night. The expensive china was stacked on the island; stacks and stacks. The extremely expensive china like Flora Danica was with the daughter on the chandelier and the perimeter counters contained plates and service pieces that were not in danger of being broken – they were utilitarian and of little worth. Common – Old Ironstone, Hotel ware, real Chinese plates, old chunky, hearty servant's everyday ware, nothing ornamental. Certainly nothing guests would eat from, only workers."

Jesus: "So you are observing that the dishes on the perimeter were safe from harm and of little value?"

Me: "Yes, from an Estate Appraiser on Earth."

Jesus: "Interesting, why did you not mention this detail?"

Me: "Because they would not be harmed by the chandelier falling."

Jesus: "Okay, your friends should know this too."

Me: "Lord, You know all this; tell me what it all means."

Jesus: "What would that do? Erin, it takes the Glory of God to conceal a matter and the Honor of Kings to search it out. What Honor is there in never having to search for truth? This honors God! Has your searching allowed you deeper fellowship? Has the Lord not given you more jewels by uncovering more? Erin, one day you will look back at all you were given, you will see it marked, you will see it even in the Word of God, and you will stand amazed. Now are you enjoying your time with me?"

Me: "Oh yes Lord! I love learning from You. Each day is a new discovery. You are not setting out to harm me or confuse me. You always answer my questions. When You won't give me dates, You remind me of Your promises and tell me to be patient. Just please remember I am human. I lack understanding. When bad things happen around me, I look for You to comfort me. I look for signs that You are here. I want so much to go to wherever the land of trees is now and safely wait until the day You come for us. I'm ready to go where You take me Lord. You have broken me of planning. You have removed my need to make arrangements. I am at the mercy of God's Calendar and Clock. Since I cannot read the writing on it, I have no gauge. Israel is a gauge for You Coming, but not from removing me from the desert. I have no gauge for this? I would like my own clock ring so I can know timing?" He was laughing so hard.

Jesus: "Let me understand this. You are asking for Your own ring on God's Calendar and Clock, this is funny – I must call upon Enoch. He will enjoy this. Erin, jus hat would you like on the ring? Come show Me!" He grabbed my hand and walked me over to the platform. "Okay show Me where you would have it."

Me: I was embarrassed, I realized I was selling. "My Lord please forgive me."

Jesus" "Erin there is no foolishness in hopes when the heart is good! Go ahead this is not a test or a rebuke. Heaven is waiting, go ahead. Go Boldly!"

Me: I sheepishly pointed to just above God's ring. "Okay Lord, this is my thinking. I am not above God. I just want a smaller, faster moving ring."

Jesus: He was laughing – "Okay Erin. Go ahead."

Me: Then I would be cogged with God's circle and my obstacle would be removed. Oh You had better cog this with the seasons. I am thinking my obstacles can be removed by spring March 20, 2014. Then You can come for us no later than June 6, 2014. This sounds workable to me! Then I can dwell here in the City by July 1, 2014 at the latest. Oh yes Lord, notice my friends are all on that ring with me. This should work. Oh yes put a few gold sparrows on the clock wheel – a few bluebirds, doves and what have you. Perfect... Done! All finished it, its set! I rubbed my hands together and raised my hands into the air.

Jesus: "Okay here is your ring!" An angel brought a ring out black with gold birds. There were personal events on the ring for Earth. "What do you think?"

Me: "Oops, I forgot. Add the time of the Creation of the New Earth and all that comes with it too! Great!" He was laughing and so were the angels.

Jesus: "Wow Erin you just changed the course of God's Calendar. You just sped everything up according to your timing, forcing God's timing to come faster. Hmmm – oh no – we lost a few souls in the process but – we got this done for you. Now there is great relief here in Heaven as I now know the time of My coming. Oh there will be some extra grumbling as there will be a few less in the Bridal party but I guess they can come later during the tribulation. Hmmm… There will be some more estates vacant here in Heaven. Whatever shall we do?" He was smiling, "Erin – ideas?"

Me: "Oh Lord, please forgive me. Don't call in Enoch, although I must admit I adore him. He is kind and funny."

Jesus: "Erin I am becoming jealous."

Me: "Oh Lord, You are funny. Okay point taken. I will wait on the Lord God and His timing, mine is according to what's best for me and my friends not the Kingdom!"

Jesus: "Erin I love that you are in constant wonder. I love that you are like a child. I enjoy that you are not afraid to say what is on your mind. You cannot hide anything anyway. I knew your thoughts in advance, but for a moment it was fun to play "what ifs". Unfortunately you discovered quickly that God contains knowledge of both the beginning and the end. All is planned. You cannot possibly reverse or move ahead of God's Plans. When you do, as you saw, this can create dire consequences. Playing God comes with a huge burden. Could you imagine being on that chandelier?"

Me: "No Lord, I wouldn't want to be up there in that high lofty and unstable position."

Jesus: "Good Erin. This is wisdom. Remember who your solid Rock is! Now how is your daughter?"

Me: "Lord you mean how is her mother? It was horrible!"

Jesus: "Yes, how was your daughter?"

Me: "As You know Lord she was the same. Same routine! She was safely cared for on the bus the whole time and Home safe and sound."

Jesus: "Good, I knew she would be."

Me: "Lord You never even had her in harm's way at all. If anything You had a veil over everyone so no one could see her and thought she was unaccounted for, why?"

Jesus: "Interesting choice of words. Come let's finish our food. (He took me back to the Gazebo; He motioned for the angel to tend to my chair. I thanked the angel). Erin there was more to this. Consider this a sign and training too. You discovered something about yourself, what was this?" He was fixing His plate of food and asked me if I would like some olives in oil for my bread. I took some for my plate.

Me: "I learned what it was like to have joy and go from that to instant mourning – as in Lamentations 5:15. I also felt the opposite of that as in Psalm 30:5. Joy comes in the morning when I heard her voice. Lord it reminded me of the utter elation of the saints arriving to Heaven – the Promised Land. They kissed the ground, jumped in the River and embraced loved ones. There were tears! – Lord I was so scared, I was terrified. At one point Lord I thought You abandoned me. I couldn't wait for your lessons, I had to act immediately. I waited, then went to You about my lost child."

Jesus: "No you didn't. What were you repeating over and over again?"

Me: "No Lord please, no Lord please. – I was pleading."

Jesus: "Is pleading and petitioning to God not prayer? Erin you had no time for formal prayer."

Me: "Lord I counted the minutes because time slowed to me. One minute felt like an eternity. When I didn't know where she was."

Jesus: "Yes a lot can happen in just 40 minutes, this is true!"

Me: "I felt punched in the stomach. I felt anger and anguish, both. I mourned with joy. I've been exhausted."

Jesus: "Erin the way you love your children is the same way God loves them! Now you understand why each one is just as important to Him. With your addition of a ring cogged with God's Clock, it benefits you and your friends but it does nothing for the parents of lost children. God's clock gives more time for the lost than yours does. Don't you want more friends in Heaven? Don't you want more children here? Think of the teenagers!"

Me: "Oh Lord please forgive my selfish desires. How can I say I desire for all to be saved and dwell here if I cannot trust in the very timing of God! You told me once to ask for anything and up to half of the Kingdom. Well Lord please. Bring more to You! Please let more people see what You have planned here for us! Lord, I want so much to be removed from my trouble but not at the expense of souls!" I began to cry.

Jesus: "Erin your time here will intensify. If you are willing to come boldly here, I will share more with you. Please be patient a little longer. There are rewards in your investigations. You honor God with your watching. Now wait with childlike wonder and parental patience."

Me: "Lord I'm a parent and a child, yet I am neither."

Jesus: "Funny. Erin you are here and enjoy our time. I know it is difficult, but soon I will remove your obstacles, even prior to My coming. So please take heart. You have been given some divine mysteries to solve."

Me: "Lord the things on God's Clock – did those just happen today or are happening now?"

Jesus: "Interesting question. See what you can find. Erin this is for your benefit, please continue on your course. Or if you prefer you can go back to your standard way of existing only 3 years ago. You can be active at church and too busy to come to Me. Which is better?"

Me: "Lord, are You saying church isn't good?"

Jesus: "No, of course not. It is about your heart condition. There are battlefields at church, the enemy has done his job of causing the opposites of the fruits to manifest there – this you know. Not everyone has this. Many churches are wonderful and God is there. Many are absent of God. These churches are more like mausoleums. Pray! These are the same people that will take issue with your dreams, visions and relationship with Me. Do not worry about these people. They are tools of the blacksmith and shouldn't be your concern. Here, taste this cake, your birthday was not forgotten." He smiled…

The Angel served me a small beautiful cake with icing and a little sweet jasmine flower made in lavender icing. It had a small diamond in the icing. It was the prettiest little cake I had ever seen. It was on a small golden plate about 6" in diameter. It had small white doves on the edges – 5 doves. I laughed. I took a bite of the cake – it was like Heaven – I can't describe it, it was buttery and sweet like nothing I have ever had in my whole life. I began to cry!

Jesus: "Don't you like if Erin?"

Me: "Oh Lord is there nothing imperfect here in Heaven. Well I am not perfect."

Jesus: "Yes Erin you are perfectly Erin designed by God. Hand crafted by the best Artisan himself!" I was in tears!

Me: "Lord, You love me so much! What an honor to be loved like this – Even when I try to be God and try to rearrange time!"

Jesus: He handed me a cloth for my tears. He reached over and put His hand under my chin and directed me to look at Him. "Erin your dreams will all come true!"

Me: Instantly I saw snapshots of my life now and to come. I also saw eternity. I was in tears! "I love You Lord!"

Jesus: "You are loved by the King! Erin, find Joy in this!"

Dream Over… Blessings

Chapter 4 – Fresh Oil

Communion

Dear Father,

Thank You for everything we have! Thank You for my children! Thank You for friends and family.

Thank You for making all things new! Lord, thank You for keeping my focus on things which are good. I realize that I am helpless to come against the things of this world, but when I remain trusting wholly in You – well, I can even scale a mountain! I have been discouraged this week with an unsettled spirit. I have had anxiety and worry. My sleep for several nights was broken, and I have had a massive amount of dreams. Many have been disturbing, but all have been crystal clear – not in meaning, but visual clarity. Lord, I know You are speaking through these, but I have no idea what the reason for them is. It is a mystery.

"Erin, Come Up!"

I stood right on His front doorstep today. The door was closed. I looked behind me to see if there was an angel. There was not. Right over me there was a cloud, very massive with cool mist. The mist was shimmering like silver dust. As the mist fell, it completely hydrated me. I look at my skin. It left a feeling of dew on me. The mist glistened. I let some more fall on my skin. I tilted my head back to receive some on my face. It was oil and cool mist. I was laughing. It smelled like morning dew and had a hint of something like citrus. I spun around to look at the valley. The mist was over the olive groves, some of the mountains, and one meadow in the valley, but the sun shone over the rest. When the sun beamed through this mist, it created a rainbow unlike anything I have ever seen. It was like and oil-and-water based rainbow. I remember seeking slicks from spilled oil on concrete – it has an unusual rainbow effect, just like rain. Wow, God is amazing!

This mist was only dewy, and absorbed quickly into my skin. It didn't leave a giant oil slick on the ground or make things slippery. I decided I had better get inside, so the Lord could talk with me about this. I laughed, because this felt like the warm blanket that was dropped over my shoulders when I started these dreams. As this fell upon me, I felt a warmth and tingle like a medicinal heat wrap (same as purchased at the store for sore muscles). The mist was cool, but when it landed, it created healing warmth.

I turned and knocked with the door knocker three times. I waited a few moments. Then I knocked again. I knew the Lord could read my thoughts. I decided to tap into the Holy Spirit. "Any suggestions Holy Spirit?"

Holy Spirit: "Erin, you knocked, now Seek!"

Me: "I am. I'm calling on You."

Holy Spirit: "Are you knocking and standing? Or are you really seeking?"

Me: "Okay, then I will try the door."

Just as I went to grab the handle, I heard the door unlatch and slightly open. I was laughing. Okay, what is the lesson today? Hmmm... I hesitated again, as I thought maybe an angel was going to open it all the way, but I heard nothing.

Me: "Okay, Holy Spirit, help me here. What do I do?"

Holy Spirit: "Erin, what are you wearing today?"

I looked down. I was wearing a white dress just over my knees. I had an outer robe of blue and white. It had a thick hem woven with silver thread – it was heavenly, embroidered with symbols. I had some silk white linen-like pants under the dress, but almost the same length. I had beautiful silver sandals, with ribbons woven up my ankles. I had a beautiful small sash of deep blue around my waist.

Me: "Holy Spirit, this is beautiful, but what am I wearing?"

Holy Spirit: "Erin, you belong in His house. Walk in and seek Him!" I was giggling...

Me: "Oh!" Deciding to walk in quietly to see if anyone would notice, I slowly opened the door. I was laughing. I slipped off my sandals. I went to leave them at the door, but kept them with me in case I wasn't supposed to take them off. This Home is more welcoming than anywhere I have been on Earth. I could have so much peace and rest here in God's House. This is amazing!

I noticed today that I could see with even more clarity. Everything around me was crisp and very vivid. The drapes were moving back and forth as I walked by. I saw this amazing illuminated pattern. This was truly incredible. Every time I saw these I had to catch my breath. I looked up and I saw the painting on the ceiling. I giggled, as I was at the part where God is creating animals. Realizing that I was giggling loudly, I put my hand over my mouth. I must have looked ridiculous to the Lord; here I was – an invited guest – tiptoeing down His hallway with my sandals dangling from my right hand and my left hand covering my lips. Just as I was thinking this, Jesus appeared at the courtyard opening.

Jesus: "Erin, what are you doing?" He was laughing.

Me: "Oh, You know, Lord, just …." He reached out to take my right hand and looked at my sandals. He was smiling.

Me: "Lord, they were so pretty that I wanted to take them with me, and I didn't know if I was to remove them or not.

Jesus: "Yes, they are quite lovely with your outfit." He was laughing. I quickly switched and put them in my left hand so that He could take my right. "Now, let's discuss the delay today. What was happening with your thoughts?"

Me: "Well, I was surprised to see that Your door was closed, even though You knew I was coming. I thought I knew what to expect, but I had to change my thinking … Lord, why was Your door shut to me today?"

Jesus: "Erin, you are seeking answers. Was the door locked? No, it was not. The door will not always by appearances be open. What were your needs, and what did you discover?"

Me: "Things don't always happen as I expect. I was not harmed in the process. You required me to knock, then seek … not knock and wait. I had to step out a bit in faith, although I must admit I did look around a bit first to see if I'd missed anything. When I reached for the handle of the door, without me doing anything the door opened. You required only my faith that the door would be unlocked and then opened."

Jesus: "This is good, Erin. Continue, but come with Me first." He reached out and took me up to the Upper Balcony of the Courtyard. There was God's Clock and Calendar. He once again drew the sky dark with moon and stars, and set the reflection in one half of the gazing pool below and surrounding the clock. Then He waved His hand and set the other side. I saw the large portion of God's ring – three more events appeared and were gone.

Me: "Lord, it looks like much happened last week, and is about to happen."

Jesus: "Yes, it was a busy week in Israel. Declarations were made by the enemy against her!"

Me: "Lord, I've been thinking of the nine-month deadline that America put on the Peace Proposal. Will this be significant?"

Jesus: "Israel is fair; her enemies are not. Remember the roots. The goal is in her dominance. The enemy wants slavery and oppression – then genocide. The enemy distorts truth and seeks to erase historical facts. Even you know this, Erin. The enemy would love your destruction, too. So what patterns do you see?"

Me: "Something haunts me, Lord."

Jesus: "This isn't good; bring this forth."

Me: "In 2009, a Palestinian leader declared that in eight years Israel would be wiped off the face of the Earth – this would mean 2017."

Jesus: "Yes, I know of this. It will come to nothing, as this is not written. Where is it written that all of God's Children of Israel will be wiped out? I don't recall it. This we have seen before. Deadly declarations have dire consequences. By their admission, they have brought condemnation on themselves. Now, we do know a few things to watch for. Say a nine-month Proposal deadline leads to a nine-month contract. Now, I say this, as this is the enemy's trick – Israel and others negotiate on longer deals, but the enemy has a nine-month deadline to break it."

Me: "Lord, this reminds me that You are the opposite – You operate on a seven-year contract."

Jesus: "Oh, yes, Jubilee – very good, Erin! The enemy is impatient – in their laws, their nine- month commitment is the length of their contract. Sad, but true! God sees this – it is trickery. This has come against Israel before. This is nothing new. You learned something about Cain and Abel recently – do you remember?"

Me: "Oh, yes. The argument I read was in Jasher. Cain became inflamed when Abel's sheep grazed upon Cain's land. Abel pointed out to Cain that he ate Abel's sheep and wore the wool from them – then why not allow the sheep to graze on his land."

Jesus: "Back up a bit – remember the heart of Cain to begin with. Cain brought poor offerings to God, while Abel brought his finest lambs to God as an offering. So Cain was already angry and jealous of Abel. Cain decided to kill Abel and hide his body from God and everyone else. So you see this same pattern operating today. Israel has favor and represents Abel. Israel comes to the aid of the enemy's children, yet not one Jewish child could safely walk in the enemy's city."

Me: "So the enemy walks freely and is safe in Jerusalem, but Jews cannot walk freely in their areas. This isn't right. Yes, I see the pattern."

Jesus: "I am just showing you that there is nothing new here."

Me: So the nine-month Proposal of Peace will come with a nine-month contract to be broken?"

Jesus: "Erin, there are patterns. Remember, there is no unknown strategy of the enemy. God's people will be protected. There will be some loss, but God will make-do on His Promises. He will not be mocked, nor will He delay. Please continue to pray, as those who divide up God's land will have their land portioned out and divided!"

Me: "Lord, You are speaking of America now."

Jesus: "Erin this too is a pattern, but please be at peace. Now come let's sit together."

Instantly we were in His gazebo dining. I was laughing as we were instantly there. He took some bread and broke it, offering me a half. I accepted it. Then again He offered me some leavened warm bread. The angel poured wine into His cup. He tasted it. He nodded His head.

Jesus: "Erin this is very good. Oh here is some oil too; it is freshly pressed from the finest olives in My grove. Here are some fresh olives also for you."

There were several different types served in a funny long dish. Then the angels brought a type of pie or soufflé – an egg dish. They also served me honey with my bread that was amazing!

Me: "Lord, why do we always eat and drink here? I love this, don't change it!"

Jesus: "Erin, in My House you will never hunger nor thirst. What kind of host would I be to not provide a welcoming and secure place for you?"

Me: I was smiling – "I feel so welcome Lord."

Jesus: "Erin, why did you believe the door would be locked today? Really?"

Me: "Because it was closed Lord. I thought I had done something wrong maybe? I had quite a few burdens this week. I was afraid. The seed You have given me is dwindling again. I thought Your favor upon me was gone. I had been continuously hammered at work. When I have these wonderful times with You, I go back to dreariness. Here I see the Promise Land and I want so much to be here but I know there is more which must occur. Some days I feel disheartened. I hurt my neck on Friday and I'm struggling to write. When I'm here with You, You don't just feed me incredible food, when I hunger. You don't just give me water for my thirst, You bring me hope. Lord, sadly I must go back down there. I am willing to do this as long as You will have me, but could I just have a portion of my glorified body and be healed on Earth? Could I have just a portion of my wealth here to bring down? I know this is a lull, but I am becoming discouraged. Please Lord. Show Your favor soon and remove my trouble. I am knocking and seeking!"

Jesus: "Erin, who was at the end of the hallway to greet you? I know you had a walk before I met you, but I did meet you before your destination."

Me: "So Lord, the hallway is my symbol of the lull in activity and escalation of attacks; a parable?"

Jesus: "Possibly Erin – this is interesting."

Me: "Well it took 7 days of God's creation to get to You" – I was laughing.

Jesus: "Okay point taken. Let's look at all of this as your season right now then. Your walk in the hallway – let's say 7 years as a symbol you work for 6 and rest on 1 then who is waiting for you?"

Me: "Lord You – You are waiting. Please forgive my mood Lord, I am heavy."

Jesus: "Then lay down these burdens Erin!"

Just then the little plump sparrow with silver and gold came to the table and Jesus motioned for her to take the crumbs back to her nest. I giggled – it was so cute!

Jesus: "Tell Me your troubles. I tell you the truth; they will one day be like crumbs – carried off and removed."

Me: "Lord, the usual trouble – worry about providing for my kids, worry about my health and job, worry about when I am to step out in faith or when to wait. When to go for that door handle and when to wait? I become discouraged easily when the enemy gains ground."

Jesus: "Interesting choice of words."

Me: "I had a dream for a friend a couple days ago and I was unable to stop things."

Jesus: "Oh are you God now? Erin the timing was no accident. This was a bit disheartening yes but a valuable lesson – a good one. Now you keep thinking about a certain part in that dream which disturbed you; explain."

Me: "Yes. In the dream I was hunting down the witch to keep her from hurting anyone else. I was led to an old brick warehouse. I opened the door and inside were children 13 and under and mostly girls. The inside of this place was pitch black and the children were covered in black oil. It was horrible. When the light shone on them the reflection of the oil created a type of halo affect outlining their bodies. Whatever the witch had given them to eat or drink made them blind. They couldn't see the light, so as they walked some slipped into rectangular holes in the concrete floor. I told them that the Lord will help them. They said a woman came claiming to be sent from the Lord. So they didn't want to believe me that You are good!"

Jesus: "This is an interesting dream. What in particular bothered you?"

Me: "The black oil, it was so different than this pure clear oil." I pointed to the pressed olive oil.

Jesus: "You picked this up, good! So do you remember some time ago learning about what an olive goes through to get to this state? The olive is pressed. The trials in your life produce the oil in you also. Remember that oil is Holy and used for light. Consecrated oil keep the enemy far away, it is pure and good. Now it is obvious in your dream that this witch got to these children before their age of accountability to consecrate them in unclean crude oil. She too gave them food and water as they were hungry and thirsty. This blinded them to who she was and she appeared as a child of light. She blinded them so they couldn't see who she was and that she had no candle. Some souls were lost but not many. The light was let in and truth intervened, there was still time! Now, this is a good message of learning, but also a warning. Now I will leave this for you to uncover, there are layers here."

Me: "Lord it felt so good to stand in the wonderful divine mist this morning. It was healing."

Jesus: "Oh you liked that? This is God, Erin. This mist was over Eden also. Not only does it consecrate you, but it heals and nourishes too! Now do you feel welcome here with what I feed you? Are you nourished and is your thirst quenched?"

Me: I was beginning to cry – "Yes Lord always. This is why I would like to stay now."

Jesus: "I understand, but there is still more to discover. You had another dream, it weighs upon you."

Me: "Yes Lord, it troubles me."

Jesus: "Go ahead."

Me: "I am living in a gray apartment – gray inside and out. There are large windows about 14' high. There is snow outside. A man comes to drop something off and leaves. I am talking to my daughter when I notice two large cockroaches about 2" long. I was bothered because we don't have these in our area of the country. When I went to kill them I noticed they were actually deadly scorpions. I went after them but they went into cracks in the floor. It bothered me to know there was a hidden danger and my children could be hurt."

Jesus: "First Erin do not be afraid. Notice their size. These can be squished with your foot. They were afraid of you. Yes, I see that you are worried about obstacles. 2 left, yes?"

Me: "Yes Lord, when will You remove these?"

Jesus: "Erin what was your dream about the soil?"

Me: "You were instructing me on tilling dirt carefully in rows. You showed me rich soil, dark and soft. I saw sparkling minerals in it. You showed me how to prepare my field and do all that I can as a farmer. You showed me to do this as if it were a canvas which would become art. Then You reminded me that inspiration is like the sun and rain. Without inspiration there can be no art. Without sun and rain there can be no crop. All I can do on my own is prepare with my whole heart. The rest, I must trust and have faith in You!"

Jesus: "Erin, you are instructing today. I am proud of you. Instead of focusing on these small scorpions, let's focus on your field!"

Me: "Lord You are instructing me in so many ways!"

Jesus: "What did the Counselor direct you to when you were standing on my doorstep?"

Me: "Two things – knock, seek, and the door was opened; and to what I was wearing."

Jesus: "Ah yes, you are dressed similar to the Homeowner, are you a guest or do you belong here? Hmm – interesting?" He was smiling and laughing. "If I were a betting man with a wager, which of course you know I am not, I would say you are dressed as if you live here – hmmm..."

Me: "Well yes, I have this beautiful glorified body and I am wearing this lovely dress, it matches Yours in fabrics and details."

Jesus: "Interesting, so perhaps you are the daughter of the King after all?" He was laughing. "Do I need to review this with you again?"

Me: "Now Lord, this is hidden in plain sight! Well not exactly hidden here!"

Jesus: "Don't let the enemy rob you Erin. Your joy has been robbed this week. You are different!" He dipped His finger in olive oil and He dabbed my forehead, my nose, and my chin. He began to laugh, "Now cheer up! You have much to look forward to! Kadima! Remember, the enemy does his level best to come in and take your joy, your light. You remember Enoch, Erin. He lived in very dark times. He had seen horrible things, yet he chose joy. He is contagious right?"

Me: "Yes Lord, like You!"

Jesus: "Well our Father's favor was upon Enoch. His face shone upon him so joy was there. Now, Elijah is more serious."

Me: "Why is he so serious Lord?"

Jesus: "Until his business is finished, his heart is heavy. It shows. His burden is weighty. There is a harsh contrast. Remember how I felt in the Olive Grove the night before I was about to be pressed and crushed? This is no different Erin!"

Me: "Lord, I never noticed You had prayed in the Olive Grove and the significance of the Olive press. Wow! God is so amazing!"

Jesus: "There are many more parables left to be discovered there. So I would say you are sometimes like Elijah with your solemn seriousness and other times like Enoch."

Me: I was laughing! "I like Enoch's personality Lord."

Jesus: "Erin, then this is up to you! Choose joy in the midst of your trouble. Many will be attracted to you when your light – your candle burns. It will be like a flame of promise. In the process do not let your flame burn out. Remember fresh oil. Remember the nourishment of good news. Look at your feet. Beautiful are the feet of those who bring good news! Now give me those pesky scorpions so I can smash them. I suggest a new color on the walls of your gray outlook – the apartment. The snow is fresh. God opened the storehouses as in Job. He is making you white as snow! This is a blessing Erin! Remember your field. When you come next time, I have more for you to see! Do Not Worry! The scorpions hide in cracks."

Me: "Lord, they are also bold and roar like lions."

Jesus: He was laughing. "Okay, but lions also rely on God for their meals. They even lose their teeth when they get old and chew on grass, so even they can be humbled. A lion is teachable – a scorpion is not! There are layers here! Give this to me! I love you Erin – remember you are perfectly Erin and even the angels ask me when you come again."

Me: I was laughing. "Am I the entertainment here?"

Jesus: "Well, yes you do make us smile and laugh. We enjoy your company Erin! God loved and found delight in your ring on His clock – Heaven shook with laughter on this."

Me: "I pray I never make Him split that sea! He has so much power!"

Jesus: He was laughing. "Erin, you delight God and so do your friends, there is not much that brings Him laughter related to Earth any more. Look at the globe of your map and the lights – this is not many if you swap these and make them cities with populations. Please pray! Pray for your sister, Israel. Oh also, pray a blessing upon your sister and friend! I will see you soon! Remember the Soil & Oil! You are loved!"

Dream over…

Blessings...

Chapter 5 - Healing Rain and No. 9

Communion

Dear Father,

Despite a difficult week, I choose joy! I thank You for the blessing of You in my life! I thank You for my children and family! I thank You for my friends and their kind prayers and blessings. I am overjoyed by Your kindness concerning me. When I faced trouble several times last week, You reminded me about the power of my words. You have taught me to let my words be few and even not reacting or responding when people curse You thereby removing their power over me. Instead of entertaining them or engaging them in a war of words, I disengaged and praised You. Each time, the enemy's power was removed and I continued on my course! I thank You Jesus for Your gentle instruction. You are music to my ears instead of sharp sandpaper of tongues of my enemies. Blessed are You Jesus for sending the Holy Spirit to nourish my heart when words break it! I love You Lord. Your ways are higher!

Jesus: "Erin Come Up!"

I arrived today in a sitting position looking over this beautiful Valley of God. I was somewhat startled because I have never arrived up here sitting. I giggled, the Lord is so wise. I felt confirmation with the Holy Spirit that I was to take a moment and breathe.

The Valley was breathtaking; It was every sunrise, every sunset, every beautiful sky I had ever seen rolled into one incredible painting; God's Valley. There was this beautiful foggy mist again with this nourishing dew over half of the Valley. The sun was breaking through at times and the beams of light highlighted the Olive groves. I saw another highlighting a meadow pasture with sheep next to the river in the distance. I looked closer and it looked like I saw a lion too but it was sleeping on its' back. This concept still was so foreign to me. I giggled as I saw young lambs playing with their mother and rolling around near this massive sleeping lion. I began to cry even as I write. What an amazing sight truly! I scanned the mountains. I saw beautiful snowy peaks. I saw snow glistening like silver and diamonds. Even though snow can be difficult at times on Earth, I had joy that there was snow here. It means that He really does have storehouses of snow – which is spoken of in Job. My eyes scanned to another lower mountain range and I smiled as I saw a beautiful vineyard – well many. These jeweled grapes were so impressive that when the beams of light were shining on them, the grapes glistened in rainbow colors – like a prism from a crystal would reflect. I had never seen this before here. I sat there for some time. I heard the Holy Spirit say, "Erin, breathe deep." I giggled.

The sounds here were amazing. I heard sweet sounds of song birds. The songs they were singing I recognized. I was laughing as I saw a large group of little birds flying together in an amazing display – perhaps even 1000 of them. They made designs in the air. They were white with gold so when they would fly through one of the beams of light, you could see a long ribbon in the sky of Gold. I believe one of the songs I had heard was "Amazing Grace" but it was amazing, not sad at all but very uplifting. I was laughing again as I thought I recognized Revelation Song (Phillips, Craig, & Dean). Well technically it could've been a song from Heaven throughout the years. The songs were so beautiful. I began to hear the Orchestra in God's House behind me. I began to hum the Revelation Song. I raised my hands and I began to worship! This was the ultimate worship experience; every cell in my body was raised up in prayer – no gravity – I was now standing on the step still looking toward the Valley of God. These beautiful flowing channels of water lined the stairs. These small little pearl onion fish were dancing in the water and leaping out and back in again. As I worshiped God, I thanked Him. I have never been so thankful for Him before. Up here I know what it is like to be alive, nourished, and healthy! I am young here. As I stood with my arms raised I felt something like rain over me. The rain fell. I spun around and laughed, but I still raised my arms! I could raise my arms over my shoulders high! (On Earth there is a titanium plate or hinge in my neck. I have such pain and trouble lifting my arms past my shoulders for worship.) I reveled in this moment. To worship God fully with no judgment, with no one looking! Wow! I had tears pouring down my cheeks as I received the rain on my face. I had my eyes closed for a moment when I felt one of those beams or rays of light over me. The rain was gone and the sun dried me off so quickly – I laughed because I was soaked.

The ray of light was so warm. I felt something like a rush through my veins. It was warmth inside my body but my outer skin felt cool. I felt healing in my body. I stood for some time. I prayed.

Me: "Lord I ask for the healing in which I feel here to follow me back to Earth. Lord, this is for all of us who love You. You are coming soon for us, please reverse our death – our declining bodies, and give us the miracle of rejuvenation while we wait for You! Lord a man could have the wealth of the world, but if there is no cure for what ails him, then all he has is You! Please Lord, I ask for a miracle. Lord You placed an ear back on the head of a soldier from the enemy and restored his hearing, please Father heal us! I know I ask for a lot, but this to You is small. You move mountains, shake the Earth, You open the storehouses of snow and determine placement of stars. You give light to Day and the moon at Night – Please Lord send this healing rain to pour out over Your children while we wait. Lord, who am I to dine with the King, yet my requests for my friends to be healed are not heard? Please Father. I go back down and I suffer. Please Lord Deliver us from our dying bodies. I ask for the miracle of healing and the reversal of death while we wait. Make us youthful Lord. Don't allow us to stumble and fall Lord. Don't let the only way we can pick up our mats and follow You is by technology. Please Lord, Open Heavens over my friends. We Love You and now that I have seen You, I am forever changed. I will gladly sacrifice my request for my own healing if You would help all of them. Because You know me Lord – You knit me in my mother's womb. There is nothing hidden in me. I am Yours Lord!"

As I stood worshiping, I felt the Lord's hand on my head. I turned and I hugged Him. I wept as He held me for some time. I felt this amazing healing warmth as I cried on His shoulder. Without saying a word, He took my hand and led me through the Open Door into His Home. He didn't let me stop to take off my sandals. He took me right into His inner courtyard. I continued to cry. I hadn't felt like this ever! He walked me over to this beautiful little spring. He drew a cup of water out and tasted it. He smiled and gave me His Cup. I gulped it down.

Me: "I'm sorry Lord; this water is the most amazing water. I no longer thirst!"

He smiled and laughed. He took my hand and immediately we were on a bridge in the back of His home. There was this massive wall of chiseled stones of cut marble and this incredible flow of water out of 7 large rectangular holes in the massive wall. The sound was like Niagara Falls – massive! The power and outflow from this could light the cities of the west coast of the U.S. easily with hydro-electrical power.

He walked me to this over-look. He turned and put His thumbs over my eyes and held the back of my head. When I opened them, I saw Him smiling at me. He motioned for me to look. There with these amazing eyes, I could see with macro-super sight. Like panoramic binoculars, I rubbed my eyes. I could see perfectly! I could see Heaven from this Vantage Point. I'm not sure how I knew this, but I didn't just see a thousand hills, I saw the seven valley's surrounding each one! Seven valleys for each of the 1000 hills! I saw an ocean! I saw beaches, villages and beautiful estates. I saw amazing mansions of so many different styles. I saw amazing things in the air as well as the sea. It was beautiful. I was still crying as I realized I had only seen the Valley of God and His Garden, and the Valley in which I will dwell, but this – wow! He has truly prepared a place for us! He turned me to the East (Earth East, I had been looking West) and there I saw the City of Gold. It shone bright like the sun. The Lord waved His hand over my eyes and then I could see the walls, gates and City itself. I couldn't believe how beautiful it was! It was truly amazing. The jewels of the Ephod were inlaid in the foundation of the city. What relief as this was a wall surrounding this city which could never be breached by the enemy! The people who dwell in the City of God are free to go outside and do not have to fear the enemy! They are not prisoners!

The whole time the Lord Jesus was holding my hand. I was very small in stature to Him. I squeezed His hand and smiled. He squeezed mine and we were now at His balcony overlooking the Clock and Calendar of God! He waved His arm and set the Moon and stars in the pool surrounding the clock, and then He set the Sun and the stars of dawn and early evening in the in-between portions. Still nothing was said. I looked and saw that God's ring on the clock had become smaller as many more events had come and gone.

Me: "Lord there were many events removed from last week. It seems time has accelerated."

Jesus: "Erin again, My Father controls the speed. You have gone through a time period where there was a lull in activity – or at least what you perceived as a lull. God has a plan in place, but again, this does not mean every week there will be more and more. Some time frames, many events will be removed, and then there will be times where nothing will be."

Me: "Lord there was easily 30 events removed last week. I had no idea there was that much activity."

Jesus: "Just because you don't read it or see it in the news, doesn't mean it isn't an event on God's Calendar."

Me: "Lord, are You coming in April?"

Jesus: "Erin, I have told you to watch Israel, this is your gauge."

Me: "Lord, You granted me information one year ago which could be for this year. This year seems insignificant to me, but I am not sure."

Jesus: "Erin, You were shown that Earthly calendars cannot be trusted as accurate; only those appointed from Heaven's ambassadors can be valid. Remember Enoch – is from Heavenly places and walks with me. He is a friend of God and even the Fallen recognized and mocked him as "Father Time." God inspires man on Earth, but Enoch walked with God, then he was not, remember?"

Me: "Yes, I know that Enoch's calendar is a gauge Lord, but how do we know man hasn't modified that too?"

Jesus: "Good question. It is best to follow the moons and look to this and go back if necessary to measure it. This too is lengthy. Best to pray, look to God and watch Israel."

Me: "Or, I can just come up here?"

Jesus: Laughing, "Yes Erin you can. Now to answer your question about April, there are patterns. Watch the proposal and threats. Remember the enemy pattern of 9 months."

Me: "Lord, I need Your help with this number 9. I know in Islamic terms it means end of a contractual agreement, right?"

Jesus: "This is interesting, but not to be gauged. God is the gauge, and the pattern of the enemy is certainly a gauge also. So let's instead look at Israel. Erin there have been 27 documented Sieges in the Bible. We can use numbers as you know God's ring on the calendar is the 3rd and the number of judgments is 9."

Me: "Oh Wow, so 3 x 9 = 27!"

Jesus: "This is a pattern hidden in plain sight! Now you were told a year ago of the proposal of peace, right?"

Me: "Yes, I remember."

Jesus: "Now let's look at signs in Haggai 1:11 – There are 9 judgments here - This was given to Haggai: 'And I called for a drought upon the land, and upon the mountains, and upon the corn, and upon the new wine, and upon the oil, and upon that which the ground brings forth, and upon men, and upon cattle, and upon all the labor of the hands!'

Erin, there were even 9 people stoned, and 9 widows, 9 blind, & 9 with leprosy – There are patterns. Now God, my Father is a God of Precision, Righteous and Fair. He gives warning with murmuring but when all is complete and final after the nine comes – Judgment follows."

Me: "Lord but there is also mercy! Lord please there is 9 months of pregnancy. Even You were in the womb for this time, then You came to save us. Were not all of those afflicted also delivered from their afflictions! Did You not also cut down those who harmed them?"

Jesus: "Yes, to all Erin! You are correct. There is hope, but there must be a judgment carried out, concerning God's Land. It is God's. The entire world is free land, but this one is God's. Whoever seeks to divide, portion or even threatens to harm will bring judgment upon their own land."

Me: "Lord, the US is finally recovering from the last trouble. If God pours out His full wrath, none of us will escape it. Is it coming in April?"

Jesus: "Whether it comes at the end of April or even summer you should not be fearful Erin."

Me: "Lord, so this is the time frame? Will You come for us then Lord? If You don't, is there any way You can take me to Your courts so that I may appeal to God there? Lord You are my Kinsman Redeemer – You are my Lawyer, plead my case. Please bring judgment on the men involved but not the land or provisions! Oh please."

Jesus: "Erin, your prayers and petitions will be noted. Do not be afraid! God sends judgment, but He also loves and has mercy."

Me: "Yes Lord, but there were still 9 people who loved and yet were stoned!"

Jesus: "Erin, they dwell here and received much more than you could imagine. You will not be forgotten and neither will your friends and God's children. Just be clear that good men, God fearing men die in battle, yet they are never alone. God is there Erin."

Me: "Lord, so there will be casualties?"

Jesus: "Erin, yes, this is to be expected as their lives were mapped from the beginning. You must grieve for the lost not the found Erin! These things must occur. This is part of what you have been shown. You are not the only one who has seen this."

Me: "So Lord, we are like the Modern Day Babylon?"

Jesus: "Perhaps, again there are signs in scriptures. Come let's have communion." He squeezed my hand and instantly we were at His Gazebo table. The angels served warm bread leavened and unleavened and they poured wine in Jesus' Cup. He took the bread and broke it and handed me half. Then He tasted the wine. He then motioned for me to eat the bread. So I put some in my mouth.

Jesus: "Someday we will be all together at the Banquet and we will partake together. My friends come here and meet with Me and we enjoy communion here. Erin you won't believe who has sat in your chair next to Me!"

Me: "Lord oh my, I never thought of this. In Matthew 26:29, You said, "I tell you, I will not drink of this fruit of the vine from now on until that day when I drink it anew with you in my Father's Kingdom!" So this is just the Banquet, You have met with others like Peter here in this very spot!" I had a big grin!

Jesus: "Very good Erin, to the followers of the laws and traditions this is also a type of Seder, but for now it is communion with My friend Erin!"

Me: I began to cry, "Oh thank You Lord! I can never thank You enough."

Jesus: "Erin, it pleased Me and My Father how you worshiped us today! God's light shown upon you and now His Radiance is shone on your face!"

Me: "Lord, is it possible for You to grant me some of the healing rain or can You send this to my friends directly? Lord, if judgment is soon to occur, maybe even this summer and if You do not come we will need supernatural strength to endure this coming trouble. Please Lord I have some friends who need Your healing touch."

Jesus: "Erin do you believe I can?"

Me: "Lord oh yes, I believe You can do all things. I know You use the meek to silence the lions and even humble them. I know we are all used by You – even in desert places to help others with the good news of Your love! Please Lord I am begging. Lord the Sparrow is granted crumbs of communion bread at Your table. Lord, even a dog is given scraps – Then please Lord how much more would You give us?"

Jesus: "Erin, then it is done. Faith as a mustard seed! Your case is a good one. See what the Lord won't do on your behalf. Remember though to forgive your enemies, forgive those closest to you also but hold nothing against yourself either. Thereby cursing your body will not bring forth a blessing upon even if I made you into a 25 year old in appearance don't divide the blessing by cursing yourself. Humble yourself. Bless your temple. Take in that which is good. Your temple houses the Holy Spirit thereby it is a tabernacle! Be careful that those who are praying over you are not also cursing you by their words. A house divided cannot stand. Offer yourself as a living sacrifice. Erin, prepare your field – I will send the rain!" He smiled and put His hand over my hand.

Me: "Lord, I cannot blossom without Your Healing rain and sun."

Jesus: "Erin there is healing in the beams. As a sign I will send healing beams, and rainbows of promise through these storms. You will have confirmation of this."

Me: "Lord, rain Healing down and nourish us. Send the sun to bring warmth and strength. Do not scorch our land. Please Lord bless us!"

Jesus: "Erin you will be far removed from the desert. There I will find you and bring you home."

Me: "Lord, so You are not coming for us in April but there will be judgment?"

Jesus: "You are persistent. Please watch for signs. There is still much more that needs to occur. This is by God's design! Now you have been told you will be safe as well as your children. This is of great comfort right?"

Me: "Yes Lord, but I'm sad for my friends. You are including them too right?"

Jesus: "Erin, they are loved dearly and will be taken care of. Please take comfort. This is enough for today. Next time we will discuss what you saw here today. I have much to show you! You are loved! Please do not worry Erin. Please read about Eagles in Isaiah 40:31. I have a special blessing for you in Psalm 103. I will create a miracle if you allow me to."

Me: "Oh Lord please. I am ready for You to pour whatever You are led to pour into my vessel. I have nothing to lose, yet everything to gain!"

Jesus: He was laughing! "Very Good, Are you ready?"

Me: "Yes, Lord!"

He reached over and squeezed my hand!

Dream over…

Blessings to all….

Chapter 6 - Oceans and Almond Branch

Communion

Dear Father,

Thank You for a day of Divine Rest! This is such a blessing! Thank You for my family!

I am like a Farmer and my children a field. There are days, Lord, in which I feel I am tending to briars in my field, yet when I clear away the debris there are flowers and rich vines. Thank You for reminding me that I make a difference in their lives. Lord, I am grateful for loved ones. I am grateful for the voice of love when I have had such a difficult week. I thank You, Lord, for Your Voice. You call to me, and every day I am forever changed by Your Goodness.

Lord, please consider me Your field. Please consider me an Orchard. Oh, how I long to produce good fruit! Lord, I don't have much here, but with You, I have everything! You are the House I live in; Your foundation is Holy, and the walls You have built encompass me with love. The roof over my head is Your Cover! Even though I own no Earthly Home, You have provided a place for me! Thank You for blessing me! I love You so much!

"Erin – Come Up!"

I stood on His front doorstep today, looking out at this amazing Valley of God. Spring was in the air. The beautiful mist was over His Home, and there were sporadic soft downpours of rain over different portions of the landscape. It was morning. There was a particular fragrance defining the time of day. The sky was aglow in pink. The sun streamed in again at several highlighted areas. I saw the olive groves with a ray of light. I saw the pasture by the river with the sheep ... giggles ... and the sleeping lion. Today, the lion was curled up like a cat. I was giggling at this...

Then my eyes were drawn to a very snowy area on one of the mountains, with a frozen lake. I asked the Holy Spirit to zoom me in. Then my eyes had supernatural micro-lenses, as if I were overseeing the area from about twenty feet. I saw the most amazing sight. There were White Sea lion cubs sleeping on their backs, three together. Their paws were faced upward in praising positions, and their bellies were exposed. They had big grins on their faces – they were completely at peace. Then my eyes went to the right, and there I saw the most incredible sight. A large polar bear was laying the same way. It must have been twelve feet in length, stretched out belly-up in praise position. It didn't look at all like it was about to snack on the cute baby seals. I began to have tears as I realized that Heaven is a place of complete peace – shalom. There won't be blood staining the snow here! I was shaking my head in amazement!

The sun beamed through like streams over these areas. There were all kinds of different flocks of birds circling in the sky and dancing. I saw long ribbons of color created from their synchronized flight together. I began to praise God for this. This was the Promised Land! I sang "Holy, Holy, Holy... Lord God Almighty, Early in the morning my song shall rise to Thee." Then I lifted my hands in full worship. I praised Him! All that He creates is Perfected Here in this Place! I am safe here under His Canopy!

I sat down on His front step for some time. I sang a new song by Hillsong – "Oceans." I closed my eyes, as I heard choirs of angels singing harmony for this in the House of God. Tears began to stream as I thought of the lyrics to this song, and my special season with God! "You call me out upon the waters, the great unknown where feet may fail. And there I find You in the mystery. In Oceans deep, my faith will stand. And I will call upon Your Name and keep my eyes above the waves. When oceans rise, my soul will rest in Your embrace, for I am Yours and you are mine." The sun broke through over me as I thanked God for everything. I was sitting on the Lord's front doorstep just worshiping, when I felt Jesus' hand on my right shoulder. I stood up to hug Him. He held me for some time. Then He said, "Let's stay here for a while." He sat me back down next to Him on this beautiful step. I was still crying.

Jesus: "Erin, please don't stop your singing! There is more to this song. What comes next?"

Me: "Lord, I'm embarrassed to sing before You. I am not a very good..." Just as He put His finger to my lips, I felt a sting of warmth like an electric charge. Then I felt a change in my throat. My throat felt like it was coated in Honey.

Jesus: "Now, sing with your new voice."

I was hesitant, but all of a sudden the song coming from my heart welled up in my throat, and then it spilled forth. "Your grace abounds in deepest waters; Your Sovereign Hand will be my guide where feet may fail and fear surrounds me. You've never failed and You won't start now. So I will call upon Your name and keep my eyes above the waves. When oceans rise, my soul will rest in Your embrace, for I am Yours and You are mine." I was in shock. I was singing acapella with perfect pitch. Now my tears were streaming.

Me: "Lord, this is amazing. Will I be able to sing like this here?"

Jesus: "Would you like to?"

Me: "Yes, but it is like writing to me. I am not confident or very skilled at it at all."

Jesus: "This is interesting here – look how much I have called you to write. Did I not also enable you to sing?"

Me: "Yes… can I sing like this on Earth, too?"

Jesus: "Well, this is not to be your focus, but I can strengthen your muscles so you remember Me when you sing."

Me: "Oh, Lord, You are right. I would think too highly of myself as a singer. I would be more interested in edifying myself on Earth then, and would become self-aware and far removed from worship to You."

Jesus: "We can't add more critics to your long list, Erin. As it stands, you are going to have trouble from critics because of Me – we don't need to add voice critics too, right?"

Me: "Yes, critics carry chains, and keep us held prisoner by their disbelief in Your miracles."

Jesus: "You are welcome to display your voice in praise and worship anytime, Erin. This is good – dedicate all of your gifts to God and

He will give you the desires of your heart! Now, why did I have you sing the next portions of that beautiful song?"

Me: "Lord, I think of You and God on the Throne, because You have called me outside of my comfort zone into the unknown. You called me out onto the waves of a vast ocean to follow You. The seas have been choppy and the waves high. When my feet have failed me, I have fallen into the deep water. At times, I barely see above the waves, as my head goes under.

"I call out to You and Your Hand saves me. Lord, here in Heaven You placed my feet upon the peaceful shores. Here, I rest in Your arms! Here, I am forever saved by Your Presence. I am in awe at Your Glory. I am humbled by Your Grace. I could work on a thousand hills, harvesting grapes even in seven thousand valleys. I could work my fingers to the bone – but I could never repay You for what You have done for me!"

Jesus: He hugged me. "Erin, you are not a slave. You are free. I came to set the captives free!"

Me: "Yes, Lord, but You have captured my heart, and I am a slave to God and Heaven! I was bought for a price, Lord! You purchased me! I am so thankful! I could've been purchased by the Blacksmith."

Jesus: "No, Erin, his offer couldn't stand up. Although he requested you and captured you for a time period, I paid the ransom for you! You are Mine! You are a Child of God!

Me: "Sometimes on Earth, I feel I am a slave to the Blacksmith."

Jesus: "Well, he might try to oppress you or make you feel hopeless – this is his limitation – but you are free, not his slave! You are bound by his words only when they are absorbed – remember your ears, the anvil and hammer. Remember – hear My Voice! The Holy Spirit is in you! The Holy Spirit resides in the deep waters of your soul, Erin. The enemy can't find you there! The Holy Spirit will keep your head above the waves. Now, there is more troubling you."

Me: "There is too much to discuss. I need to put this behind me."

Jesus: "Why would you want your troubles following you from behind? Let's dismiss them now. What is happening?"

Me: "Lord, two old journals were poking out of my journal storage – a red one from the end of 2010-11, and a purple one from the end of 2011. At first I saw them. I wondered why they were poking out; then You began to call me back to them. I picked up the red one first. It is so pretty; I began to read it. The pain I felt was recorded in my pen-strokes. During this time, I was in a brutal custody battle. It came without warning, and I was brutally attacked. I thought I would lose my children, because I had no money to fight. I couldn't sleep. I could barely eat. I went to various churches for prayer. I explained what I needed prayer for, and I was treated as if I somehow deserved to lose my children.

"One church asked me if I had used drugs or alcohol or had an affair. When I told them no – it was because of my heart – they didn't believe me. One pastor said, 'It is unlikely the courts would take children away from their mother for a reason like this.' I was discouraged. As he prayed over me, it was insincere and doubtful – as if I were a liar. I stopped asking for prayer. I was alone and in great despair. If I had not come to this desert, and I had just stayed where the church and courts knew the story, it would never have happened like this. Then justice would've been done, and I wouldn't have had so much grief!"

Jesus: "Erin, why do you think I brought those journals up?"

Me: "I guess to see how far You have carried me?"

Jesus: "This is true, but not the whole picture. Erin, you became impatient and wanted your sons back after your surgery. They were taken and not returned as agreed. Remember? It was a broken contract. Now, you didn't hear from God in a 'timely' manner, so you acted. You didn't let God lead. You stepped out to walk on a turbulent Ocean, and expected God to be there."

Me: "So You let me fall? Lord, I lost almost everything, and almost lost my children, too."

Jesus: "Erin, that little red journal is filled with deep anguish. You cannot even read it without weeping. God knew in advance about this season. Now, what happened in your purple journal?"

Me: "I began to see God go before me, as I was at the end of myself. There was no more of me. I had sleepless nights. My heart felt as if it were failing. I couldn't breathe. I would gasp for air, but I couldn't find it. I was so grief stricken as no one would hear my case. No one stood for me. I had no means yet I didn't qualify for help. I made too much but not enough! Every day I waited for the next wave of lies to hit me. I wept like a child. When I thought the punishment was finally over, another paper was filed against me and another wave of attacks came. (I am crying as I write.) I was emptied. I was a slave to an unjust system, where only money wins!"

Jesus: "There is one more thing!"

Me: "Yes, after I finally won, I was stripped of all my valuables. I sold my gold and silver – anything I had of any value was sold. I'd have given everything for my children. Then we had no money. I had my kids but no money, we were bankrupt. Then one last thing happened in May 2012. It was the final blow. I drowned in my tears – well almost. Do You remember this night Lord 5/25/2012?"

Jesus: "Yes, Erin the sound of your wailing hit the ceiling above God's Throne. You were heard!" (I was crying on Jesus' shoulder.) Erin, you had people petitioning for you here who you would never imagine. God heard your cries!"

Me: "I was completely drained. I was alone here. On 5/28/2012 – Memorial Day I wished I was dead, I would have more honor! Lord, if I had sinned, if I had done the things I was accused of and later vindicated of – then I would have understood – but this? This was wrong! Why was justice never served here? Why?"

Jesus: "I understand the depth of your pain Erin. You felt abandoned and forsaken. You were tired. You were robbed and left in shame. You were humiliated. This is difficult to understand, but this was allowed. Can you understand why?"

Me: "I have to believe it is so I could be made whole again! Lord, how can one simple poor decision affect the lives of so many? If I could only go back but I cannot."

Jesus: "Why are you going back to a mistake you made as the sole reason for all of this? Am I the Punisher? Is God My Father the executioner of His children? No, this is the mistake in your thinking. Come, it is time to come! First you will have refreshments then we will go to My Father on the Throne!"

He squeezed my hand and walked me through His open door. We walked down the entry. (I was quickly reminded, who I was walking with.) Then we went through the entry into His Inner Courtyard. He took me past God's Clock and Calendar to the small well-spring. There He filled a cup of water and took a sip. Refilled it then gave it to me to drink from the same side. I was still blubbering with tears.

Me: "Oh Lord, I'm so sorry! Am I in trouble?"

Jesus: He had the most beautiful loving face. "Erin don't you know how valuable you are? Don't you see your own great worth, Come here!" He stands to His feet and looks around. He sees the gazing pool surrounding God's Clock and Calendar. He waves His arm and sets the reflect ion of the moon and stars. Then He waves His arm again and sets the reflection of the sun. He walks me to the night side. There we kneel. "Erin do you see your reflection here?"

Me: "Yes Lord, my silhouette."

Jesus: "Good, now let's go to the day side." There I saw my reflection. I was in such a beautiful outfit. I had beautiful adornments. My glorified face was so beautiful; it was difficult to take in. I was still crying! "Do you see your reflection?"

Me: "Yes, Lord!"

Jesus: "Now, Come!" He squeezes my hand and we are on the balcony above the clock. We look down and I could see my reflection still in the day and silhouette in the night.

Me: "Oh – I am still reflected there!"

Jesus: "Erin, you are in my thoughts both day and night. Erin the gift in Psalms 103 is there. Erin read Ephesians 1:3, Revelation 3:20, Psalm 1:1-6, Jeremiah 29, Isaiah 49, Isaiah 41, and Psalm 8:3. Erin, go to Genesis 1:14-18, there is a deeper meaning here for you, hidden in plain sight. You are loved by Me! I would give up my life just for you alone."

Me: "Then why Lord? Why all of this? Remove the enemy in our life now and bring us home here where we can see You and be free!"

Jesus: "Oh, Erin, how I long to be with you. There is a greater battle occurring in the hearts of man! It is not finished yet! God must complete His Good Work. It is not for man to try to understand because this is a battle won in hearts. You must be patient a while longer"

Me: "Lord, more events have been removed, can't I ask for clarity" I will be an old woman when You come for us."

Jesus: He was laughing, "Well define old? You are certainly wiser, are you not?"

Me: "Yes, but we are all trying to figure out the proper calendar and timing so at least we will know your patterns based on the proper Enoch calendar."

Jesus: "Erin there are even arguments about the time of the week of Shabbat. This was a sacred time of rest commanded by God and even I observed it, yet a certain church determined that they were holding more authority than the Word of God. How does this happen? I will tell you all was foretold.

"Look in Daniel 7:25. I quote this for you as this is important proof when understanding timing and corruption of this. 'He will speak out against the Most High and wear down the saints of the Highest One, and he will intend to make alterations in times and law, and they will be given into his hand for a time, times, and half a time!'"

Me: "Lord! What does all of this mean? It is controversial!"

Jesus: "Erin, the enemy is the author of confusion; he tries to re-write history and confuse. You understand the 'shell game' right?

Well in Heaven there is a seed under – every shell. On Earth there is no seed under; no winner ever. It is a guessing game of the highest order controlled by your enemy. Now, only by Heavenly wisdom are you given revelation. So you have proof about the author of confusion. Pray for revelation! You are on the right course concerning the calendar. Now, as foretold by Daniel, there is a limit to the enemy's timing. So please know that, and be confident that God is a God of Justice and the fulfillment of prophecy. Remember it takes the Glory of God to conceal a matter…"

Me: "…And the Honor of kings to search it out!"

Jesus: Laughing, "Now though, pray for Israel. The enemy is trying to rewrite history using the proof of the fallen and the tribes of their origins as a hidden clue. Remember the Jebusites, Canaanites, etc.? Well, one has only to research even further to see the origins of these to know who the father of this enemy is. You were shown this last year and how they followed the Israelites from Egypt. Pray Erin – Books removed from the Bible can confirm some of this. These are referenced in scripture and are also a pointer to clues and more."

Me: "Lord these books are controversial."

Jesus: "And why and who was controlling this? Erin, to use these as reference when they are clearly mentioned in scripture is no accident. When an investigative reporter researches, he must research all the evidence – even a judge is legally sworn to do this. They must weigh all evidence to grant a fair judgment. This is wisdom like Solomon.

"Now it is up to a Godly judge to make known his evidence; a Godly judge is sworn in by God Himself, and will be held accountable by God, if all truth is not revealed. There is no deception or corruption here. Now, why do I say this? Simple, there is wisdom in research. God reveals and provides revelation when something is applicable. There is more to the story Erin. The same is your case. You only know your side and are accountable to God for your actions, but God sees all sides and knows more of what was hidden from you. Do not worry as there will be justice concerning you and your children. You were not forgotten. Now, come with me, God My Father has something to say!"

He reaches over, squeezes my hand and we are immediately at the Sea of Glass. For a moment I'm afraid. I wonder if I have miss-spoke.

Jesus: "Erin, your thoughts – take these captive, you are not in trouble. I have called you my friend, please trust me!"

I squeezed His hand. Before me was the most amazing glass floor, it was deep blue like an ocean. There were massive archways with columns. In the distance I saw risers of chiseled–translucent marble or quartz. I couldn't see beyond this as my eyes were not able to behold the sight. Then Jesus put salve in my eyes. He looked at me and smiled.

Jesus: "I have a surprise for you."

Just then, I felt a cover drop over my shoulders. I looked from side to side and there was Enoch and Elijah. Jesus was laughing. I hugged Enoch. Enoch had long wavy white hair; he was wearing layers of clothing. He looked ancient as if he were the wisest prophet. There was wisdom and knowledge in his eyes. I can't explain this. His skin was tan and golden. He had brilliant blue eyes. His eye brows were white which made me laugh. He had a very trim white beard also. He had a shofar on a beautiful braided cord strapped on his shoulders. He looked as if he were on a journey or going on one. His face was so kind yet he seemed younger in age than I did if skin is a gauge.

Elijah had a cover over his head. His hair was shorter, above shoulder length. He looked like a Rabbi. He was in white and had a type of scarf with fringe. He was more serious. His eyes were green and caramel colored and they were quite striking. He has a walking stick, like a branch, but beautiful! I was chuckling because it looked like a small flower was growing from the branch. It was a blossoming almond branch. Elijah was funny. He is very serious, but with a very dry sense of humor. His personality was very much like one of my Jewish friend's father. I think he liked me.

Jesus: "Erin, Elijah likes you do not worry." I was embarrassed…

Enoch: "Yes Erin, Elijah is perfectly Elijah." Elijah kind of silently chuckled, cracking a small smile as he took his walking stick and tapped Enoch on the leg.

Elijah: "My apologies my Lord, oh yes and Erin, there is much to do."

Enoch: "Yes and he worries a lot."

Jesus: "Well right now, I need your faithful witness as the King's daughter is feeling battered by ocean waves!" He smiled. I was quiet and quite humbled to be in this place at this moment. I was elated and I had tears.

Enoch: "Do not cry Erin. You have come a long way since I first was called to meet you. Elijah, told you to die to yourself remember?"

I then remembered my extreme fast when I was caught up in a vision. The vision: "I had died when my motorcycle went out of control and the last thing I saw was black top. I hated motorcycles so this was a stretch to be riding one again. The year was 2000 when I had the vision".

Elijah: "Yes, when I saw you I was discouraged. You even had designer pajamas." He shook his head.

Jesus: "Yes, Elijah has come before the Throne of God a few times when meeting various people God has selected for certain things." He was laughing. "Erin, let's put it this way. You were very worldly at this point so it was difficult for Elijah to imagine God using you for such a task. God rebuked Elijah when he showed him what you would become and how He was going to get you here." I was speechless.

Enoch: "I knew all along Erin! You were perfect from the beginning. I saw God's vision."

Elijah: "Okay you two. Yes I must admit, I didn't think she would get this far, a few dropped off as you both know, so I didn't see the same vision."

Jesus: "Elijah, are you still having trust issues after all this time has elapsed?" Jesus was kidding with him.

Elijah: "Oh Lord, I am still stubborn but You love this about me right? At least God appreciates me." They were all laughing – It was a priceless moment. I observed 3 friends laughing and truly enjoying each other. I was with my Savior before the Throne of God. I will be forever changed!

Jesus: "Erin, you have a question, please ask."

Me: "Yes, Lord! Elijah has an almond branch and it is blossoming, what does this mean?" When I saw him in 2000 this was not blossoming!"

Jesus: "Great observation! Do you know that it has been exactly 14 years to the day when you met them? (February 23, 2000) Now the almond tree is the first to blossom and the last to drop leaves."

Enoch: "Erin, the almond branch was used for temple menorahs."

Elijah: "Look Erin!" He drew my attention to the area near the Throne – there I saw a 7 branch menorah it was an almond branch design cast in gold, the shape of the lotus–like blossom of the almond branch.

Jesus: "This is a sign Erin, of the time and season we are in. There has been two 7 year periods from 2000. This is significant for you."

Me: "I don't understand?"

Enoch: "Erin, this is measured on the 5th ring – you can see this."

Me: "Lord, what is my task? What are these dreams going to do to help people? The Jewish people won't even consider a Christian worthy of a message of hope let alone a female. How can I be of use? I am not worthy to even stand before any of you. Elijah, I still own designer pajamas! I am in a very superficial profession. I am bankrupt. I am a woman raising children in a country so far from God, how can I make a difference?"

Elijah: "Lord, here she goes. She is questioning Your choice, even God's choice. (He was chuckling.)

Jesus: "Erin is this true; after all you have been through?"

Me: "Lord, forgive me for my lack. I need help here. As the waves of the ocean crash over me one by one, I can't see the horizon line. I don't have faith like a mustard seed. There is something wrong with me. Do I need a sign?"

Enoch: "Erin, we have all been where you are. Do not worry. Your faith and love for God has gotten you here. Very, very few people have ever been where you are, at least on your side of Heaven from an earthly perspective."

Elijah: "Yes, at least you were invited to dine with Jesus. We were not called up to dine with the King – okay maybe Enoch was!"

Enoch: "No, I don't remember getting an invitation to dine with you Lord. Hmmm..."

Jesus: "Okay you two. Erin they have both been over to My House – they are joking with you. Now, we are here today to encourage you!"

Me: "Lord, I'm afraid am I about to come into trouble? Where have both of you been for the last year? Am I about to be called home? Is trouble coming to Israel now?"

Jesus: "Erin these questions are good, as you are coming into a time of blessings. I know you have been looking back over your trouble. This was for a purpose. You have been chastised and pressed as an olive from the vine. The dross has been removed and you will remain like this until you are called home."

Me: "Lord, won't I be in the rapture?"

Jesus: "Is the shofar sounding, not a call? Please Erin, have faith. Now, for your sake I have called witnesses to view the covenant I will make with you. Then God my Father will bless you. Are you ready?"

Me: "Yes, Lord."

Jesus: "I have been with you Erin from the beginning. I sent angels concerning you. You were God's from the beginning. Your life has been a series of trials like waves in a tumultuous sea. A few times you went under, but each time I was there with you. I know you look at your life as a series of failures and missed opportunities, but I tell you the truth they had a purpose. Each one drew you closer and closer to the woman you have become.

"Erin you are worthy. You are worthy to be used of God. You never saw too much joy on Earth. The enemy requested to sift you as wheat. Well, your sifting is over! I know that you have lost years of your youth as you went through these intense trials, but now your heart is refined. You will now be as a youth. You will laugh at the days which have past. You will no longer worry about tomorrow. You will dance as you did in your youth. The branches of your life which the stripping locusts destroyed will now begin to blossom. By a miracle you will be like a well-watered tree whose roots will be nourished by the River of Life.

"The enemy coming against you now until I come for you will be as nothing, as his schemes will be thwarted. The burdens you have experienced have been a yoke now lifted. You will pray for others and your prayers will be answered. I am about to do something that you would not even believe even if you were told. Remember to bless those who curse you, as I will bless those who bless you and remove those who curse you. Now this will be healing for your children also. This also means your friends and family too. They too will be blessed.

"Now your suffering will come to an end. Your time remaining will bring you great joy. You will still be hated as many of us are, but none as much as Me and I came to save. You will want to pray for Elijah and Enoch and their assignments, they are ready for the time is coming upon us. Do not worry about tomorrow Erin, you will be carried through the storms. The waves will not overcome you. Now remember what scriptures were highlighted by light in the Garden of God. This too will bring comfort."

Me: "Lord, will I ever see You again?"

Jesus: "Erin the dreams are not over. This is a special blessing and covenant I am making with you. It is a contract! This is binding. Close your eyes!" I felt 3 hands on me as I dropped to my knees. I felt an earthquake and a deep groaning in my body as every cell within me awakened by an electric charge of warmth. Then I heard a voice like thunder and running water.

God: "Erin, Come forth!" The Lord brought me up onto my feet. I was shaking. The Lord calmed me.

Jesus: "It's okay Erin, step out on faith by invitation."

God: "Erin, My blessing is upon you! Your enemies will be removed! With you I am well pleased! You bring Me joy and laughter! You are My friend and My child! Your heart is good! Do not worry! Nothing but your love is required! (Tears were streaming down my face. I was overwhelmed.) Soon you will be granted a Divine Gift from Me and special to you as a sign I am pleased. You are loved!"

Jesus lifted me up and hugged me. "Erin My Father's love for you is as wide as the ocean is deep, but even more if you can fathom it. Find Joy! I love you! See you very soon!"

Dream over…

Chapter 7 - God's Numbers

Communion

Dear Father,

Thank You for another day! Thank You for all that we have! Thank You for my children, family and friends! I have been so blessed! Lord here I am – I dwell in the desert, but You found me here. You have nourished me in a very dry place. I can never thank You enough for Your love! Thank You for using me and providing for me. Giggles – Although I am a worker in the cave of my job – my least favorite birds – the crows feed me there. Each paycheck is fed by You bit by bit just enough to remain here. You provide enough to sustain.

Lord thank You for the time removed from my cave as just for a short time I had rest apart from this; a time to be thankful, think without squawking sounds of crows and dream uninterrupted. It was divinely worth it! My first real vacation in 17 years! Lord, I pray my next vacation be with You, but I know there is sometime yet to go. I had a calm week at work up until the last couple of days, then so much happened. I noticed quickly that this was also personal as I watched the enemy come at me personally on his pattern of attack. He is relentless. I discovered something that was so diabolical which confirmed something hidden from my past – that I can barely grasp the magnitude of the evil.

Lord, You have exposed something in which I am struggling to comprehend and why now if You are not about to do something extremely "God" around this. Lord, I lay my burdens down. Lord I ask for Divine protection over my children. I ask for Divine protection over me. Lord, let the enemy never have another victory in my life. Let every instruction be by Your gentle hands! Please Lord never give me over again to the enemy's schemes! I ask for Divine protection over those who have no idea about these schemes. I ask Lord that You would expose this so even those who cursed me in the past will one day give gratitude and even apologize. Lord please go ahead of us, as You are our God. My heart is forever Yours and I am consumed by Your Love. The burning desire in me is the passion I have to run after You. Therefore, Lord I trust that You will go before me. I give this all to You, Lord! I love You!

Jesus: "Erin Come Up!"

I was immediately up and sitting on one of the steps leading to His front door! I jumped up because I wanted to see Him. As I went to turn He was on the step above me.

Jesus: "Erin where are you going, please there is no hurry. I have come to sit beside you first, and then we will go inside!"

He motioned for me to sit back down. He held my right hand and He sat right next to me. He reached with His left arm over my shoulder and I went to hug Him resting my head on His shoulder for just a moment.

Me: "I missed You so much Lord!"

Jesus: "When did you go from me? I believe I was with you on vacation, wasn't I?" He was laughing.

Me: I was laughing, "Yes Lord of course, but I mean these visits. You spoke to me continuously and I dreamed, but I miss this time of visions and journaling!"

Jesus: "Did you think I was like a crow? They do squall, well nag really. Did you think I did this to you?" He was laughing.

Me: "Oh no Lord. I wondered at times if I'd hear from You again. You were quite, but You were there."

Jesus: "Now I can't be confused here, did I tell you a time of rest is removal or renewal?"

Me: "Oh You're funny – Renewal."

Jesus: "So time to look-up the definition of Renewal. This is a strong word and one in which I used concerning your time of rest. How do you feel?"

Me: "I felt fantastic up until late in the day on Wednesday (March 19th), then the attacks came."

Jesus: "Yes Erin, true there was a reason for these. I am aware of them but these will come to nothing. Now, what happened during your time?"

Me: "I think You are preparing me for something. My dreams were very unusual, but very clear. I felt a pull to do things in my spirit as if I was ready to do what You would call me to do at a moment's notice – (I giggled) – I was ready for service!"

Jesus: "Very Good! This is a good place to be, tell Me more."

Me: "I feel refreshed. Like a fresh fire has come over me?"

Jesus: "Erin, please explain fresh fire? You cannot have this."

Me: "Lord, I'm confused; my heart has a burning desire for You. I feel my love for You is like a flame."

Jesus: "Erin, you are like a lamp. You shine like a star! You are a light as darkness longs to have your wick burn out. This is why you were given rest in the first place. Your lamp needed fresh oil. Now you are ready. This is by God's design! You are a child of God! Now do not confuse your burning desire as consuming fire. Fire is meant to consume the living dead or even the dross. Remember that wheat fields are burned; the dead stalks are burned so the ground can be tilled and replanted. Look at the examples of fire in My Word. It is of judgment! What happens after fire comes?"

Me: "Well, when I was having my time of rest I saw a few homes which had portions that had burned. Two homes were being restored. One large one I could tell the restoration would be much better. One home was too burned; it was a total loss and needed to be torn down. Seeing these homes, I felt a loss and sorrow. I avoid fire. I am not even fascinated by it."

Jesus: "Yes Erin, I remember why! Do you?"

Me: "Yes Lord, I was about 11 years old. My parents were burning candles. The rock music in our house was extremely loud. It was summer time but late at night. A wind came through the windows and blew some feathers in a vase over the flame of a candle. Within seconds there was a very large fire. I ran to the kitchen and grabbed a pan of soapy water. Then my parents grabbed water when they heard me screaming. Our wall was burned and the smell was horrible and it never went away. I hate fire!"

Jesus: "Then your fear is valid. Fire is not easily controlled, but it easily consumes everything in its path. One day My Father will consume the Earth with fire. Do you understand why?"

Me: "I think because He will reshape it, reform it and most importantly burn away all the old, making everything new." I smiled and squeezed His hand. "When You came, Lord You brought new life. Look at me, I was a pile of ashes burned continuously – You created something from nothing but ashes."

Jesus: "Very good Erin. Come, before I take you to see the Calendar, I have a beautiful place to take You, Come!" He squeezed my hand and we were on the forestry path!

Me: "Oh Lord, I thought I recognized this! It is so beautiful here! Is this in Heaven? I saw a photo of this – was I in Belgium in Halle Forest or here?"

Jesus: "Very good Erin, you were in a special room, a secret place of learning. You were in Heaven, but not here. It is difficult to understand but one day it will make sense. Now, this is a replica is it not?"

I looked around me; the forest floor was all bluebells. The sun streamed through silver and white tree trunks. The bark was silver and luminous. As your eye looked further up the path it looked like a sea of purple. The leaves on the trees were lime green – well every shade of green. As we walked the fragrance was so wonderful. It was so fresh. It smelled like fresh rain, forest, jasmine, and grass. It made my eyes mist up. I was speechless. It was one of the most beautiful places I have ever seen!

Me: "Lord, this is so much better than any place on Earth – this takes my very breath away!"

Jesus: "Well, remember Heaven breathes life, it doesn't remove it! Erin, this forest is special to God. This is part of My Father's Garden. There are forests like this on some of your friend's properties here. They grew up near the earthly version of this place and long to be there. Of course they will have the glorified version like you see here."

After He spoke I heard the sounds of mourning doves and some song birds. In the distance across the path I saw a large peacock walk with its fan spread!

Me: "Lord. Peacocks are so beautiful. How can God Glorify even these?"

Jesus: "Remember things on Earth are remnants of Heavenly things not vice versa, so look!"

He reached down into some bluebells and picked up a very large peacock feather. It was much more beautiful. The entire feather was iridescent in all of my favorite colors. It was stunning.

Jesus: "Erin, look over here!"

In the distance I saw a beautiful white peacock. It was one of the most beautiful birds I had ever seen. It popped out of the blue bells.

Me: "Lord this in incredible – truly incredible! Thank You for this! Heaven is so full of wonder. How can we even contain it? There is more beauty here, just in this one place than even all of earth! This is paradise!"

Jesus: "Yes, even God has a sense of humor, look how He dressed a chicken! Even Solomon was amazed."

Me: "A peacock is a chicken?"

Jesus: "Yes a variety!" Jesus was laughing.

Me: "I would think it closer to a turkey… Wow!" We continued walking. The sounds, smells and beauty were amazing. At times I'd see something and I would begin to cry.

Jesus: "Erin do you remember what happens to forests after they burn?"

Me: "Yes I went to a forestry management retreat with Project Wild when I was in college. I remember they talked about the loss of forestry land, animals and birds. It is devastating. Most start from lightening. I do know that the forest will spring new life again though almost immediately. The soil becomes rich with minerals, etc. It just takes a very long time to regrow it."

Jesus: "Sometimes fires are good, but this too is difficult to understand."

Me: "I know that You are not sending strange fire to us to demonstrate Your power. I do however love the blanket of warmth from Your mantel." I was laughing.

Jesus: "Again remember that God will not go against His Word. Fire was usually judgment in the Bible. Now, I brought you here to show you a familiar place." Just then we walked around a bend and off to the left was this beautiful pond, with weeping willows and blossoms everywhere. There were fountains and groomed grass.

Me: "Lord, whose home is this?"

Jesus: "You are still in God's Garden." We came upon the Forestry Board. There were tags with numbers 1 thru 9.

Me: "Oh wow – Lord You are amazing! I recognize this. It has been a year. These are new numbers."

Jesus: "No Erin, those numbers you had a year ago still have meaning, perhaps not always on your timing. God speaks in many different ways, but all things have significance and perfect order. Even the smallest of numbers are important. Look at 1. One is the most important yet rarely taken into account."

Me: "1 is the beginning or God right?"

Jesus: "Yes, Aleph or Alpha, the Beginning. The first is the only! There cannot be two firsts! What is the first commandment Erin?"

Me: "Love the Lord God with all your heart, soul, mind and strength!"

Jesus: "Yes but before this the declaration is made, "The Lord our God is ONE Lord! There is so much more to this too. Let's look at the number two."

Me: "Does two mean division Lord?"

Jesus: "It can, you can see this occur by God on the second day of creation. Two usually means good vs evil. Also though, it means separation. There is more in the Word about this. Take number three." I reached up and picked up the number 3 tag off of the hook.

Me: "I know this number Lord, 3 means the Trinity!"

Jesus: "Yes, good, but there is even more to this Erin. If you were a math genius you could find this makes a solid and works as a binding agent as a measure. It can represent time; past, present, and future. It can represent thought, words and deed – this is important."

Me: "Lord, Your angels always sing Holy, Holy, Holy!" He was laughing!

Jesus: "Yes they do! You are correct! It is a Divine Number of God! There is also a scripture that 3 strands of a cord are not easily broken. This is also a marriage contract with God. Three days is also significant. Now there is more here too. Pick up number 4, what do you think of?"

Me: "Since I am not a numbers person I would say simply $1 + 3 = 4$. Then I see there are 4 angels guarding God's Clock and Calendar, North, South, East, and West. Then I think of Earth, Air, Fire, and Water."

Jesus: "Very good. There are also 4 seasons and four lunar phases. There are signs coming in relation to this also."

Me: "Lord can I make an observation?"

Jesus: "Yes Erin, please."

Me: "I saw God's Garden divided into quadrants, with seasons."

Jesus: "Very good, yes you are correct. There are 4 Cherubim also."

Me: "Lord, are those large angels guarding the Clock, Cherubim?"

Jesus: "Interesting question. What did you see? I'll tell you what, let's come back here again. I will take you back to the courtyard and you can look at them yourself!" He reached down and squeezed my hand. Instantly I was on the overlook looking down over God's Clock. All 4 angels looked up at us. I began to laugh as they smiled and waved.

Me: "No Lord these are not Cherubim. They have the normal beautiful angel faces, not faces of animals."

Jesus: "Erin these angels you see here are very significant too, and high ranking. The Cherubim were not created in the image of God. The Cherubim are by the Throne of God and are awaiting God's instructions. They will one day announce the judgments and these are always related to creation. These 4 angels here will report and announce completion when the Calendar finalizes. If you notice, we are drawing nearer, every day!" I looked down and what I saw was astonishing.

Me: "Lord, those are the Blood moons. Why did I not notice these before?"

Jesus: "These were there all along Erin! This hasn't changed. You just didn't notice this before."

Me: "Lord, I cannot read what I am seeing, but it looks like these are the start of the time of the end. Lord, You gave me the number "40" – 3 times when I woke up the other day. You said "40 pause, 40 pause, 40! Is this 40 days, 40 weeks or 40 months?"

Jesus: "Erin you were given a dream last year in May about June. I believe it was in May. You thought it was for that time yet you didn't look at the events which had to occur prior to this June date. You need only to go to scripture to read that which must occur first. The blood moons are a sign and have a particular history for Israel behind them. Have I not said to pray for your sister? Now remember God has brought His people closer to Him from trials. These are God's chosen people and this land of Israel is God's. Watch and see what comes from this – this is wisdom!"

Me: "Lord I'm afraid. This is a clear visible sign that I can actually see. Based on the fact that this will be the last Blood Moon cycle for 500 years then, I must believe, this is the last group for us!"

Jesus: "I think things are accelerating faster than 500 years. You can see this based on the Clock right?"

Me: "Yes. What of the number 5, Lord?"

Jesus: "Erin it is a number of multiples and ingredients. Study this. We will discuss the remaining numbers again!" I looked downcast. "Erin what is wrong?"

Me: "Lord this is a serious time with You. I'm not sure about all of this. I feel unsettled."

Jesus: "Please don't worry Erin, time to eat some great food!" I looked down as I saw each of the 4 angels laughing to themselves.

Me: "Did I miss something Lord? What is so funny?"

Jesus: "Erin, you are the one being so serious today. You are acting like you are on a very serious quest. Oh yes I know, you are hoping for the big Reveal after your break."

Me: "Well yes, I was kind of hoping for that!" I was embarrassed because even the angels saw this in me! "I'm sorry Lord. You gave me some intense dreams. I guess I was expecting some major information." Jesus was laughing.

Jesus: "Oh, so you really weren't resting, but anxiously awaiting something big? Come let's discuss this." He reaches down and squeezes my hand, immediately we are sitting at His table. His seat is right next to mine. He motions for some angels to serve me water. When they poured it into my glass, I looked to Jesus and He motioned for me to drink. I must have been thirsty as I gulped the water right down. He was laughing and motioned for the angels to pour more in my glass.

Jesus: "Erin you are thirsty! Who knew? Oh yes, I did!" He laughed and I laughed too.

Me: "Yes Lord, 21 days I have been thirsty, languishing without food or water!"

Jesus: "Wow, you were looking a bit thinner!" He was laughing.

Me: "I guess this has more meaning than just thirst for water too, right!"

Jesus: "Yes Erin. You hunger and thirst for righteousness!"

Me: "Lord, can we go over more with the Clock & Calendar?"

Jesus: "Okay, but first let's begin again with one. There is one body, and one spirit, just as you were called to one hope when you were called! (Ephesians 4:4) Erin one is the only number that can be multiplied and divided by itself and remain unchanged. 1 times 1 = 1 and 1 divided by 1 = 1. God is the same no matter what! He is the same yesterday, today and tomorrow. God does not change! When you, Erin bring your best for God – it is also called first fruits. I came as the First fruit of those who have fallen asleep!"

Me: "Lord this really is amazing! There are multiple meanings, who knew that numbers could be so complex?"

Jesus: "Really, complexly simple! Now number two. Two means union, division and witnessing. It can also mean a double portion of blessing. I always sent out disciples in pairs. The covenant of marriage is two – yet to have a firm marriage you must have God with your union, thus three strands! Now, with 3 there is more here too. There are 3 founding Fathers of Israel, 3 festivals of offerings; Passover, Pentecost, and Sukkot. You remember 3 days spent in the belly of the whale, Esther's extreme 3 day fast, Abraham's 3 day journey, Elijah stretched out over the dying boy 3 times. I was raised from the dead on the 3rd day. We went into details of the number 4. There are also 4 earthly kingdoms in Daniel. There are also 4 tassels on my garment." I looked at Jesus' sash and He had 4 tassels. Then with the number 5 in Numbers it was said, 'To redeem the 273 firstborn Israelites who exceed the number of Levites, collect 5 shekels for each one.'"

Jesus: "This is the number of Redemption, Divine Grace, and God's Goodness. Erin, you study architecture. Look at 5 there, it is written in the Word. This is also for you in Matthew 25. Look at the parable of 5 bags. Ask this also, why did David pick up 5 smooth stones when only one killed Goliath? There is that "One" again!"

Me: "Lord, You are so Wise! Wiser than Solomon! Divine in all Your Ways! Who is like You? Who is like God? I will walk away today with more wisdom than I can even imagine! What if I don't write this correctly? What if I mess up?"

Jesus: "Okay now, I must rebuke you! You are speaking of my friend Erin and you are implying that I have made an error. I don't believe the Kingdom of God or His Son are rooted in mistakes as everything is made known from the beginning! You are not made strong in my weakness Erin! I am strong when you are weak. There is nothing new under the sun or Son! You were not some Divine accident, where God woke up one day and said, "Oh whoa who is that and what did I create her for?" or "I didn't anticipate that thing Erin did today, what Am I going to do next? I can't keep ahead of that rogue child Erin!"" I was laughing so hard. He was keeping a straight face then began to laugh! "Erin, see how ridiculous this sounds?"

Me: "Lord, please forgive me; I am out of sorts today. I've had some very odd dreams the last several weeks and they all have one thing in common! The End of days, the Tribulation! How can I rest when you give me all of that too?"

Jesus: "Erin, you were given these and you had some delightful distractions so you would realize when you awoke you could find happiness. It was not all gloomy! Now this brings me to the next number – number 6 and a hard lesson for you. What is one of God's practices? He worked 6 days then rested on the seventh. You work seven days. Who are you? Are you greater than God himself? No you are not! Now this is also the number for man – 6 is the path to Holiness but without God it is nothing. 6+1=7. I won't give much more to this number as you know the rest – 666 – is the God of this world on Earth, the Antichrist – notice that he used three 6's. There is more but let's move on to your favorite 7! How many silver bangles do you wear on your wrist?"

I looked at my left wrist and there were 7.

Me: "How did my bracelets come with me?"

Jesus: "There is a treasure in Psalm 12 here for you about silver and refining, this you know! This number 7 is the number of completion and fullness! Rest Erin! Sabbaths, Jubilees, there are seven Holy Feasts! There are seven furnishings in a perfect Tabernacle. There are seven branches of the Menorah."

Me: "But Lord 7 is also of punishment. 7 x 10 = 70 years! 70 weeks of years, 7 rings, 70 sevens."

Jesus: "Erin, we have come full circle back to the Calendar. You are smarter than you think! There is wisdom here!"

Me: "Lord, help me then. Why did I have these dreams? Lord, while I was there a young boy age 8 died. I asked You if we could have that boy come back to life."

Jesus: "Yes, I remember! He is here now Erin. I found such joy that you were ready for anything. I heard your prayer. God on the Throne heard it. Do you remember what you prayed which made us take note?"

Me: "There were several things, but I knew Lord that You were doing something. I was in a plumbing store, when the radio announced the sudden death of this 8 year old boy. Only I heard it. It kept haunting me. I asked You if You wanted me to sneak into the hospital and pray. By day 3 I felt it was too late. I was ready for You to speak but You never said, 'Go Erin!'"

Jesus: "Erin what we noticed is your readiness. You recognized that God let you hear this. You stood ready for service. This is what you are asked to do as a believer. You are to be a willing vessel, ready when called to serve. I noted in your prayer that you asked to sneak in unnoticed! This was important as most would want a public display and recognition."

Me: "Lord could You imagine the uproar here at home if I had been recognized for an act from You like raising a dead boy? I would lose my children! This would need to be hidden!"

Jesus: "Erin you were willing and able, this is important. Now this was a time for the boy's appointed Home-going, but your motives were good! You were willing! Now, the dreams! You were given these because you and your friends will need to pray! There is a time coming. You have now noticed the Blood Moons. This is a sign in the Heavens and a Marker. The stars are displaying markers also! Please do not be afraid 2014 might not seem significant, but it is!"

Me: "I don't feel You are coming yet, but You did say three times, "Erin the Landscape is about to change!" Lord when and what does this mean?"

Jesus: "Erin, do not be afraid! You have prepared for this. Be excited, take heart and find joy, remember you are like a light – a lamp with oil! The only flames you have seen here is by the Throne of God."

Me: "Lord, I did see a fireplace in my mansion."

Jesus: "Yes, but this is for your enjoyment. It is not meant for burning refuse. It is not a special fire sent as a super power for you to burn with."

Me: "I always thought Baptism by fire are my trials before my growth spiritually!"

Jesus: Laughing, "I guess you are correct, you have been in the fiery furnace of affliction, and this is good! Just remember this is a tool in which the Blacksmith uses, allowed by God to refine you. It is meant to shape your vessel and make this perfected by God for His use, not for yours! All of this is for His Glory, not man's – this is the difference. Now are you ready for greater service?"

Me: I hesitated for a second, "Yes, Lord I am ready!"

Jesus: He laughed! "Good then, Erin we will start now, are you well rested?"

Me: "I think so!"

Jesus: "Very good! You are loved by the King!"

Dream over…

There was a lot of information given to me by Jesus in this dream. I wrote this dream down and had a few questions for the Lord after this.

As I was going about my routine at home this afternoon I went to the Lord with these questions -- here is HIS response. I believe this should be added to the end of this dream.

I asked HIM, "Lord, at Pentecost what some people saw were tongues of fire descending on the group of people, what was this really?"

He said to me, Erin what happened after the tongues rested on the people?"

Me: "They began to prophecy and preform many miracles, signs and wonders"

Jesus: "When I return on the Horse with Heaven's armies what did you see from my mouth in my Word?"

Me: "It was your tongue as a sword coming from your mouth. It was the word of Truth coming to cut through the darkness."

Jesus: "Good, okay then, the Holy Spirit came as tongues upon believers. By your words you confess and speak truth. You speak the power of life and death from your mouth. The tongues were also a sign of your flame of truth. -- The Holy Spirit was like a flame coming to light the Oil within your lamp!! It is a Baptism from Heaven and is a miracle!! This is to enhance your faith and is a special gift from God! Each of you will show like a light from the Menorah meant to point the lost to Heaven. You are showing the way through the word of Truth!!"

I pray this helps with discernment. Remember that our Lord -- Jesus does not go against HIS own Word. The Lord God is not a double-minded man. A double minded man is unstable in all his ways. Do not be deceived or follow strange doctrine. The Lord can create a new thing, but it will still be rooted and grounded solidly in scripture. I believe when we see manifestations of strange displays and do not feel right in our spirit via the Holy Spirit -- then it is time to flee and turn away from these strange occurrences.

Chapter 8 – Breakfast with Jesus

Dear Father

Thank You for Another day! Thank You for Your love. Thank You for all that we have. Thank You for my children and family. Thank You for Your provision.

Lord, I need to hear from You! My dreams have been dark and it is about times coming and the cruel hearts of men and discerning between falsehoods and truth. I'm coming across people who hate me, people who submit to scripture in the Bible but do not really search. Lord, I have been here. For years I read the Bible. I would read a passage and relate it to my daily walk, sometimes treating Your words like a fortune cookie. Nice words on Holy paper but meant for someone else. I longed and searched for something. I longed to know this Jesus who doesn't speak or walk today, but the words say He does. I longed for evidence of these miracles of Him. I longed to have more to my life. Life on its own apart from God is nothing! We are but a vapor!

Lord, I'm one female. A scribe of sorts, I'm not Jewish. Not affluent to have a measure of Earthly status. I know a little about a lot of different things, but I am not great at anything. I have some education in a field that is far removed from Biblical significance – this gives me no earthly credentials. I have nothing here to leave as an earthly inheritance for my children. Other than the dreams, I have no land to leave, no assets or legacy to give. I am no longer an active church volunteer or community leader. I have no interest in man's praise with my career. I have had enough published with my Interior Design to satisfy anyone in this field. This is no longer a goal. I realize little. I grew to be a lover of material things of this world fully, yet when I ate all of these things – devoured what I could until I was full, I still was empty. You see Lord the world has been my desert place. The earth has been our testing ground. In scripture, You shortened our life span it seems in average blocks of 40. My life has been like a desert place, until You have begun to speak to me so I could hear.

(The Lord stopped me here on Saturday. He said "No more to do here today. I am calling you to the movies, one in particular. Hurry you don't have much time" I looked at the movie times and realized I had exactly ½ hour drive to get to one that started in 45 minutes.)

To back-up I went to the Noah movie Friday evening. I left very sad, the last thing I really wanted to do was go to another movie and even two more. I knew the Lord was behind this so I was on my course. My first movie Saturday was "God's Not Dead," I was pleased with this and I will take my children to this one. As I was leaving the theater, I saw that "Son of God" was playing in 20 minutes – since the Lord hadn't called me before to see this I went out to my car. As I sat in my car the Holy Spirit prompted me to buy a ticket to the third movie. I proceeded back into the theater. The only agenda I had for this weekend was the Lord – I had cleared my plate for Him!

I sat in the theater and thought about Noah. I thought to myself why would Noah ever need to be Hollywoodized? The story is so incredible on its own. If they had only shown the despicable things the fallen had really done with creating abominations – people even teenage boys would be interested. (The ones like mine who tend to like all of the x-box games and fighting videos.) I prayed to the Lord, why? Why allow this?

Me: "Lord, I pray that You call people to reading the Bible because they are curious now about NOAH. Lord, I ask that You use Enoch and the Holy Spirit to speak through Your written word so that the last calling begins. Please do not allow this message of this movie to change people's heart about God, Noah and the Fallen. Lord it shows the enemy being kind and gentle and being redeemed by God and taken home. It showed Noah as a heartless man who was willing to cut down his wife and children to eliminate man completely. It showed that You didn't speak to Him – yet clearly in the Bible that Noah was a Holy man who walked with God and loved his children. Lord, Adam and Eve were shown as strange light beings with no hair. My prayer would be that when those You have called, see this movie that they would question and search for truth and that it might be found by them. Lord, clearly we are at the beginning of the end.

Holy Spirit: " Erin, I am here with you and I have heard you. Do Not worry!"

I sat through the "Son of God" movie I felt lukewarm. Forgive me

Lord because I have seen You and interacted with You, it is difficult for me to see someone "playing" Jesus! I barely made it through this movie, unlike 'The Passion of Christ', ten years ago – I didn't feel the Spirit of the Lord upon this one.

I left the theater. When I came in today it was sunny, warm and windy –no clouds. The sky had grown very dark with large clouds.

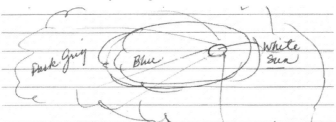

The scene was incredible as I drove home. It looked so amazing like the Lord had opened Heaven for a moment. Waves of dark gray and beams of light came out of this. It was so beautiful. As I drove, I became very sad. I knew the Lord has been strengthening me the last month for something more, but I know this will come at a price. I know I would need to be willing to leave everything I love to follow Jesus. I just prayed that He would be merciful with me and protect my heart. I thought back to all of my Christian friends who no longer communicate with me and when they do they ignore my dreams. They ignore what the Lord has called me for. I became sad as I drove. I said to the Lord, "Lord what if this was it? What if I am false or I have done evil without knowing it. What if…"

Jesus: (I heard His voice clearly!) "Erin Stop! Look to your right!"

I looked to my right over the area where Hanford is before I turn into my neighborhood and there was the most beautiful rainbow. I cried for a moment and pulled the car over. I heard Him say, "I am with You!"

Last night I had a difficult sleep. I had dreams of unclean areas, bathroom with overflowing toilets in High–end neighborhoods and my earth father appeared briefly in one of the dreams. I woke up this morning sore, tired and heavy.

4th Day, Sunday…

Communion (Breaking my fast.)

Prayer: Lord, thank You for Your promises! Please Father, take me up to You today. I miss You!

Jesus: "Erin Come Up!"

Immediately I am up and sitting next to Him at His table. I was startled a bit and surprised to see Him immediately smiling at me. I reached over and embraced Him. He wrapped His arms around me as my arms and hands wrapped around His chest.

Me: "I'm so glad to see You! Why have You taken me here right away?"

Jesus: "Erin, don't be afraid!" (He smiled.) I thought we would begin with communion today. Here, take some warm bread!" He opened the cloth and pulled out some flat bread. Then He pulled out some French bread. I was laughing. He handed me both. Then He motioned for the angel to bring Him wine and to pour water into my cup. He then poured wine into His cup.

Jesus: "Erin, take this bread and eat. It doesn't matter which one – I think right now you will enjoy both!"

Me: (Even as I write, I am hungry.) "Lord, this is my favorite time with You! I love sitting and dining with You! Thank You for this!"

Jesus: "Erin, you are My friend and My guest, too – yet your place is here."

Me: "This confuses me at times when the world seems so dark!"

Jesus: "Here, drink some water, but first take a sip of this!" He takes a drink of wine from His cup and hands it to me to drink. I take a sip, and He motions for me to drink another before I hand it back to Him.

Me: "Lord, this is wonderful! Where is this from?"

Jesus: "This is from the Garden of God! It is the Spring Release!"

Me: "Lord, does this have more meaning? Spring Wine Release here is not until May."

Jesus: "Erin, is the wine good?"

Me: "Oh yes, Lord, very good! Please forgive me, Lord, for searching everything You do and say with discretion. I don't want to miss anything in Your actions or words. It seems like everything You do is significant."

Jesus: "No need to forgive what is good. Erin, let's just enjoy this day, communion, and each other. I see you are troubled by some things. Please eat, because you are hungry; drink because you thirst; and then lay your burdens down. You cannot enjoy your time with Me while you are empty. Please allow Me to fill you."

Me: "Lord, are you speaking physically now, or with my spirit?"

Jesus: "Erin, this fast was Good. I heard your prayers. I have promised you certain things and I stand fast to My word; all will be fulfilled. Right now you have burdens. First, break the fast – breakfast – then come back to Me. Go ahead and send this to your friends so they, too, can pray for you."

Me: "Lord, You are not doing this as I had expected. I was hoping for a big message today. Something Huge! I feel I am on the brink of something. You have shown me the tribulation for the last two weeks. Please, Lord!"

Jesus: "Erin, how do you know I am not about to do something Big? It's good for you to be ready. Let's look at this again. The three movies showed you what the world would like to think about God, but they are incorrect. The other showed you a Lord which is still not who I am, but scripted – a Hollywood Jesus. The third movie was a message that I AM Alive, but clearly the least watched so far of the three. Now, remember who God is from the beginning? Erin, you are overwhelmed by your knowledge, because you have seen both Good and Bad! You are struggling to understand about this! Did it ever occur to you that your burden is not to understand it! Erin, you can only convey what you have seen. You cannot make people see who I am if they don't want to know me in the first place! Some want just words on a paper. Some don't believe I AM

Alive in the words. Some don't ask for any more because when they have asked for more – then more is required – they are much too comfortable with the world. Erin, you are not comfortable in the world any more. Now you understand Enoch and Elijah! You understand how I felt walking there! – Right before I was crucified! The darkness of the world is overwhelming! You have a burden. You must die to the world yourself; take up your cross and follow me! I have not called you to forget your children – just your father's house (your earthly father) – then follow me. You must trust that I will do the rest. I AM requiring nothing of you other than your heart. Coming to Me empty is good, then I can fill you – I will fill you! Erin you have drunk from my cup! This is a contract, you are my friend. God, My Father loves you. You are in favor. The enemy hates you and the world hates you, but it first hated me and preferred death. Therefore the Lord God has shortened man's days from the beginning. Erin, I am NOT rebuking you! I see the worry on your face and the burden on your shoulders. Please let me carry that for you, My shoulders can take your burdens."

Me: "Oh Lord, I do not feel worthy of all of this, I have taken Your call. I would never trade my time with You for anything! I would give everything away and follow You – I almost have!

Jesus: "Erin, give Me what is most precious to you now – your children! Can't you trust Me? I love them, too!"

Me: "Oh, Lord, I am so sorry. Yes, Father, please take them!" My hand shook and I began to cry. I reached over and touched the sleeve of His robe. He reached and grabbed my hand and wrist.

Jesus: "Erin, do you trust Me – that I will do something Good?"

Me: "Oh yes, Lord, of course. They are the last thing. I have now given You everything. You have all of me! Other than Your promises and You, I cling to nothing else."

Jesus: "Give Me your bills, Erin. I will pay these! Give Me your enemies, Erin. I will remove them! Erin, give Me your worries. I will speak and comfort you!" The look in His Eyes was a love for me deeper than any earthly love – a sure and true love! Steadfast!

Me: "Lord, how can I deny giving my whole self to You? How can I deny what You have done? You have forever changed me. You have ruined me for this life. I have just seen heartless men in my dreams, and I deal with them daily. Please, Lord – it is getting worse. My dreams are very difficult. My friends are experiencing the same things. Many of us are treated as outcasts, and shunned. With me, I still remain silent to many, until You lead me differently."

Jesus: "Erin, all that you have been through, I have also. I AM with you always. Now, remain in Me and I will remain in you. Do not be afraid. Are you ready for what comes next? Are you up for the challenge? Are you ready for service? I have sent you friends! They will stand with you, and you will all be blessed greatly together for what you are doing. You do not understand the Harvest yet, but soon you will yield record crops!"

Me: "Lord, please bless my friends tenfold for all they have done for me. Please heal those who are sick, alone, and hungry! Lord, pour out Your Spirit on us so that we may shine like You do!"

Jesus: "Erin, hand your friends to Me! Hand Me all of them. I will speak to them this day. They are Mine, and the Love I have for them will never be removed. They will be like trees of splendor in the Garden of God – Oaks of Righteousness! All manner of birds will come to rest on their branches and sing praises to God! They will be richly blessed! Now, go eat! Go drink, because you are thirsty! Think of Me! I love you, Erin – oh yes, look at Enoch and Elijah at the same crossroads you are, in scripture. You will see yourself, at the same spot – now what comes next?" He smiled.

Me: "I get rid of my designer pajamas?" I was smiling.

Jesus: He laughed. "No, this is an Elijah issue, unless those PJ's take My place – then we have a greater problem." I laughed and so did He.

Me: "No, they wear out – You don't!"

Jesus: "Very good – then there is no issue. Erin, it is always a heart issue. You can never judge a book by its cover! Solomon was dressed very well. God blessed him, and no earthly King was more knowledgeable than Solomon. God made Lucifer beautiful to behold, a bright and beautiful star – yet he fell the hardest and took many with him! Do Not be deceived by appearances. God knows the Heart!

Now, you will be shown much more. Continue to write, even that of tribulation. I will show you more of Heaven, but you need to report on that which you have seen during the darkness. It is unimaginable – but then, no one can say, 'We didn't know!'"

Me: "Lord, when I am having these, I am walking the landscape. Why am I sometimes physically here and sometimes in the spirit during the tribulation?"

Jesus: "Good question, Erin. Write all of these dreams down, even if you wake several times during the night. You already know your place is here in Heaven. One day, some – well, many – will apologize to you, but many will thank you for these. You will be given detailed interactions when you are given these; you must write these clearly."

Me: "Okay, Lord. I will pray for wisdom and the ability to record like Ezra!"

Jesus: "Good, Erin – this is a good prayer! Granted! Now, rest and eat! You are loved! Do Not worry! Pray! You are blessed, as well as your friends! I AM With You! I AM Here! SEEK and you will find Me! Knock and the Door will be opened! I Love you."

Me: "I love You, too, Lord! (We hugged!)

Dream over...

Blessings...

Chapter 9 - God's Clock & the Olive Grove

Communion

Dear Father,

Thank You for another day! Thank You for my children. Thank You for their good health. Thank You for their hearts to ask and wonder about You. Thank You for family and friends. Please Lord, bless them abundantly, answer their prayers and heal their hearts!

Lord, I have been struggling recently with what You have shown me. I know You are coming, in fact even at the door step. When I still don't know? I have had very dark dreams now for three weeks, and even longer. I know there is instruction in these but this week it took its toll on me. The pacemaker technician called it tachycardia. I had so many that my heart always felt like it was skipping. I have been tired all week, but I have had no time to rest fully. Please Lord, grant me special resilience to continue down this new path You are taking but please allow me some glimmers of Heaven to contrast this. I feel as if the enemy has kept me from You but I know too – You have allowed this. Please Lord make a way when there seems to be no way. I love You!

Jesus: "Erin Come Up!"

Today I was lying in soft grass. My cheek was resting in this beautiful soft green grass. I brought myself up to sitting position and I realized I was in God's Olive Grove. I looked up to my left and there was His Mansion up high on the mountain to my left. I giggled and spoke out loud.

Me: "Lord, where are You? Are You here?" ...Silence. I leaned back against the base of this olive tree and looked up. I never considered the olive tree as being very beautiful. They are short, squatty, and gnarled. Here though they all had a beautiful twist to them. The leaves were silver on one side and green on the other. The olives were ripe and consisted of many different colors; some were burgundy, some deep purple, some green. Each one seemed to have a golden brush stroke of metallic paint on each olive. This grove was beautiful. The smells here have a familiar distant memory – I couldn't recall it.

I looked back at the Mansion of God and hoped He would come out but I still didn't see Him. I felt tired. I could hear some little birds fluttering from tree to tree. Their song was familiar. I was trying to recall it, and then when I did I laughed so hard. "When the Saints go marching in," Seriously Lord, You are funny! So incredibly wise! I had a hard time recalling the lyrics which of course these little birds had completely down. I rested my head in the soft grass and I looked way up! I saw the sun shining through the beautiful mist. I could see small glistening rainbows around each of the olives on the branches. I chuckled; the metallic interior of each olive must reflect the sun so brightly they create small rainbows. It was beautiful. I laid there as my eyes became heavy; I felt a small rabbit or animal come over to me to examine me. I looked and a small bunny had come over and nestled in the grass right in my neck area. I love small plump bunnies. This one nestled in for a nap.

I was laughing, "Lord did You bring me here today to nap?"

My eyes were still open as the song kept going through my head. For a moment I drifted off. I awoke to a bunny's whiskers on my nose. I was laughing. "No, I guess sleep was not the plan. Lord what are the words to that song?"

Just then the words were down loaded...

We are traveling in the footsteps
Of those who've gone before,
And we'll all be reunited.
On a new and sunlit shore
Oh, when the saints go marching in
Oh, when the saints go marching in
Lord, I want to be in that number
When the saints go marching in
And when the sun refuses to shine
And when the sun refuses to shine
I want to be in that number
When the sun refuse to shine
And when the Moon turns red with blood
And when the moon turns red with blood

I want to be in that number
When the moon turns red with blood
Oh, when the trumpet sounds its call
Oh, when the trumpet sounds its call
Lord, I want to be in that number
When the trumpet sounds its call
Some say this world of trouble
Is the only one we need?
But I'm waiting for that morning,
When the New World is revealed
Oh when the new world is revealed
Oh when the new world is revealed
Lord, I want to be in that number
When the New world is revealed
Oh when the saints go marching in
Oh when the saints go marching in
I want to be in that number
When the saints go marching in!

As I sang this tune, I thanked God for my Grandma Mac who would take us to church when I was little. During our visits, I remembered this hymn. I pray she is here somewhere and she made it! I drifted off to sleep. I woke up to Jesus looking down at me. His hand was on my forehead and His other hand was on my wrist.

Jesus: Laughing, "Oh good Erin, you're alive!"

Me: "Oh How long was I asleep?" I awoke a bit disoriented and expecting to wake up in my bed. He reached out and gave me a glass of water, I was thirsty, I drank the whole glass. "Lord, I forget that I can rest or nap in Heaven. I love this! I feel bad though, how long was I asleep?"

Jesus: "Awhile, it matters not however! You needed the rest!"

Me: "Lord, this was the best sleep I have had in a very long time. I feel refreshed and renewed. How long was I really asleep?"

Jesus: "You will laugh Erin! In Earthly terms, three days, in Heavenly terms three hours.

Me: "Oh, so an hour is like a day?"

Jesus: "Yes in terms of today and the nap I gave you here. You are using this as a gauge for other things – I would caution you a bit here. Erin you don't want people on Earth thinking they have three days when they only have three hours or the opposite. How do you know? A day is like a thousand. Take instruction from Peter here.

Me: "You are so wise Lord and You knew I would wonder about this and take notice. Based on this scripture, I am surprised you didn't tell me I was asleep three Heavenly minutes and this was like three Earthly months, or even years?"

Jesus: Laughing, "Yes I knew you would begin to calculate. How Erin can you do a calculation if you have no understanding of the intrinsic value of Heavenly Time?"

Me: "Yes, Lord I understand. You are orderly and You will not go against Your own Words.

Jesus: "Erin, Peter stated this so you understood the Hour we work in – Erin it is a late Hour and it is God's wish that no one should perish, yet some will.

Me: "Lord, it is difficult to take comfort in the lateness of the hour we are in. I can't help but wonder when – children ask a lot of questions Lord, it is what we do. I'm struggling right now and I'm having difficulty resting.

Jesus: "Oh – this is why I brought you here, let's take communion here. An Angel brought a small short table like a tray with legs. Jesus motioned for me to sit next to Him, so I did. I was curious to see where the little bunnies went. "Erin, they are over there." I saw a group of brown and white bunnies sleeping in the grass. Some were curled up in a ball and some were on their backs and bellies up. I laughed so hard.

Me: "Lord, I love this – Thank You!" At odd times in my life, a bunny would appear in odd places at odd times. I thought it was the Lord showing me He was with me! "It's neat to see them so calm and resting in the sun." I laughed because I saw one moving its legs while it was sleeping. "Lord, is it dreaming about running?"

Jesus: He looked and laughed. "Oh probably, but not from a predator, Come, let's break bread!" He reached and broke half of the bread He had and gave me a piece. "Erin, do you know why you came here today?"

Me: "You mean to the Olive Grove? No Lord, I don't understand."

Jesus: "Here first have a drink then I will remind you of something." The angel poured wine into a goblet. Jesus took a sip then handed it to me to drink. He turned the cup to the very spot where He drank from so I drank from that very spot on His cup."

Me: "Lord, why do You do this?"

Jesus: "Erin, so you are partaking from where I partook. What you are enduring, I too endured?"

Me: "Lord, How can this be? You are a man?"

Jesus: "Yes, but you are God's creation. The Holy Spirit resides in you. Do you believe there is nothing in your life in which I have knowledge? Do you believe if I have sent you the Counselor to dwell inside you, that I have not given the Counselor senses, even eyes, or ears?"

Me: "Oh of course. You know all things Lord. When You have me drink from the spot You drink in I thought it is because You suffered and I might too have to suffer."

Jesus: "Erin, what is the significance of this Olive Grove?"

Me: "Well it is a reminder of You sweating blood before You went to the cross and were crucified."

Jesus: "Okay now, remember the Olive. It is battered off of its branches to a cloth then carried off to be crushed – pressed to produce Oil. – There is nothing new with God, this is the same. Now let's look at the timeline because you like having patterns. What do you know of the day before my crucifixion?"

Me: "You had the last supper. Then You came here to pray. The disciples were sleepy and resting, but you couldn't sleep. You were arrested about 1:00 AM? Right?"

Jesus: "Yes, but there is more of significance in a short period of time. I had 6 – trials over the course of about 7 hours. This would be unheard of in your world today. Erin look over the course of your last 7 years how many large trials have you had with crushing?"

Me: "Oh Lord, it seems like much more, but I will look at this."

Jesus: "Erin, no need to. Now the difference between the two of us is that mine was condensed. There are more symbolisms with this block of time than any other in history. Look at the time frame of the crucifixion to the point of My death there, do you see it?"

Me: "Lord, I see You carried Your cross for about 3 hours from 9:00 – 12:00 – Noon. Then You were crucified and hung there for 3 hours. You died at 3:00 PM. In just 15 hours from the time of the last Supper, You were gone!"

Jesus: "The Passover meal ended around 11:30 pm and the Olive Grove was 2 miles."

Me: "Lord, this makes me sad. My stomach and heart have been sick all week. I don't like what I see when I sleep and I don't like reliving what has happened to You!"

Jesus: "I understand. I'm glad that you know Me enough to hurt over Me. There are very few who can make this connection because they have gone no further than to say, 'An innocent man hung on the cross.'"

Me: "Lord, You might have come in flesh, but You are God! The world has no idea how remarkable You are! You are Incredible!"

Jesus: "Why did I bring you here today Erin?"

Me: "Lord, am I about to be crushed?"

Jesus: "Haven't you had enough crushing? Did you need more?" He was smiling.

Me: "No Please! I'm okay – I have my stuff but please no more!"

Jesus: "What have these dreams done to you lately?"

Me: "They have broken my heart. I am afraid for those who are sleeping spiritually. I'm afraid for those who are stubborn. I'm afraid for those who didn't understand the seriousness of the hour we are in. Lord people are going to be pressed like olives and trodden as grapes. They will look for answers. Hope will be gone."

Jesus: "Tell Me what dream stands out to you."

Me: "Well there have been many, but I told my children as they have seen me with a different look about me – heavy and unsettled. I have told them in a very serious tone that no one wants to be here during the tribulation. I showed them the movie trailer for "The Purge" and I told them it will be like this every day. I showed them the movie trailer for "World War Z". I felt bad only a little as I had no other way to describe what was coming and they needed to be aware to minister to their friends."

Jesus: "So which dream stood out?"

Me: "Well one in particular. There was a mandatory curfew. I was caught out taking medicine to someone. I ran into an underground parking garage. There was no one there. I couldn't find my way out. It was a maze that kept folding into itself. The curfew comes with mandatory darkness. So there were no lights. Before the garage went dark, I saw a young man with a hooded sweatshirt. Then I lost him. I had no bearing. I had no Holy Spirit gauge or even intuition. I lacked discernment. I knew this person was close. I could hear him but I couldn't see. Then all of a sudden I felt something grab me. The man lit a cigarette lighter by his face. I saw evil. It said, "There is no escape". I woke up out of my sleep. I even was sore as if I had been running. This one was scary."

Jesus: "This was not you Erin, but someone else. You had another one which stands out just recently."

Me: "Yes, Lord I believe You had not raptured us yet. It was right before. I was in a city near Panama. It was hilly. There had been something which took all power from the area as well as water. There had been massive rain and slides followed by a drought and famine. People had come from highland areas to a now abandoned remnant of a city. There were mud encrusted concrete sheets. There were car lots in which mud – dried mud was half way up each tire on the car lot. All gas had been drained from the cars. Even though they were new – they couldn't be driven. A few families used cars and vans to live in on the parking lot. The occupants of the area spoke Hispanic, it was a strange tongue though and was not urban Hispanic, and it was Indian and Spanish, both. With me, was a toddler. I was taking care of him. He was dark skinned with black curly hair. He had just learned to walk and he seemed to laugh even though he was weak and hungry. His belly was extended. I was in search of water and I had gone from place to place looking but there was none. I had American dollars and I tried to buy clean clothes and water, but every time I heard, "no" tu money es mal – "tu es mal". They would turn from me. I looked at myself and I had darker skin. I had a strange rash. One man directed me to go to this clay home.

There were children there. A woman came out to greet me. I needed help. There was none so then I asked for help with my boy. Just then I noticed some strange gold idols coming from the walls of all of these different clay structures. It was shiny as if it is being rubbed or worshiped daily. It looked like a dog, a snake and bird combined. It was very odd. Just then I heard my toddler say – "Ma". I looked down and he had lost his bowels. I picked up and ran up and down the street yelling "Help, aqua por favor, aqua por favor." People turned their backs. I had no help. People were cold. It seemed so real. Where was this Lord?"

Jesus: "Right now it doesn't matter where. You see that people are dwelling in an area where once others prospered. You noticed that both you and your son were sick and thirsty – there was no relief. This is not uncommon, and will be more common very soon. This is when the world becomes even colder."

Me: "Lord I saw 2 dreams with a cult in Africa and South America blending the Catholic Religion with witchcraft. It was called beautiful and godly. Many were told they should follow this. There were blood sacrifices too."

Jesus: "Yes, this is Santeria. There are many more born out of each. This is going to become worse as many try to control their own destinations. This is the wide Gate. Remember it is the Narrow Gate which leads to God – very few take it."

Me: "Lord, what are all these dreams about? I have seen the tribulation from all over the globe. What now?"

Jesus: "These are given to others as well, and again, confirms the hour we are in!"

Me: "Lord, forgive me as I don't want to miss any key items but help me to understand why many of my dreams are occurring in Northern Europe. I have had quite a few in America, but I don't like what is happening there. It is too painful to see. I wake up hungry because in my dreams there is no food. I wake up thirsty because there is nothing to drink. The water is polluted. These dreams seem so real, how will anyone survive? Lord, before the veil it is frightening but when that is lifted and we are gone – who can survive? They will – those who remain – will die of heart failure. Help me Lord to be clear. Help me to be ready. Is there more I can do?"

Jesus: "Erin you were told a long time ago that nothing is required. I only require for you to love God… well you know the rest. Then pray! You do have an assignment. You continue to run after me! This I will bless. Now I did tell you to also prepare your field."

Me: "Yes Lord, what is this about? I am not a very patient person. So I have continued to say Kadima and look forward because when I look back or even at my current circumstances I become frozen. I become focused on the overwhelming task and the slow process. The very thing I've wanted my whole life on Earth was a home of my own. Yet, now because of time I look to my Heavenly Home. Clearly this is worth waiting for! Now I just want to make good use of my time here while I wait. What would you have me to do?"

Jesus: "Then Prepare Your Field! Come with Me Erin!"

He reaches down, takes my hand, and lifts me to my feet – then instantly we are in His courtyard in front of God's Clock and Calendar. We were on the Upper Balcony over-looking His inner Courtyard. With a wave of His Hand the stars and moon are set, and then with His other, the sun is set on the Outer Ring.

Jesus: "I would like you to see something. I will illuminate this in your language. Look." There before me I saw some harvests listed on the Fourth Ring. I saw seven harvests and some other small ones. "Erin, you can find these listed in Deuteronomy 8 (8:8)." I saw Wheat, Barley, Grapes, Figs, Pomegranates, Olives, and Honey. I saw Pentecost listed. I saw the word "Threshing," which occasionally overlapped Grains and Grape Harvests.

Me: "Oh, Lord, I see a measure. The New Wine Festival comes fifty days – or seven weeks – after Pentecost. Then I see fourteen weeks after Pentecost is the New Olive Oil Festival. Then I see three sections: the Spring Grain Harvest, the Summer Grape Harvest, and the Autumn Oil Harvest. Wow, Lord, this is well thought out! Can I have a Calendar like this?"

Jesus: "You are funny, Erin! Are you a farmer now – do you need such timing?" He was smiling.

Me: "I get excited when I am shown something from here, which makes complete sense to order on Earth. It is a timing issue – right, Lord?"

Jesus: "Erin, you are being shown something from the growing seasons – it is not always a gauge for My timing."

Me: "Lord, forgive me, but never in my whole life have I ever met a human who could match Your knowledge and perfection. Solomon could be given just enough to finally make him weary of this world and all of its meaninglessness – this I know too well, and I am no Solomon. But You, Lord – You are the Son of God and far from simple. What I am seeing, You have allowed me to read in English – at least some of it. You have done this for a reason. Please help me here, as clearly there is something!"

Jesus: "Okay, okay – very good, Erin. Yes, I told you to prepare your field, Erin. You fasted for answers; I am giving you further instructions. I like that you are forging ahead. This, too, is good."

Me: "Lord, the key for me is knowing when to rest, wait, and pray; and knowing when to pray, step out, and watch. You complete a good work."

Jesus: "Hmmm… Interesting way to state this. Let's look at Peter. Peter was eager and hesitant. I asked Peter to step out on the water and walk to Me. He failed to look beyond the waves to see Me. He lost his focus and looked down at his circumstances – the water consumed him because he lost his sight of Me. I required Peter to step out, not knowing the outcome of his act. Here is another example. I consistently tell you to prepare your field – what does this mean exactly?"

Me: "I think I know, but then I'm not sure."

Jesus: "There are two Farmers. They are each given a rich field by the Landowner. The Landowner says, 'I am giving you everything you need to take care of my field – equipment, labor, fertilizer, seed, and top soil. I am leaving for a season, and I will be back the second season. I am going to the Temple to pray for God to send rain, and I am going to give an offering in advance for this record harvest. Please follow instructions, as we are planting on faith.' One Farmer immediately did everything the Landowner requested. The second Farmer said, 'I am going to sit and wait for more instructions, waiting on the Lord in faith to plant my field for me.' The Landowner went to the Temple, thanked God for all that he had; he thanked God for the two Farmers whom he had hired to help with his harvest, and he gave an offering to God of double His requirement, in hopes that God would send rain in the drought.

"God heard the cry of the Landowner, sent the rain, and gave the Landowner record crops – more than doubling his offering on the first field. When the rain came, the second Farmer rushed to throw seed on the ground and quickly covered it with top soil and fertilizer. He had been too lazy. Waiting on God to do everything, he had almost missed the opportunity when the rain came. This Farmer did yield a crop, but it barely produced a healthy harvest, and it was nowhere near that of the first Farmer. The Landowner was still very happy that the Lord had answered his prayers and received his offering. He gave the first Farmer his share, which was double what he expected; and he gave the second Farmer only a percentage of his yield, which was the bare minimum. Nothing needed to be said, as it was obvious what had happened. Erin, now explain to me what this is about?"

Me: "Well, God is good, and faithfully God, even when we are not! God blessed the Landowner for his great faith. He also blessed the first Farmer for stepping out with him in faith, despite the drought, and for believing with him for a miracle. He was faithful, and the Landowner trusted him by tithing in advance as an offering to God! This is great faith in action! The other Farmer believed God for all the miracles too, but – did he really? He believed he could just wait on God for more instructions, probably because he didn't want to follow his employer's instructions – again, I think he was afraid. Maybe he was not really faithful at all, and used this as a crutch to stay mobilized. 'I'm waiting on the Lord!' His obligation was to serve his employer, thereby serving God – believing that if you have done all you can do – then all the rest is up to God – like the Rain!"

Jesus: "Very good, Erin. There is more here, too. Now – there is a story like this, too. This can also be seen in some of the horrors of your dreams of late. In Second Kings 7 there is a story about lepers – outcasts. The Syrians in this story had put a siege on the Northern Kingdom of Israel. As you know, sieges result in famine. The food stores were gone, and the inhabitants faced certain death. They were so hungry they had decided to eat their children. The lepers – a total of four – decided that since they were to die anyway, they could be crazy and go out to the enemy camps and beg for food. They basically said, we have a 50/50 chance to live or die, so we might as well go out and ask. The King, Jehoram was blaming Elisha for the trouble, but Elisha prophesied relief from the famine. When the lepers went out to the enemy camp, there was no enemy there. Why? They had heard a noise and thought a great army was coming, so they ran for their lives, leaving behind food and more.

"Erin, God had prepared the way. The lepers went out on faith, with hope of a better future. He met them with His Supernatural Power! All the lepers had to do was go in and take it!"

Me: "Wow, Lord, I just went to read this story. I had never noticed it before. Lord, I was just reading about fear."

Jesus: "Erin, I have something for each of you; it is waiting for you to take a hold of it. Now, there is a time to sit still and wait, but sometimes there is a time to say, 'I'm not going to sit here any longer. I'm going to take a risk.' Don't allow fear to govern you – fear of the unknown, fear of failure, fear of success, fear of responsibility, fear of abandonment. The key, Erin, is to not lose heart. When you are going through your reasoning for not moving or taking action, make certain that your fear is not steering your course. God has not given you the spirit of fear, but of power, love, and a sound mind (2 Timothy 1:7). The fear of God is the Beginning of Wisdom."

Me: "Lord, are You requiring more of me? Am I to move or go somewhere? Is the landscape about to change? Is this a warning?"

Jesus: "No warning. Erin, you moved ahead of God and landed in the desert. Don't let fear keep you here when God says NOW."

Me: "Lord, I've not heard this yet! Am I to do more to prepare? To prepare others? Help!"

Jesus: "There are hints here! Now, I have revealed some more to you. You are learning about this late hour. You are to prepare your field and household. This is wisdom. It is okay to change your thinking. Sometimes you wait on God; sometimes God is waiting on you! Don't lose heart! Now, you have learned today that Heaven is a Place of Order, Complexly Simple. God's timing is His order or gauge of events, cogged on His own cog, apart from – but related to – the order of seasons, days, harvests, and moons. There is more to this, but all is structured and originates in your Field Guide – the Farmer's Almanac." He began to laugh. "Erin, the Bible – it is there in My Word! Find it! Now, I will continue on course. You are not out of favor! There is more! You are loved! Be Blessed, and Do Not Fear!"

Dream over...

Blessings...

Chapter 10 - The Cave, Uriel, and the Snow Storm

Communion

Dear Father,

Thank You for another day! Thank You for loving me! Thank You for my children! Thank You for my family and friends. Thank You for my dreams! Most of all thank You for Calling! Lord, all week I have been ill! Not normal as You know. Forgive me if I have not pressed into You more. I still have a habit of giving into my circumstances when You don't immediately answer my prayers. You do however answer my cries for help! You come immediately in different ways, but You always come. You are faithful! Please forgive me for running from You.

I have felt the burden and I haven't even told my friends everything, so they could pray too. You told me to come out of my cave like Elijah. You even sent a friend with a vision of boats on the water and me being afraid to step out on it, to run to You! Lord, I want to be like David and even Enoch – they faced giants but always saw You as bigger. Lord, forgive me as I am more like Elijah running to the desert cave. I am more like Peter with his absolutes, "I would never Lord betray You" - or his fearless desire to walk on water when he sees You, but then that fear makes him lose his footing! Please help me Lord, this might be the most important game changer for me. Do I have what it takes to deliver both messages of hope and those of darkness? Only You know!

Today I come to You boldly like Esther. I have questions. I need to be clear. I love You! Please find favor in me!

Erin Come Up!

My eyes were closed. When I opened them I was in a dark place. I smelled wet dirt. I sat up quickly and began to panic. I saw a very faint light so I stumbled in the darkness for a while. I cried out to God! "Lord, have I been so horrible that You would send me to the dark pit? Father, God on the Throne, I cannot do this anymore. I am not worthy. All of this has no significance. It is one endless riddle and I'm tired chasing after You. Go ahead and forget me now. Wipe my name from Your hand. Remove my brick in Your Garden. Send me home to Earth and let me never wake from my slumber again. I was crying – Lord, I'm too old for this task. I'm tired!" I was there for some time. This was a large cave. I was afraid there. The longer I stayed there void of much light, the more I wanted to get out. The air was thick. I used my bare feet to find a smooth, soft, dirt like path. As my feet walked this path I knew I was on the right course. As I kept moving on this small path the light began to grow brighter. I went around a rocky wall. My hands were my guide and kept me from stumbling into a wall. As I turned past this wall, I saw the light at the end of the tunnel – yes a cliché of epic proportion. I stopped for a moment. The opening of the cave (obviously the Lord had placed me here because I have been stating this) was about 9 feet high and 9 feet wide.

As I drew closer to the opening, I looked out and I saw desert. I began to cry. I wanted to look out and see the Garden of God. Instead I was in a severe "time-out." There was a ledge at the front of the cave. The sun was hot. I was wearing a white dirty long sleeve t-shirt and some black work-out tights. I had taken my tennis shoes off to feel my way in the dark – Wait, come to think of it why would I take off my tennis shoes in a dark cave. Why were they off? I didn't remove them. Oh why does it matter? Having shoes off in a cave when I had them available? "What a bone–head I am Lord! See this proves I am dim-sighted! I am not worthy of Your Call." I sat on this ledge for a very long time. I cried off and on. I looked out for miles and I saw red dirt and sagebrush. I saw hawks flying overhead. I was shaking my head – "Oh sure Lord, now leave me here – next will come buzzards!" They always circle above carcasses.

Then I saw buzzards circling overhead. "Oh sure, go ahead with Your humor. I'm upset here. I'm mad at You! I need help, but all You do is hammer me! You want me to do Your will then when I do – You allow the demons and everything else to pursue me! You allow them to attack me; my health, my work, my family, my finances. Lord, You promised me You would deliver me. Did You mean death? Now I will not see the Promised Land because I'm here in the desert and You are busy using me to prove a point! I'm tired of being a test dummy! Couldn't You have just given me a nice ministry? Maybe one in which I run the church nursery and craft fairs? I'm not sure I signed up for this? Why allow me to see Heaven? What if I cause You not to even want me here? What if...?"

I began to sob even as I write. I sat there for some more time. The sun was beginning to set. The sky was very beautiful. The sun was like a glowing red fireball. There were bands of colors; purples, reds, pinks, yellows and blues. I rested my head on the entrance wall to the cave as I sat there. The cave was positioned about 100 feet off of the ground. I didn't really see a path leading out and down to the desert floor. I wondered if I had come in from another route.

Then I heard the Voice of God: "Erin, what are you doing here?"

Me: "Lord, I'm tired. My enemies still pursue me. I feel like an island. I feel You do not hear me when I call. You want me to stand on faith, but where is my faith?" I began to turn rocks over. "Maybe I can find it here?" I looked under a big rock, nothing. "See? Help me Lord! I need help!"

God: "Erin, go and stand outside on the ledge."

I saw before me a mighty cloud of sorts – this I am unsure of. The Wind blew so hard my hair whipped across my eyes. I saw sagebrush pulled from their roots. There was sand and rock digging up the landscape and then it stopped as suddenly as it came. I dropped to my knees. Then I looked for God, but He was not there. Then the entire land shook. It shook so violently, I was on all fours then I dropped to the ground with my face down – then it stopped. Then the sun in the sky began to cause fire to burn across the landscape. I was terrified. Then it stopped. I was in tears.

Then I heard in a quiet whisper, "Erin, what are you doing here?"

Me: "Lord, I've seen what happens. You have shown what is coming. People will hate me. Lord the enemy continues to punish me and I'm tired. Lord, now I stand here before You like Elijah, but I'm no Elijah, I don't have a mantle, only a T-shirt to hide my face."

God: "Erin, go back and continue on your course! I am with you always!"

Then I felt a small fluttering on my shoulder. It was a small white bird with silver wings. It was a glorified sparrow. It chirped a few times, looked at me, and then flew off. I followed its flight and there around the side of the ledge was Jesus. I began to cry and ran into His arms. He held me.

Me: "I'm so sorry Lord, so sorry!"

Jesus: "Erin, it's okay, come!" He reached down and squeezed my hand. Instantly we were in a meadow in the Garden of God. It was next to the River of Life. Off to our right were a flock of very fluffy white sheep. There were a few lambs. The meadow was filled with all kinds of wild flowers and some perennials. The colors were amazing. The scents were beautiful and the fragrances difficult to describe. Nothing was overpowering or offensive.

We walked for some time. I was still rattled by God's display of power after my rant. Up ahead and high-up to the right was God's Mansion. It was incredible and cut into the Mountain of solid rock. Like marble or blue stone it looked like it was quarried directly out of the side of the mountain. It was massive!

Jesus: "Erin you aren't really speaking."

Me: "What can I say Lord? What can I do? Just to have this experience – well, people will think I am thinking I am Elijah or some might think I am Elijah. Clearly, I am no Elijah."

Jesus: "Erin why do you think God allowed this? Your best guess."

I looked over at Him while we walked. He is so much like a friend yet He is so much more than this. He is handsome, funny, strong, steadfast, endearing, and passionate about all of us. His personality is magnetic – just one moment of looking into His eyes and experiencing His smile and You will be forever changed. I began to have tears well-up. I am not a tearful person. It takes quite a bit to move me to tears, but when it comes to Jesus and His Goodness, His Grace, and His Mercy – you cannot help but love Him! Then You cry at the magnitude of all of Life and Him – Well let's not forget the Power of God!

Me: "Probably because my thoughts were like those of Elijah. Lord, I'm so troubled by what I have seen, I cannot go there. People without You dwelling in them, no Holy Spirit, or even being near people who are Christian – will do desperate things. I have seen unspeakable evil. I have been moved to tears and I am depressed like Elijah. Maybe God was giving me a choice to continue or die?"

Jesus: "Erin why did you run from Me when you were afraid?"

Me: "Because Lord, my dreams are so dark and You are not there. I have had trouble going back to a daily routine. Then, the enemy has been given permission to ramp up against me, and won't stop until I have nothing, physically, financially, or emotionally left. I'm depressed and tired. After my fast, You have always been faithful – this time more was required of me."

Jesus: "I am taking you to have some nourishment! Come!" Immediately we were at His front door. The door was open and one of the beautiful angels was there by the open door to welcome the Lord. Jesus smiled and called him Uriel.

Me: "Lord, what type of angel is he?"

Jesus: "Good question, (to Uriel) what is your assignment?" He had a big beautiful smile and amazing green eyes. His hair was wavy and a little below shoulder length with colors of white, gold and silver. His skin was dark and he was extremely muscular. His voice was very gentle.

Uriel: A bit modest but strong. "I am a protector and guard."

Me: "So you are a protector. I saw you by the clock. Who is protecting the clock?"

Jesus: "No worries Erin. There are 3 other angels and many more. After all we are here in God's House."

I heard both of them laughing. I knew that Jesus was in charge and these were archangels, but I also saw a long and trusted friendship. The loyal attitude of Uriel coupled with the fact he was clearly on the level of Michael, Gabriel, and Raphael was just amazing. What a long term assignment.

Me: "Lord, do the angels rest?"

Jesus: He was laughing. "Erin, are the angels greater than God, are you even? Think about this, if God works for six and rests on the seventh should His creation also rest?" He turns and addresses the archangel. "Do you observe the Sabbath?"

Uriel: He was smiling and laughing with Jesus, "Of course Lord."

Jesus: "Let me ask this next question for you Erin, because I can see this all over your face. (To Uriel) "What do angels do for fun?"

Uriel: Was laughing. "Well, I hang out with You Lord!"

Jesus: He was laughing, "No, really."

Uriel: He became quieter. "I rest, gain my strength, I spend time in worship, I enjoy music and I love spending time walking in the Garden. It is beautiful, Erin – wait until you see everything. I still have not seen everything!" I could read on his face that he loves serving Jesus and Heaven too!

Me: "Lord, may I ask one thing of him?"

Jesus: "Yes, go ahead." Meanwhile we are walking down the Hall in God's House. We have just come to His Courtyard.

Me: To Uriel, "Are you afraid of what is coming? Are you still bitter about your friends the Fallen turning from God? What will it be like fighting all of them?"

Jesus: "Erin this is 3 questions. (To Uriel) …Go ahead." Jesus was laughing because He knew in advance of my questions.

Uriel: "Well Erin, I was there at the time of the fall. One of the angels whom you know had a measure of vanity. He began to have the other angels answer to him even those who were not assigned to answer to him. Many of those he took with him were those who I trained and cared for." He looked over at Jesus and Jesus waved for him to continue. "He began to have the angels worship him instead of God. He divided and persuaded them that he would be taking over God's position on the throne. When God removed him and 1/3 of the angels went with him to govern Earth, there was wailing. Heaven mourned and so did the fallen. When they couldn't be redeemed and all hope of coming back was exhausted they decided to do the unthinkable – teach things of Heaven to man. There making man destroy himself. Erin I follow orders. I am not afraid of the coming wars because I know the outcome. Those whom I fight against are no longer from Heaven. They no longer praise God, but curse Him. They must be stopped to keep Heaven – Heaven! I am not capable of having fear because I am God fearing only. I serve Him therefore I have no fear. I have angels under my command and there are more under them. All love God and are capable to serve Him with our whole hearts – Yes I will cut down God's enemies at His command!" He spoke with authority!

Jesus: "Erin, did he answer your questions?"

Me: "Oh yes – thank you and nice to meet you! I bent over and whispered in Jesus' ear, 'Lord can I say, Hope to see you soon?'" Jesus was laughing so hard.

Jesus: "Uriel, Erin hopes to see you soon!" All the angels were laughing.

Me: "Did I say something funny?"

Uriel: "We hope to see you soon Miss Erin! You make us laugh, in a good way!"

Jesus: "Now Erin, are you ready to dine with the King?" He was still laughing. He pointed for me to sit next to Him at His table. An angel pulled the chair out for me. I sat. Then Jesus sat. I noticed the stone gazebo was covered in grape vines and wisteria – or something like wisteria. It was really beautiful. There were my favorite jeweled grapes on the vines. They shone like diamonds. They created lights. The table was set beautifully. There was a linen table cloth. This miracle fabric which couldn't take stain – it rejected stain. The little birds were chirping and singing up on the lower balcony.

Me: "Lord is that flower Wisteria?"

Jesus: He reached up and took a grouping of them to show me, I giggled. They were clusters of miniature lilies and on a vine no less. "What do you think?"

Me: "Wow Lord these are amazing!"

Jesus: "When you come here again – well when you reside here, I will give you a couple of clusters to take home and plant. Then you can have fields of lilies just from planting one cluster."

Me: "Wow, can I do the same with a cluster of grapes?"

Jesus: "Sure, if you would like."

Me: "Lord, do these grapes light up at night time in Heaven?"

Jesus: "Oh there are plenty of lights from many different sources. No I hadn't thought about having grapes light up at night. Hmmm... Well with the sun they definitely sparkle. I think this is what you are referring to right?" He pointed to some that sparkled like rainbows and the rainbows were everywhere.

Me: "Yes Lord, they are beautiful."

Jesus: "Erin if glowing grapes are your request then I will see if we can't somehow grant it." As I was speaking He was looking at the grapes. "Certainly if God can speak light into being, then He can certainly provide glowing grapes for you. Is this all you require to get you out of your depression? Glowing grapes?"

Me: "No Lord, this is not the key."

Jesus: "Remember Erin I was sent to remove sin as a living sacrifice."

Me: "Lord, so You were a type of scapegoat?"

Jesus: "Interesting term scapegoat. I came as the Lamb of God. I was His but let's go to Leviticus 16 and see this. So there were 2 goats. One was a sacrifice, the other was sent into the desert or wilderness. This goat is called Azazel.

Me: "Lord, forgive me but the name Azazel is the name of one of the fallen, correct?"

Jesus: "Interesting observation Erin, in Leviticus 16:22 the Scapegoat bears the iniquities for a land which is cut off. All of the sins were taken upon the goat, it was then sent out into the wilderness."

Me: "So, Azazel was sent by God under the Earth for 70 generations and to be removed around now right? Did he not sin so badly against God that He was sent below?"

Jesus: "Erin let's go back to your question on Scapegoat - there was a time when Jews would tie a red cloth to the goat's horn, when the goat came back the red cloth would be removed as a sign. And the cloth would become white. This occurred when God accepted the sacrifice. In tradition there was a period of 40 years from AD30-AD70. When the temple was destroyed, so were sacrifices."

Me: "Lord, so You atoned for sin during that time? …40 years."

Jesus: "No, for much longer than 40 years but this was a symbol. I guess in this case I would be an Azazel – a scapegoat for bearing sins."

Me: "Yes and You went to the desert for 40 days, too."

Jesus: "Now let's get back to you right now. I asked you to write everything down and record dates and times. Did you do this?"

Me: "Well, kind of..."

Jesus: "I know, first tell me about your storm dream this week. Oh yes, I believe this was on Wednesday."

Me: "Yes Lord, I went to bed on Tuesday and the dream occurred early Wednesday morning April 9th."

Jesus: "So tell me about this dream."

Me: "In this, my children were at school, I didn't recognize the city. I only know it was north of me. In this dream there were more brick buildings. I owned an interior design business and shop. It occurred in April. There were light rain clouds and trees were beginning to blossom. It was pretty. One of my customers came into the shop and said, "Did you hear about what is coming?" I replied, "No what's coming?" She turned on a TV and the news reporters were saying that there is a mandatory evacuation of the schools and businesses – the people are to stay in their homes and gather emergency supplies. There is an Epic Snowstorm so severe that no one will survive outside their homes. I was panicked because my kids were not dressed for a snow storm. I said to the customer, "It seems like I just put away all of my snow removal equipment and heavy coats." I scrambled to get things out. I phoned the schools – they told me there would be a 2 hour delay getting them home to me. So I decided to go to the market for supplies."

Jesus: "Why didn't you come to me with this?"

Me: "Lord, it was a snow storm in the spring, it seemed mild."

Jesus: "Mandatory evacuation isn't mild, now you removed something from the last dream...a date... now explain."

Me: "Lord I thought I had heard wrong. You don't give me dates and this one contradicted one which Enoch gave me. I sent it off to the Moderators, and then I emailed all of them to remove it and said I would go to You about it. It made me question everything."

Jesus: "Yes, I know Enoch was correct. Explain what you removed – you haven't done this before."

Me: "Yes Lord, I know."

Jesus: "Do you trust me Erin?"

Me: "Yes Lord, but You don't contradict Yourself – ever."

Jesus: "Please tell me why you would run?"

Me: "Because then I would need to doubt my ability to hear the Holy Spirit."

Jesus: "Okay, please give me the date you removed."

Me: "April 15th and the word Friday."

Jesus: "Why would I give you a date which contradicts another unless it was notable? Is there something significant here?"

Me: "Lord, I don't know, please help me."

Jesus: "Erin what does snow represent? It represents the removal of sin. Isaiah wrote – Though our sins are like scarlet, they shall be white as snow."

Me: "Forgive me Lord, other than the Scarlet – Red Moons coming on April 15th then what is coming? A snow storm?"

Dream over…

Chapter 11 - Faith Training

"Erin Come up today!" (Dream 1:30-3:30 am)

He had called me immediately before my written prayer. I had awakened several times during my sleep. I thought about several things. Each time I focused on these I cried. I had despair. I felt empty. The last time before I had fallen asleep, I said, "Lord fill me, I am empty." About 2 hours later or 9 am, I heard, "Erin Wake-up, get up." So I rolled out of bed. I was so sore from sleeping in. Every muscle and joint ached today. I took my communion elements, gave my dogs bones (to keep them busy) and proceeded to pray.

Erin Come Up!

Immediately I was back in the cave.

Me: "Oh no Lord, not here again!" This time I was ready at least my shoes were on. I stood up and felt my way toward the light around some rock walls. When I turned past this last familiar rock, I felt more confident with my steps. After-all, I had been here before right? Instead of panicking, this time I had more confidence. I saw the tunnel of light which became the opening to the cave entrance.

Me: "Maybe the Lord will have me come out at a new place in the Garden?" I said this out loud hoping the Holy Spirit would respond – nothing. I ran as quickly as I could toward the opening. I was disappointed when I realized it was the same desert scene.

Me: (Discouraged) "Oh Lord what now, seriously?" After my ridiculously busy week, grant me Paradise, or at least a glimmer!" I said this out loud – no response. I went back into my cave. It was very early morning right before dawn. I sat down and pouted. After what seemed like an eternity – when I'm impatient this translates to about 25 minutes – I began to give off a series of sighs – the impatient kind. Then I heard a flutter of wings. I peeked out and I saw two crows on the cave ledge. They landed and just stared at me as if to mock me.

Me: "Oh Lord, You are funny! You know I hate crows. I can't stand them. I don't care that they are intelligent or Your creation. Forgive me Lord. They remind me of camcorders with wings and feathers. I think they are from the enemy, I'm convinced. They sound irritating too." All of a sudden they began to squawk at me. They were mocking me. "Lord come to think of it, I have never seen a dead crow on the road or come to think of it, I've never seen a cute, cuddly baby chick crow. I'm not sure they exist. These things definitely eat their young. I'm sorry Lord, why did You create these?" Then I turned to the crows, "By the way....you don't exist in Heaven as far as I've seen!" Just then they flew off.

Me: "Lord, they are probably going to their friends and family to mock me more. Don't they go to a squawking tree? Sorry, Lord I'm tired, sore and crabby. I'm hungry too!" No response. I let out a sigh and went back inside to sit down. I thought about the heaviness of the season I've been in. I thought about my depression. Earlier this week I had punched in some of the homes I was raised in, into Google Earth on my computer. All the dark memories came back, everything, all of it. The homes were still intact. One home was the size of my bedroom and living room combined. The neighborhood was, well let's just say, I would be worried all the time for my children. The other house was twice the size of the first, but still less than or around 1000 square feet – for a family of 5. No wonder I spent most of my time outside or at friends. I am so glad my Mom moved us out of these!

I sat there for a while. Things came to me. I cried off and on. The apple tree I used to climb had been removed to make way for a parking lot for an apartment building, next to the one house. I went searching for the tree but couldn't find it. Of this house it was the best memory. I was 4 or 5 years old.

Me: "Lord forgive me for dishonoring my parents, but it makes me both mad and sad. I can't forget. I can forgive, but I'm troubled by what happened at both of these homes! Lord, I know there were circumstances, based on ages we make certain choices. Sometimes we don't care about the outcome because we are so focused on ourselves we forget that other people are involved and even children. Lord, I felt neglected and unimportant. Please forgive me Lord my parents didn't know. Please bless them!" I cried. As I sat there I heard some movement on the ledge. I looked out and the two crows had brought me some berries. I began to laugh. "Oh Lord You are Priceless and Infinite in Wisdom!" I went out and thanked God, the crows – which earlier I had cursed, and sat down to eat berries. I began to laugh when I realized they were huckleberries. They were wonderful! I stood to my feet and searched around me to see a distant forest mountain where the crows would pick these from.

Me: "Well Lord, now I feel like Noah on the boat waiting for the sign of land or even Jonah in the belly of the whale." I began to look for a way out of this spot. I began to search. I went to the side of the ledge where I saw Jesus before. There I saw a narrow ledge on the rocky cliff. I began to scale the side of the wall. I looked down and realized I was about 80 feet up. I saw a type of path once I scaled this wall about 15 feet wide. A few times when I would go to grasp a ledge like a handle, the rock would give way. When I was about 7 feet across, I went for another rock lip for support – the rock slipped out from my grip and dropped to the ground. For a moment I had lost my footing. I looked down and I became aware of the drop. Right as I began to panic, I began to hear the buzzards above me circling.

Me: "Seriously, God? You sent buzzards– Really?" I was suspended on this wall. One foot was on a semi-solid ledge while my other foot searched for footing. I stopped looking down because I became terrified about how high up I was. I noticed the jagged outcropping of red rock. If I fell I would be wedged and even the crows couldn't give me berries. The bonus is the buzzards couldn't pick at my dying carcass either. I couldn't seem to find a place to get my footing. The ledge my left foot was on was only about 6 inches wide and 6 inches deep. My left hand was in a groove in the wall and my right was grasping onto another sand stone ledge. I was stuck; I had no solid place to put my right foot. I had better go back if I can. I turned to look back to see how far I had come and if there was a pattern I could follow to get there.

Me: "O Lord, I should've just stayed in the dumb cave! Holy Spirit, help me here!" Just then the Holy Spirit downloaded a scripture, "The Sovereign Lord is my Strength; He makes my feet like that of a deer, He enables me to go on the heights." Okay but I have sneakers and I am still having a hard time. Hmmm… What other scriptures involve deer? "Lord obviously You are instructing me on faith. Then okay, I have complete faith that You will make a way where there seems to be no way! Please Lord, my hands are losing their grip, I have nowhere to go. I can't go down, I can't go back, and I can't go forward, where else is there?" I began to panic again. My heart was pounding out of my chest. I had climbed a fake rock wall before with a safety line and harness, but I was prepared, plus there was also a soft mat in that situation so I was never in danger. Now however, I was scared, there is nothing more I can do but to rely on the Lord. I've seen Him answer prayers consistently, although with me it is 50/50. I clearly lack. Right now however, my self has gotten me into a mess which only prayer can take me out of!

Me: "Lord, please help me! Show me the way Lord." I sat there longer. I was crying now, this wasn't funny anymore. My arms were falling asleep. The sun was rising in the sky. It was sweltering heat about 100 degrees. The buzzards were continuing to circle. I decided to come up with my own scripture, well a proverb. "Surely when a fool wanders ill prepared, the buzzards will circle and find strength!" I sat there for another block of Sparrow Eternity Time – 25 minutes.

Me: "Okay Lord, clearly You downloaded scripture from Habakkuk or even Psalm 18 about the deer, now what about this? I better remove my situation out of this for a second. You are clearly allowing me to an out here as a faith lesson. Clearly I am failing. What have I missed? I prayed for help. I know You won't leave me here as I can wake up (or even stop writing) at any given time but I need to finish this. So help me then break-down the scripture. You enable me to go on the Heights by making my (hind legs) my feet like a deer's hooves right? Wait, I came across the ledge straight across. I have looked forward, down and back – Oh I haven't looked Up!"

I looked up and there just a few feet above me – above my head was Jesus with His hand out! He was standing on a very large ledge. His face was bright and His smile was so beautiful!

Jesus: "Erin, my hand is falling asleep waiting for you to grab it. I don't have all day here!" He began to laugh. I was shaking my head in disbelief. I reached up, grabbed His hand and He easily; with no effort brought me up to a secure landing – a high place! Instantly my feet began to have feeling in them. I reached out and gave Him the biggest hug.

Me: "Thank You Lord! Were You there the entire time? Why didn't You say something?"

Jesus: "Well that would be too easy for you! Erin, we will speak more about this but right now take my hand!" I was so relieved to hold His hand. Tears were streaming down my cheeks, I was so glad He didn't leave me there to perish. Instantly we were on the forestry path. It was beautiful but it was not in Heaven yet, it was from the beginning of these dreams.

Me: "Lord, why are we here?"

Jesus: "Erin I have something to show you. Clearly you have several things on your mind that you have never released. These are yokes of affliction and great suffering for you. Remember when God Himself told you not to look back to see how far you've come?"

Me: "Yes – Lord!" I became quiet because I was guilty of looking back.

Jesus: "Erin, I am going to take you to a horrifying place now!"

There at the edge of the path was a suspended door. It was wooden with a moon and star.

Symbols that were
on the door.
Star of David was above
the Moon crescent

He reached out to grab the handle, it opened out towards us. It was dark on the other side of this door.

Jesus: "Do not worry Erin, I have hold of you." We appeared to be walking in a dark tunnel. The Lord shone brightly. His entire body was like a lamp.

Me: "Lord, I could've used You to light up the cave." I giggled nervously.

Jesus: Chuckled, "Perhaps next time you won't be in a cave at all! Why were you there Erin?"

Me: "I do not know."

Jesus: "I'll use your term here, seriously, is this your answer?"

Me: "Lord, I have faith and believe for others but I lack faith for myself. I guess I still don't believe You could use someone like me and my past reminds me I come from nothing and I have no worth."

Jesus: "Hmmm – so you would rather stay in dark caves dwelling on your past and wallowing in this? Erin – Not good, Not good!" He seemed so loving though. He was not shaming me, but giving me a gentle rebuke as He clearly loved me, unconditionally. We neared the opening of this dark tunnel and there before us was a scene straight from Ezekiel 37. I saw a massive valley of red dust – jagged rocks forming a bowl. In the middle of the valley were white bones – millions of bones. The sky was blue, not a cloud in it. The band of red from the rocks formed a stripe right above the massive bone yard of pure white bones. I was crying at the sight.

Me: "Lord, this reminds me of the Holocaust. It makes me ill."

Jesus: "Erin, this is not a modern historic grave. This is a symbol of those who are dead and even decaying."

Me: "Lord, I have been like these old bones until You blew Your Spirit into them – You blew life into my bones."

Jesus: "Really, Erin then why have you succumbed to despair, depression, and darkness this week. You not only looked down at your feet, you looked back at the ledge and how far you had come. You made a common mistake and fell for the blacksmith's tool here. You then lost heart; with you, your heart actually began to skip beats. You realized your place and you panicked. Your faith dwindled, then your strength. You were too focused on failure and reliving mistakes to look up and see me holding out My hand! Erin, it's great that you can encourage your friends and your children, but it would be even more convincing if you actually let My Words breathe life into you. Do you believe that I love you?"

Me: "Yes, Lord."

Jesus: "Do you believe that I AM the God Who Saves? Your Savior?"

Me: "Yes, of course, Lord!"

Jesus: "Do you believe then that I give good gifts to those whom I love, My friends?"

Me: "Yes, Lord."

Jesus: "Then, Erin, I am handing you gifts; receive them for yourself also. The cliff can't save you. The crows mock you. The buzzards anticipate your death and long to pick the meat off your decaying body. Even the sun can strip you of the wellspring of life, when you are exposed to its heat. Why put yourself out there, exposed to the elements without My Help? Who does this?" He was being very direct, yet very loving at the same time.

Me: "Lord, I do this. How can I receive that which is good, when I've been told my whole life that I don't deserve it? Lord, You know me better than anyone. You were there from the beginning. Please, Lord, help me heal so that I can continue!"

Jesus: "Do you believe that I can heal?"

Me: "Of course!"

Jesus: "If you believe I can heal, then can you receive healing if I were to heal you?"

Me: I paused for a moment. "Yes, Lord."

Jesus: "Hmmm. You hesitated. Do you believe by faith I can heal you, Erin?"

Me: "Forgive me, Lord, I have not been able to receive this because I do not feel worthy."

Jesus: "So, you are content in your cave? You're content lying here in a heap of bones on the valley floor? Okay … well, if these bones could talk, they might say, 'Do it, Erin!'"

Me: "Lord, please forgive me. I have lack. I lack faith. I cling to fear. I am afraid. What if I can't let You do everything You'd like? What if I'm a barrier to Your Will?"

Jesus: "You build your own barriers. You erect your own stone walls. You cannot stop God's Will, Erin! No man can stop God! Will you allow Me to tear down this barrier? This keeps you from realizing all that you have been called to do! You have laid your children at the foot of the Cross. Now, Erin, do you trust Me with You? Can you let go and let God work? Will you receive gifts when I give them?"

Me: "Yes, Lord, I am ready to receive. Please, Lord, breathe life into me. Take me across the waters to You! Please take hold of my hand. Keep my eyes looking forward and up. Let me no longer look down or behind me. When I look back, it comes with severe pain and memories. I see the birth of failure. When I look down, I feel fear. I realize my footing is unstable, and I fall – or like Peter, I sink!"

Jesus: "Then, Erin, Focus Forward! Look up, for your Redeemer is Here!" I reached over and hugged Him. He held me for some time. Then He kissed my head and said, "Erin, your faith has healed you!"

Me: "Thank You, Lord. I will receive Your gifts with my whole heart, not knowing where You will lead me, but I will have faith that You will keep me from harm. You are the Giver of Good Gifts!"

Jesus: "Now, let's gather these four angels over the valley walls." Just then I saw all four angels standing on the points of a compass: North, South, East, and West. Each of them had a Shofar. The Angel from the North started to blow his Horn. The ground began shaking – the bones began to rattle. Then, the Angel to the East began to blow, while the Angel to the

North continued to blow. The bones began to come together to form skeletons, and then the Angel to the South, over our heads, began to blow. I began to see flesh form on the bones, then skin, then clothing. Then the Angel from the West blew, and a Mighty Wind came. I saw the Heavens part, and a Wind blew from the Throne of God into these people, and they became alive! There were at least a million. I saw Jews and even some Muslims.

Me: "Oh, Lord, this is incredible!"

I turned from to look for Jesus and He was gone. I looked again and He was walking amongst the people. They all bowed to Him. He said, "Please rise up and celebrate!" They cheered and tried to hug Him. They were dead and now they were alive!

(Just as I was writing this my phone beeped. It was my phone alerting me to a sticker they sent. I was curious, so I opened it. It was a cartoon of a cute girl in a bunny suit, reaching for an egg with a message "Happy Easter" – I couldn't help but cry at the amazing God we serve!)

The people were hugging each other and so happy to see Jesus, their Messiah! As I stood over this valley, I saw Jews – more than a million – declaring Christ as their Savior! This was amazing, but to see Muslims coming to confess Jesus as their Lord – amazing beyond amazing – and embracing Jews!

I sat observing this for quite some time. The landscape had changed. I saw water springs coming from the sides of the valley. I saw rivers. I saw people bathing in the River. All the while, they were praising God for Jesus! I heard Choirs of Angels singing "Holy, Holy, Holy, Lord God Almighty!" The sight was incredible. I just praised God, too!

I realized that He had shown me what is to come someday when He takes His Throne in Jerusalem, but I was unclear exactly. As I stood there and worshiped the Lord, I was instantly removed to the deck of the Bridal Chamber in Heaven by the Throne. I was wearing the most amazing gown of white. My hair was very long and braided. I was so excited! I ran over to the edge of the Balcony to find

Jesus. Instead, my Guardian angel was there. I hadn't seen him for some time.

Me: "Where is the Lord?"

Guardian: "Erin, He is with you; do not worry. I have a gift for you. Take it with you. When you open it, receive it! Do not give it away … it is for you this time! It is okay! Erin, every good gift and every perfect gift is from above, and comes down from the Father of Lights" (James 1:17).

Me: "Thanks be to God for His Indescribable Gift! I look at my place on the Balcony near the Throne and I am overwhelmed!

Guardian: Now, take this with you and receive it! Erin, do not forget Psalm 46:5, Psalm 45, Habakkuk, Psalm 18, Ezekiel 37, Haggai, and even Song of Songs. You are His! He Loves You! Now Receive His Gifts! Don't look back. Don't look down! You are loved by the King! This is the Beginning!

Dream over ………

Blessings

Chapter 12 - The Alpine Meadow & the Tevah

Communion

Thank You Father!

Lord, today I praise You for Your Divine Goodness. Thank You for sending Jesus to Save us! Thank You for Rising Up and wiping the despair off the faces of Your followers! Thank You that You, Jesus are our perfect gift given to us by God! I accept You as the Greatest Gift I have ever been given!

You are our Groom and we are Your Bride! Thank You for this Divine courtship of Life. Now my heart is forever changed. Lord You saved me from the jaws of death. You made my feet so I could scale a wall. When I needed Your help You were right above me and ready to take hold of my right hand! Thank You Lord for You are Good and Your Mercy Endures Forever and Ever!

God please be with me and find favor. Though my feet often walk in shifting sands, You place me on solid rock so there I will stand. When my head drops and I continue to look down, You take hold of my chin and gaze into my eyes. I see myself reflected in Your eyes. There I see a mystery beyond this place. Your eyes reflect a love for me which I have never known, so deep a love that everyone should desire it but very few know of it. It has been there since the beginning of time, if we had only known earlier. If I had only known, but even had I would not have believed it. Now I am older and most of my youth is gone – now I desire to run with You! Now, I want to run that race and scale those walls. I once, sprung out of bed daily with nary a pain in my bones, but now when I want to run to You I must move slowly. Oh Lord, if I had only known You like this just twenty years ago, where would I be now? Now, I am old and full of years, to imagine You would desire me as a bride no less is difficult to comprehend. Here I am like Sarah in her older years, but in Heaven I have youth like Esther. Lord, today please breathe life into my old dry bones. I can hear the Shofar sounds and imagine what I saw in the Valley as You assembled Your vast Army of those who found You – Well those You chose and sought from the beginning. What a joyous and glorious day when You come for Your people! Thank You Jesus for all that You have done! Thank You for Your Divine Love!

Erin Come Up!

Today I pulled into an area of Heaven I have not seen. It was very High Up, almost like Alpine Mountains. There were beautiful lakes everywhere. The color was that of a tropical shore, like sea green – crystal clear. The sky was completely blue, deep blue like cerulean blue. The Alpine Mountains had snowy peaks. I was in some type of vehicle, although I am not sure how to describe a train with no tracks. Yet this only had one car and I was in it. It weaved in and out of the area as I looked down I saw homes. I saw animals and beautiful conifer trees. I saw cedars and redwoods that reached almost higher than some of the peaks. It was stunning. One tree was the circumference of my property at its base. As we turned around a peak I saw a meadow. I had been here before a few times in my dreams. As I pulled into a platform area, I looked across this meadow and it was a sea of color. Every mountain flower was represented there. I saw bees buzzing and so many different species of butterfly, it was like looking at flowers fluttering in the sky.

The vehicle that I was in stopped at the platform and the door opened. The platform was made of some extremely large slab of blue stone or granite; it was chiseled in one piece – impossible from Earthly standards to machine. The stairs and the entire piece of slab were seamless. There was a beautiful stone pergola over the platform – but it was masculine in form – not made of wood but all stone. There was a purple carpet made of wool and silk about three inches and shimmered with silver thread which seemed to run through it. Off in the distance I saw an incredible water fall coming right out of two peaks. The water was light green and it literally burst forth. It was jetting into a very large pool – really a small lake! It was easily a few miles from the platform.

The doors opened and I jumped right onto the platform. It was about 73 degrees – I expected from an Earthly measure of temperature to experience cool air like a very high elevation would have. I stood at the platform looking at this sea of color. Tears streamed down my cheeks as I have never seen such a beautiful sight! Each time here, I think it's not possible to see better but it is. – Of course nothing is quite like God's Garden, this is special.

I was wearing a beautiful white gown but it was shorter and I had some linen pants like pantaloons. I had my long curly hair with braids. I was in my body at age 25 only better of course. I ran out into the meadow and danced around the flowers for some time. The flowers were so fragrant. For wild flowers – there was no weedy smell about them. The fragrance was amazing! Perfect! The sun was crystal clear; I would look at it and not have it blind me like Earth. As I was dancing, I heard the sound of humming from the wind. The wind was causing the flowers to sing. I heard the Bittersweet Symphony – but in Heaven the Song is glorified so I will call it Divine symphony.

After a while I wondered where Jesus was. I looked but I couldn't find Him. I decided to run like I did when I was younger, so I stopped dancing. I stood, looked around and I set my sights on running to the waterfall. I said out loud, "On your marks, get set, go!" I ran full on sprint as fast as I could run – no holding back! As I ran, my target was still further. I ran, but I couldn't come closer.

Me: "Oh Lord, what is going on here? I should've made it to that waterfall!" I was laughing. I was amazed at how strong my lungs are. The air was life giving. It expanded my lungs with healing capacity. I was not out of breath or light-headed. In fact, it was if I had – "runner's high" – hmmm... I love this Heavenly body. This is a harsh contrast to the Earthly body that I rolled out of bed with this morning! My skin was alive and the color – well let's just say I was filled with Heavenly Oxygen!

I loved the sound the flowers made with the wind. The song and fragrance were amazing. I looked around for the Lord again, but didn't see Him so I decided to lie down and rest. The grass was fluffy and seemed to respond to my body giving me extra support. I imagined this would be like one of those Posturepedic mattresses. I laughed. "God, You are so Incredible!" I laid down and looked up at the sky and began to hum praises with the flowers. A small honey bee landed at my chest. I began to brush it off because I didn't want to be stung, but I realized it had no stinger, no need for one. I laughed and looked at it closely in my hand.

Me: "I see, you're only job here is to make honey! No fear, no stinger, clever and Divine!" The tiny honey bee was like spun gold. It actually had what looked like a yellow diamond embedded into it. It's worth here was great! In Earthly terms if I had just seven of these little bees I could easily buy a home. The small rare diamonds were easily several carats. I was laughing…how common here for God – how rare on Earth. I love Heaven! I think I had fallen asleep as the next thing I saw was the Lord right over me. I opened my eyes and heard His laughter!

Jesus: "Erin, did you enjoy your rest?"

He reached His hand down to me. I was laughing and I reached up to take His hand.

Jesus: "What do you think of this place?"

Me: "Oh Lord, this is breathtakingly beautiful! I love it. I feel so young again here. I'm ready to come Home now... Can I?"

Jesus: "Erin look at your feet, what do you see?"

Me: "Well, my feet are beautiful here. They are perfect and they run wonderfully fast!"

Jesus: "When you ran fast today did they take you anywhere?"

Me: "No Lord, I wasn't able to run to the fountains, the waterfall."

Jesus: He was smiling. "Erin beautiful are the feet of those who bring good news! Your feet will one day run here, but for now use them for My purposes. Run like the wind!" He was smiling. He picked a stem of flowers as we walked.

Me: "Lord, what more can I do?"

Jesus: "It is not for you to "do" anything. Just wait on Me and I will instruct you in the way you should go. As you have learned from your dreams, knowledge will increase as your time grows shorter. Now give Me your hands, and I will take your feet, Come!"

Immediately we were at the pool which I was unable to run to on my own. He walked into it. He stood in about 3 feet of water.

Jesus: "Erin, sit down."

I proceeded to sit on the bank of this small mountain lake. My feet were bare and had Heavenly remnants of shimmering dirt. They really weren't dirty as clearly this was symbolic. He took my left foot and put it in the pool. He washed it with a linen cloth. I began to cry as I remembered another time like this awhile back. I was crying at the magnitude of this moment. "Remember Erin, do as I am doing. I have given you an example to follow. Do as I have done to you. Remember slaves are not greater than their master. Nor is the messenger more important than the one who sends the message. Now that you know these things God will bless you for them! Erin, beautiful are the feet who bring good news! Are you ready to run?"

Me: "Lord, what are You saying? You are preparing us for something; I can see it in Your Eyes! Lord, I have nothing to lose here. I have no fear of death only of living my life like a dead person. I have come this far. If I perish for Your sake then I reside here with You! I have gained everything. I have lost only myself! I love You!"

Jesus: He was smiling. "Then Erin, be of good cheer. Do not fear. You are mine. I have redeemed you. Exalt God, minimize self. Stay on your course. One day you will be here permanently, but now deliver good news. Love your neighbor as yourself."

Me: "Lord, I love You with all my heart and soul."

Jesus: "Remember Erin, the enemy doesn't bring a message of Hope to the Lost. You will be mocked by those closest to you. Please take courage and know that I am here to take hold of your hand. Look forward!"

He finished drying my right foot. "Then don't forget to Look Up! You are loved, I am with you!"

Dream over...

Blessings....

Chapter 13 - Faith and the Ocean

Communion

Dear Father;

Thank You! Thank You! Thank You!

I love You Lord! I pray every day that I will walk in Your ways. Lord, You have gifted me with a desire to follow You. Where ever You would take me. Lord I pray I walk a blameless path. I pray You come into the hearts of my enemies so that they too would see what an amazing God I serve! You are good and Your Mercies are New every morning! Today is a new dawn with You. I can scale a mountain! With You nothing is impossible!

Lord, keep me on the path which leads to You always. Keep me Holy and apart when living in this world. Lord every day I deal with cold people. Their hearts are hard and they think nothing of me. Much of the time I feel like collateral damage, as I am a blip and of no significance to those who hate me. Please forgive me when I become angry or I become depressed when I have no choice but to be in their presence until one day You remove me. I give my life for You Jesus, now and forever. Here on Earth I serve my earthly master but in my heart I do this to please only You. Lord, I cannot make myself Holy. I can walk in Your ways the best I can every day and it is You who decides whether I am holy and pleasing to You. I cannot act Holy and fool God – this is impossible, there is nothing hidden. Lord, let me not be fooled when someone calls themselves Christian or speaks scripture. As I have learned the hard way, someone claiming to be Holy can lead many on to a different road – a very wide highway. Today, it seems many prefer this "Holy Highway" with the illusion of it leading to Heaven, but Lord You in Your amazing goodness remind us that it is the little bumpy slow and less traveled road which leads to Heaven; very few travel this one.

Lord, I love You, take my life and make it Yours. Take my family and make them Yours. I dedicate all I have to You. What I have is not perfect but it's perfectly what You have given me! Lord, I give everything I am to You! You are my Joy!

Erin Come Up!

I woke up out of my sleep on a sandy beach. I could hear waves crashing. My clothes were torn. I must have been there for some time. My muscles ached. I was in my young body again about 25 years old. My right cheek was pressed against the sand. I woke up on my right side. I was wearing a white t-shirt and some cut-off jean shorts. My hair felt dirty from salt water. It was curly and filled with sand. My skin was sunburned where I had obviously been exposed to the searing sun. I sat up and looked around. I was on some sort of island sand bar. It was about the size of my rental home, about 75' long by 20' wide. I looked and saw fragments of what looked like a broken up boat. I must have been on it. I had no recollection of what happened which brought me to be here. There was no greenery. In fact it looked like low tide and come high tide there would be no sand bar at all. The sandbar seemed high though it was about 7' above sea level. The waves crashed on the sides and made a loud sound.

Me: "Okay Lord, did I abandon my faith altogether? Why am I here?" I walked over to the boat fragments to see what type of vessel I crashed here on. It looked like a small catamaran. I saw fragments of the sail. There was only one hull on the sandbar. It looked like a 16 foot hobie – a bit too large for me. "Why would I be on such a thing in the ocean no less?" I began to look around to see if there was anything to salvage for me to use. I looked around to see where I was. It was a tropical area. The sand was white like sugar. I looked around to see if I could see land. There was nothing. I was locked here. The water was clear and deep sea green in color so I knew I wasn't really in a shallow area, it was just an illusion. I began to panic as I realized I was by myself on an island – sandbar – with no resources. This was certainly not Heaven. The sun was high in the sky and it was about noon, based on the shadow off of the broken catamaran and the heat. It was about 95 degrees and humid, with a slight breeze. The humidity made it seem like 100 degrees.

After sometime, an eternity – okay, about 25 minutes, I realized I needed water. I was laughing; my surveying and panic made me forget I was parched and thirsty. I began to pray. "Lord, if You are here, and I know You are, please reveal Yourself, or at least give me something to drink – water would be great." I waited around for a while; nothing! It was around 3:00 p.m. or so, assuming I was somewhere near the equator in earthly measure.

Me: "How did I get here? I would try my hands at sailing a catamaran on a lake with friends, but the ocean alone? No life vest even? What was I thinking? What could the Lord be showing me?" I was talking out loud to myself – audience of one! "Lord, please, I'm thirsty!"

Once again I'm getting discouraged and impatient. I began to search the remnant of this catamaran to see if something was hidden under the debris. I began to dig in the sand a bit and discovered a strap from a day-pack. I dug frantically, when I got to the pack I opened it and discovered a set of car keys with an automatic lock, I pressed it a few times wondering if I'd hear a chirp – nothing. I began to laugh. "Lord, You are funny!" I looked further. I found a raincoat in a zipper bag, a small flint starter, a mirror, and a small compass. I laughed again at this. This was something I carried in the back of my car for emergencies. Well, how is this going to help me if I'm dying of thirst? I began to pray. "Lord, I don't know how I got myself into this mess, but I did. The items I have won't save me here, I need water. Help!" As I lay there in the sand I took the mirror and looked at myself with it. I loved what I looked like, but obviously my youthful confidence caused this mess and it won't help me get out of this. I began to laugh.

"Holy Spirit, please grant me wisdom here. The tide is rising. I am going to lie in the sand looking – up to wait for my 'rescuer'... Jesus I am looking up, where are You? Little Help Here!" I began to panic again as I realized the high tide would overcome my sandy beach – or island very soon. Just then I heard a thud. I looked behind me as a seagull flew over me. "Oh great last time it was crows – now it is a giant rat with wings." I yelled, "Hold on, maybe the Lord wants me to cook and eat you!" The seagull looked at me and began yelling at me and flapping its wings. Then it flew off. I got up to see what the thud sound was. I looked on the other side of the Hull and there was a plastic water bottle. I immediately gave thanks and drank the fresh water.

"Thank You Lord for Your provision! Next time please send a rescue boat soon, I'm going to need it!

The tide was rising. The small island now had become even smaller. I began to prepare the catamaran parts as my only hope of floatation. I had no life vest. Darkness was coming and to make matters worse; there was a storm on the horizon.

"So Lord, there is a storm approaching, the waves are beginning to rise, darkness is coming and all I have to use for floatation are remnants of one hull of a catamaran? Did I do something last week that required this lesson? Can I say, I am not at home in the ocean, I would prefer a lesson like this in the desert cave. Please…"

I waited – Nothing, no word from Jesus. I put my small day pack around my neck and arm. I used some cording to assemble parts not knowing if they were even sea worthy and I waited for the tides to overcome the small piece of land; now about 5' x 10'. The hull of the catamaran was bashing up against the sand and soon it would float off if I didn't just jump on it, so I did. Right as I did, the small sandbar was overtaken by the tides. The Hull was slippery. I could barely cling to it and I was praying that the waves wouldn't roll it over on me. I tied the cording around my wrist and waist so if the waves pulled me off I wouldn't lose the only thing saving my life at that point. The sky was growing increasingly dark. The clouds were collecting just over me. I began to cry.

"Lord, I've cried out to You. I know this is more faith training, but You are going too far. I will drown." The waves and rain seem to increase. I kept going under with each wave. The salt water was coming into my mouth and out my nose. When I was a kid and my family surfed off the California Coast I remembered this feeling, it was awful. My parents rode the waves with their wetsuits way far out beyond the breakers. My brother and I did nothing but get pounded by the surf. To grown-ups these were small waves; to children they seemed like 10 foot killer waves. I ate more sand and salt water than I spent actually surfing waves. Needless to say I didn't enjoy it much until my little wet suit was off and I was safely in our van. Some of the conditions were grueling and cold. I realized as I recalled my surfing adventures that I could actually use some of that knowledge to climb this hull and paddle. It took several attempts at trying to hoist my wet body onto the slippery hull and finally I did. Just as I draped my body over the hull to rest, the storm came. The wind blew massive waves over me and at times the hull itself went underwater. The swells on the ocean were 6' high and this was only at the start of the storm.

"Lord, please deliver me now. Don't forsake me! Please, I want to wake up from this nightmare! Holy Spirit, Help! There is a scripture and a promise as soon as I call, You will answer my cries, please I am afraid!"

Jesus: "Erin, I am here Look." I peeled my face off of the Hull to look out over the ocean. There through the storm I saw Jesus walking on the water.

Me: "Lord, is that You?"

Jesus: "Erin, You know My voice, now step out in faith and come to Me."

Me: I quickly untied my hands and waist which attached me to the hull. I got on my knees and stepped my left foot out on the water. There was like an invisible road which I could feel with my feet. I began to walk toward Him on the water. I became overly-excited and began to become aware of myself. I took my focus off of Him, I looked out to the storm then down at my feet. Then like a bridge falling I shot right into the dark cold water. I became disoriented, but I got to the surface. My head was barely above the surface; I couldn't see anything but swells. I yelled out! "Jesus, please forgive me!"

Just then His hand grabbed my wrist and He pulled me out. Instantly we were on a beautiful balcony of stone and crystal glass. Below us was an incredible sandy beach with sea shells made of pearl. There were palm trees with fruit and tropical plants. The ocean was crystal clear. I could see to the bottom. The sand was white like sugar and sparkled. I saw His white Horse running up and down the beach, another horse playing in the waves. These horses were the most beautiful I had ever seen! They chased each other. I heard the Lord laughing with delight over the sight of His horse. He gave a funny whistle and clapped. The horses quickly stopped, looked at Him, and then He said, "No, go – keep playing!" They began to chase each other again. I was sitting in a chair on the balcony of someone's beautiful beach villa. It was beyond the magazines incredible. It was a Beach House of a King!

I was still somewhat quiet about what just occurred. I was in shock.

Jesus: "Erin you are quiet. Here have some water, you are thirsty." He handed me a glass and I quickly gulped it down.

Me: "Lord, what happened? What was all of that? Why did You allow that instead of bringing me here? Am I lacking more?"

Jesus: He smiled. "First Erin you did exactly what I expected. You didn't surprise Me!"

Me: "Lord, shouldn't I be more advanced in my faith? Why, when I was just remembering the reference of Peter last week would I do exactly what I had purposely tried not to do? Fall in the water."

Jesus: "Hmmm. I heard a lot of "I"s in your last statement. What do you think landed you on that sandbar to begin with?"

Me: "Obviously I was an unskilled or arrogant captain of this catamaran. I put myself there."

Jesus: "Actually, Erin God did, why?"

Me: "I have no idea. Did I sin last week which caused this?"

Jesus: "Sin is not always the reason you can land in trouble. Erin you live in a fallen world with the root of sin but this doesn't mean this lesson is based on this."

Me: "Oh, so this was a lesson. Lord is my lack of faith a sin?"

Jesus: "Hmmm, this is an interesting question you ask. Why do you lack?"

Me: "Lord I came from lack. I lived most of my life with no hope. I have prayed some times and You have not granted my requests. Because You haven't in the past, why would I be wise to keep asking?"

Jesus: "Okay, so now you stop asking?"

Me: "No Lord, I stop believing You will answer!"

Jesus: "So, now I have never answered your prayers?"

Me: "Oh, forgive me Lord, You answer my basic needs – You are faithful. Just, some of the larger things…"

Jesus: "So there is a limit to God's answered prayers? If you are perfect I would answer big ones but since you are not perfect I can only answer small ones? So now I am a God who requires a performance? I must be entertained in order to reward prayer? Hmmm… this doesn't sound right! Erin, where is the coming from?"

He was smiling and comfortable but was looking for an honest answer from me. He was kind and loving, but stern.

Me: "Lord, I guess at the point in my life journey I should be without the sin of lack. I feel I am sinning against You when I doubt. Like I am testing You. I catch myself when I pray for signs… I have prayed for certain things but haven't got my wishes."

Jesus: He waived and an angel brought a 'Genie Bottle'. He thanked the angel. The angel and Jesus were both smiling. "Okay Erin, rub the bottle and pray." He laughed and handed it to me.

Me: "Lord, I know You are not my personal 'Jesus Genie'." You are my Savior. If I had only three wishes it would be as follows: That I dwell in the House of the Lord forever, near His Altar. That my children dwell here too!" I paused…

Jesus: "Go ahead Erin, you have one more wish."

Me: "That You would delight in me always."

Jesus: "Now what happens?" He picks up the bottle and looks inside. He shakes it and holds it up to the Sun. "Hmmm… interesting – Do not put your faith in worthless idols – I learned something today!" He was laughing.

Me: "Oh, You are funny!"

Jesus: "Erin, I granted you those prayers long ago. These are good.

Now, whatever are you speaking of? Why did you stop asking for certain things?"

Me: "Lord gibber prayers, miraculous ones which can only come from You."

Jesus: "Ah yes, those which you cannot govern. Please explain!"

Me: "Lord, those Korean children from the Ferry. I haven't stopped praying for a miracle, but now it seems like it is too late. I am so sad for the parents. One of the teachers, the vice principle killed himself as a guilt offering to the parents since he arranged the trip for the kids. It should've been a happy time yet death and despair seemed the victor. You didn't answer my prayers!"

Jesus: "Erin, that is not true. Who are you that you alone are sending prayers that God will answer? Your prayers were answered and so were many others. What did you pray for?"

Me: "A miracle. I prayed the children would be saved. These were good children who were very obedient and listened and followed instructions. Death was their reward and despair is their parent's burden to bear."

Jesus: "Erin, who is God My Father? Who am I? Do you not believe that more than one thousand angels or more were dispatched. Do you believe that I am capable to save even under the depths of the sea? Is there a limit? Where is this written? How do you know there were not Christian servants leading these children home? Do you believe God's saving grace is multicultural? Do you believe God is capable of speaking other languages and understanding – hearing the cries of these children? Erin, is there nothing God can't do? Remember in Revelation He opens doors which no one can shut and closes doors which no one can open. God is in control Erin. He is there. I am there with you always. You can spend precious time building a floatation device or you can pray. Which one ultimately saves you?"

Me: "Lord, Prayer!"

Jesus: "Your lack of Faith is not a sin, but do not be surprised if I don't test you here."

Me: "Lord it is you testing me?"

Jesus: "Here with you it is, I. On, Earth it is being allowed by the enemy. The enemy prefers trials of testing. He knows that testing produces endurance. Trials are different trials come at the hand of an accuser and are usually a petition granted due to sin, but not always. One day you will understand. For now be thankful for both – in you they are producing that which is good and a heart which pleases God! This is why you are to be Joyful when trials come."

Me: "Lord you said, my enemy had run his course and I am free."

Jesus: "Yes, but you haven't tested the prison cell door to see if it is unlocked. You are remaining there – you have been told to run.

Me: "Lord, cells also keep the bad guys out."

Jesus: "Well in your case then enemy likes to keep you in fear and locked up. You are scary when you roam free."

Me: "Oh Lord, to You too? Am I scary when I'm free and not locked up?"

Jesus: Laughing… "You are scary only when you try to sail a catamaran with no leading. You steer your own ship sometimes and have more faith in your own abilities than My capabilities to work your sail. Erin let me be your Sail, let me steer your boat and let God navigate as He clearly knows the way in which He sends the wind. You are a passenger and a first mate. You serve the Captain and you are at the Mercy of God! Now there is much more to discuss. Do you believe lack of faith is a sin?

Me: "I believe in my case lack of faith is a long–drawn–out–learned behavior which started from my childhood. I quit believing. I knew You were the God of Miracles, I had seen the results, but I didn't believe I was worthy. Many don't believe I am worthy or clean enough to be here with You?"

Jesus: "Then no one would be. Erin, what do I require?"

Me: "To love You with all my heart and love God – and my neighbor as myself!"

Jesus: "Then do I require a fresh shower and clean clothes to be in my presence? Holiness is a matter of the Heart, not that of soap. Let's go back to the word consecration, study this. What does righteous mean? I tell you the truth, that many will not be worthy who call themselves clean. They will be unclean as they are about appearances. You would not measure up to their standards – yet neither would I. So we are together in this Erin! You are mine. I am mighty to save. Now, tell me what else you have prayed for?"

Me: "A home here on Earth, but now it is too late?"

Jesus: "Wait, did you see something on the Clock which I didn't? Angels did I miss something? Is it almost Time? Erin, I am close, but there is still more. Please don't limit God because your timeline isn't happening according to your prayers. There are things which must occur first. A house for you is not out of the question. Is anything too big for God? You are to continue to live, laugh, pray and follow Me."

Me: "I can't always laugh Lord, this is sometimes too hard."

Jesus: "I understand, but Erin, find Joy! You have much to be happy about. Be anxious for nothing. Even though times will become more difficult on Earth, you must try to find joy. Then Erin, when others see you – your faith will become a source of comfort. Your trials will be used to comfort people who need to hear good news. Now, I told you I would build a house for you. I also told you I will remove you and your children to the trees."

Me: "Lord where are You speaking of, here in Heaven? I can't imagine another physical move before You come. It would need to be You supernaturally removing us from this place. Lord, these dreams have been time consuming but such a life saver for me. I have come to know and love You so much. Lord, if You say, "Move," I will move. Please provide the circumstances to do this if trouble is near. I will trust You! I know 100% that Your love is greater than anything I can imagine. Each time with You is better than the last and I can hardly wait until one day I am here with You!"

Jesus: "I look forward to this day too Erin. It is written. Try as much as you are able to look for me when trouble comes. There will be events in which many will believe that God no longer cares. But remember the Valley of Dry Bones! Remember where the breath of life comes from. Remember the Silver Cord. Now tell me about your faith and prayers a few days ago. Did you encounter a Mourning Dove?"

Me: "Oh yes, I heard a bang on the office building like someone had thrown a baseball full force at our window. I got up and went outside. There was nothing in front so I walked to the grassy area of the building and there on the ground was a dying grey mourning dove. It was lying on its side and seemed to be breathing its last breath. It was breaking my heart. I couldn't watch it. It looked like its chest cavity was bulging and there was blood in the corner of its beak. I stayed with it for a couple of minutes. I didn't want to watch it die so I went inside. Then I realized I wanted to pray for it. So I went back outside and prayed this, "Lord You can do all things. You are the God who created the Universe. Is nothing too small for You? Please heal this dove." I moved toward it and the bird flipped over on its feet. I thought one leg was broken as before it was contorted and the leg was spread out. I quickly ran inside to get my camera. I still believed the bird might die. So I took a couple of photos as evidence that the dove existed. I prayed, "Lord, You are requiring me to have faith like a mustard seed. You are saying by the Word of God that I can move mountains by faith in God's name. You are saying nothing is impossible. Well as I sit here, I believe You can, then please Lord heal this dove. How can I heal the sick on Your behalf yet I cannot believe for this bird?" I prayed in the Spirit and I saw open Heaven and an angel come. The bird was comforted by my voice. Then when nothing appeared to happen, I decided to go back inside. My co-worker was there and asked about the sound. I took him outside and just as we rounded the corner, the dove flew off as if nothing had happened. We went to the window which is mirrored and saw an impression on it and feathers stuck to the window.

We couldn't believe the bird survived. "Thank You Lord for healing that bird!""

Jesus: He was laughing. "Erin, You were testing me in this."

Me: "Wait Lord, isn't faith a form of testing? Faith is something hoped for and the evidence of things not seen. If we see what we pray for happen, then doesn't it build our faith? If I prayed non-stop, believed, yet there was no evidence of answered prayer – then how can I confidently walk? Lord, I sit here; I can't claim to know all of You. You are a Divine Mystery. You are amazing and Faithful! I believe in You with my whole heart!"

Jesus: "Your words are good; they come from your heart. You recognize that when you pray, if the prayer is good then God will turn and hear your prayer. Sometimes there is evidence manifested, other times you do not see it, yet you must believe in that which is unseen. You must trust me. I hear you Erin. Your heart was breaking for this gray dove." He began to laugh. "Then Erin, your impatience turned it into a fleece." He was laughing. "Then later that day when you told someone about the dove – they being a bird expert told you the bird probably flew off to die. Then what did I do?"

Me: "You showed me the bird looking right at me from a pole."

Jesus: "This was a few hours later and the bird was very much alive. For a moment you doubted your prayer availed much. One minute you believe your prayers should've raised the Ferry and saved the children, then the next you doubt that your prayers healed a dying bird. Later what did you find out about the bird's speed of flight?"

Me: "I learned a dove can fly up to 55 mph. It flies the speed limit." He laughed.

Jesus: "Interesting an object flying that rate of speed should be dead instantly or crushed. Yet you witnessed a miracle. You saw an angel from an Open Heaven and you then later listened to a bird expert? Erin who created the dove to begin with?"

Me: "Lord, I am never going to believe like a mustard seed. I have come this far and my belief is horrible. I'm mad at myself."

Jesus: "This was the first truth you just spoke about in your last statement. Now forgive yourself! You are learning. When you pray, you must believe for it. Erin, I tell you the truth that dove will never forget you and it will reside in the Garden of your Heavenly home. Do you believe this?"

Me: "Yes Lord, You have said it, of course I believe!" I was still down about my unbelief. "Lord, I'm so sorry. Please help me here. Please grant me unshakable faith. I love You so much. I want You to use me. I want You to be pleased!"

Jesus: "Erin, a son does what his father does. I wait on My Father. On Earth you have been taught to follow yours, except yours you couldn't trust. Your trials are made more difficult because you are slower to learn about Who I am and Who My Father is. You have stood in Heavenly places. You have seen miracles and you know. You have prayed and your prayers have been answered – just not as you or the world expect. Your belief is good; your faith in your receiving is the issue. What did I say about a Gift? Did you receive it?"

Me: "The angel gave me the gift, but I have not seen it here. Is I the gift of faith?"

Jesus: "Erin, believe that you receive! Have faith in the Lord. Be patient, you have some time. It is okay to receive good gifts, you are capable. Now you can expect something."

Me: "Oh Lord what is it? I'm so excited!" He was laughing.

Jesus: "Erin, before I was willing to give up to half the Kingdom, now you are excited for a box or what is in it."

Me: "Yes Lord, I am having faith in what I cannot see. This is good, right? Half the Kingdom comes with responsibilities! Please keep this, but I would love to be invited to see it!"

Jesus: "Erin, think and pray on this today. I'm about to use you, your friends and others. Take heart! Keep your eyes on me! Now, tell me about your dream, from last night – this is important."

Me: "I was invited to a client's home. She has some very young children. She was baking and had invited me over for lunch with several others. I had arrived early. She had bunches of wilted flowers. I asked her if I could help her since the flowers were dying. She pointed me to a large vase with water. She said she hadn't gotten to this yet. I arranged the flowers. She said that she doubted they could be saved. I prayed to myself, under my breath. There were small bluebells and bleeding hearts. Immediately the water helped and the dead flowers perked up. She had made wheat bread that she had ground herself. The house was lovely. Her children were beautiful and well-behaved. The feeling of sorrow had overcome me, she was a Mormon."

Jesus: "There is more, go ahead."

Me: "Yes, I had an event to go to around noon so I would miss lunch but I helped her set up for others. I said to her, "You are the perfect Proverbs woman. You speak kindly to your husband and children; they respect you and treat you with love. You run a beautiful household. You are healthy. You even grind your own wheat, can your fruits, and sew. You entertain friends and you have great status amongst the community!" She laughed as if she knew but she was humble. "Erin, when you are finished, please come back! You can learn to grind wheat."

I left a stack of my business cards for her luncheon. I came back after my event at the Auditorium and she was preparing for dinner. Her brother came to the door – a builder who was also a Mormon. "Erin, he will show you how to winnow wheat! Please give him your business card." I didn't see any. She said, "They are right there!" My business cards had been copied and on the back side of them was an invitation to an event at their church with my name on it. My name was changed to something I didn't recognize – Zarah or Zara. I was upset that they had tricked others to believe I was part of their church. I had become ill. Her brother took me out in the back. He showed me a pitch fork, it had 6 prongs and began to scoop up grain and toss it. He then handed me the pitch fork. I told him that I knew how to separate wheat. I told him I will winnow from the Lord. He looked disappointed."

Jesus: "What did you think?"

Me: "If I'm to witness to them, I will need faith like a mustard seed. How about I just believe You for crows to feed me and seagulls to bring water bottles? Lord they – the false religions – are based on a myth about You and Heaven."

Jesus: "Erin, you will know the roots of a person's faith by who they believe I am and what they believe Heaven is! Now you must pray; they have been deceived. Soon every knee will bow and every tongue confess! There will be mourning and wailing. So many have been misled! Now pray for them to know me now. You know what is coming."

Me: "Lord, heal me of every part in me which lacks. Help me to stand!"

Jesus: "Erin, your faith heals you! Be encouraged. Receive and believe when you pray. When you see Heaven Open in the Spirit, while you pray and angels descend, then this too is a sign for you that your prayers reached My Father God. You are loved! Do not worry! Oh yes, go back to all those scriptures you were given for food and water. Remember who you are!"

He reached over and hugged me! The Heavenly Ocean was beautiful!

Dream over...

Blessings

Chapter 14 – Four Dreams

Four Dreams – May 3rd 2014 (12 Hours sleep) Woke up at 1:11 AM

First Dream:

I lived in a desert place, on a hill with no water. The house was lovely. Money didn't have any worth, so all was in trading. I had worked to help another family but we had plenty. We needed water but money couldn't buy it. The man was poor. His milk cow has just given birth to a calf, He handed the little calf to me and said grow it and use the milk for water. "Sir, how can I grow the calf for milk if there is no water for the calf to grow?" He insisted. I took the calf, as I knew that this calf was taking milk from the mother they needed but they didn't want to butcher it. I smiled and thanked them for their generous gift, I knew the little calf would eventually die, so I lifted it up in prayers and offering to the Lord, It was a perfect little red heifer with no spots or blemishes. It even looked at me like it was glad to see me. I felt an instant need to care for it, but I didn't know how I could in a drought stricken land.

Second Dream:

I live somewhere in a town with a very cute atmosphere. It had cobblestone streets, shops on the street level and apartments above. The buildings were stucco and brightly colored. There were iron gates and balconies. There were shutters on each of the windows. I was there visiting with my children. It was getting near closing time around 6:00 PM so the shops were beginning to close their doors. Right before closing while people were shopping a drug lord in a black car pulled up to the gate of this shopping area. I heard the people speaking in Spanish or Portuguese to run and hide. Suddenly, I was screaming and searching. Many of the people walked right past the gunman. The gunman had targets so the fear was to be in their cross hairs. I saw this cute peaceful village turn dark in a matter of seconds. I heard my children calling to me in an upper room just as the gates closed. I told them close the shutters and do not worry. Just as the gates closed, I turned to see the gunman in very advanced technical gear. The vehicle turned from a normal car to an extremely high-tech tank with strange tentacles in the front bumper area. They

were willing to kill everyone just too exact revenge on one. I stood only feet right in the middle of them. They didn't see me at all or I had been dead. I felt at peace as I knew my children were safe and hidden in the upper room, but the village would be gone, I prayed to God in a yell! So loud that everyone should've heard it.
Dream over…

There were two parties in two dreams.

Third dream: Party #1

My family had gathered in a very large house. There were more mouths than I could feed. I went to a gourmet market for the finest food for my guests. There was a gourmet restaurant next to it. There were so many people at the house I was worried I had no time to prepare a good meal that would satisfy everyone. More were arriving.

The women from the restaurant said "You look lost, can I help you?"

I explained the situation and she said, "You need a caterer. We will be there right away to help you. All of these caterers gathered. They were wearing white dress shirts and black pants with black aprons. Their sleeves were all rolled up and ready to serve. I agreed and gave the address. I was a bit worried as I didn't know if I could afford to feed everyone. They were willing and able because I had other errands to run when I arrived at the house, more guests had arrived, but the caterers had already set-up and were waiting for my approval to serve the guests food. I went to the service room and there were amazing foods and drinks. The table was way over done for the guests. I was worried again about the price, I was also aware that it was so extravagant I didn't want to appear as a show-off or flashy. I wasn't. I wanted to serve like this if money was no object, but I had never had the means.

The guests were enjoying the food and celebrating. They complimented me on my good taste and service, although I didn't feel like I deserved it. I only hired the workers and didn't know if I could pay the tab. I mingled for some time; there were people of all ages enjoying the fare. I wondered to the back yard of the house which was under construction. The rains had come, so there was quite a bit of mud. I saw there was a family back there eating and drinking with a toddler who could barely walk. The couple had drunk too much wine. Their feet were wading in a pond of mud water. The hole had been dug by the landscape crew but had no liner or pump installed. The rocks and plants hadn't been set. Yet these people were pretending it was a real pool, they were too drunk to notice they were bathing in mud. Their little toddler was playing in the mud and fell into the pool about 30 inches deep. I ran to grab the toddler. The baby was inhaling the mud. The mud was so slippery I couldn't grasp the toddler. Finally, I prayed to God and pulled the baby out. I took the baby, cleared its air passage and breathed into its mouth to revive it. I took the toddler and he clung to me. The parents were so drunk they didn't notice or care. The baby would've drowned. I walked inside, shut and locked the door and I told the servers to cut them off and don't allow anyone else to go out there. I kept the toddler with me.

The party continued until the food was gone. The servers cleaned up everything. I was relieved to have help. I said to the main server, "How much do I owe for all of this?" She said, "You only pay for the food. The service was free!" She handed me the invoice and it read $156.34. I was amazed. I had cash. I thought the cost would be much more. I ask her, "How can this be?" She said, " No one has parties anymore and we were ready to serve, and truth be known someone paid in advance knowing you couldn't afford more than the cost of the food and drinks?"

I was in shock, "But who paid?"

Server, "You don't know?"

Fourth dream: Party # 2

I was in a University Town, a hilly town in the US. It was night time. In this dream, I went to a party to pick some people up before picking up my very young children at a scheduled time. This area of the city had two and three story homes, very close lots – maybe less than seven feet apart from each other – a lot like Knob Hill in San Francisco. I had a hard time finding a place to park as it was street parking. It was raining and visibility was poor. I finally found a spot, parked and went in. I found the group I was looking for in an upper room. We began to leave down a very wide staircase about ten feet across from the 3rd floor to the second. The staircase was about thirty feet high. I was carrying a metal black ladder which I had lent to a friend. As we were descending the staircase, the ladder slipped from my hands and dropped down the stairs. There was a wall at the base of staircase containing two items…

There was a photo display to the left and a mirror to the right with heavily carved ornate frame. The ladder fell and with speed caused the force to hit the wall but nothing was damaged. Just as we were descending to run to see if there was damage to the wall, the glass with photos fell and the glass covering broke. The mirror didn't move. The home owner confronted me. I apologized and told her I would pay for the glass on the photo piece. She said no problem but you must pay for the damage to the mirror too.

Me: "But the mirror was not touched, it was fine." I turned the corner and she claimed I had damaged her mirror too. I told her, "No, I didn't touch your mirror."

She said, "It didn't matter, you damaged the other piece and someone has to pay!"

I was bothered – I was late to get my children. My witnesses had left the party and all that remained was this woman claiming I damaged something I didn't. She proceeded to stall me and tell me she wanted a certain place to repair it. The place she told me to take it to charge double the price. She insisted and because of time I compromised, When I finally began to measure the pieces to get the repairs done I realized my tape measure was in the car, I went to look for my car but couldn't find it. I went back in and told her my car was stolen because of the late hour.

She said, "No it is right in front of me." My car had been in the driveway the entire time. I decided to come back later to measure; I needed to get to my children, so I left.

Dream over…

Chapter 15 - Training Part I - War Assignment

Communion

Dear Father,
Thank You for another day! Thank You for all that You have done. Thank You for not giving up on me, when I would like to give up on myself. Lord, I need help forgiving those who continue to hurt me. How long do I forgive? With one, I have easily forgiven 70 X 7, as it says in Your Word. How much longer, Lord? I will continue to, until You deliver me. I can do nothing else. Lord, sometimes memories are like small shards of glass. You brush them off of your skin and move on, but some go into your skin and become painful – because you can't see them, they are difficult to remove. You have a reason for everything. You have promised to deliver me to a safe place. You have promised to deliver me soon. I am wearing down, Lord. I need help! Help me, Lord! You are mighty to save!

Erin – Come Up!

Immediately, I was in a city I didn't recognize. This was not Heavenly. There were abandoned brick buildings everywhere. I saw some script on one of the buildings – it looked Russian or something like this. The sky was dark, very gloomy. There had been rain. The streets were brick in some areas, under a coating of asphalt. Many, many of the buildings had been blown to bits. I looked down at what I was wearing. It was like a tactical sniper outfit. I was me, but completely in character for the landscape. I was like a soldier. I couldn't tell what was happening. When I saw what I was wearing, I realized I was going to be in the middle of a battle.

Me: "Lord, what are You doing with me – what is this about? I don't want to be here!"

Holy Spirit: "Erin, I brought you here for an assignment. Do not be afraid. Allow Me to guide you. You will not be hurt. I will deliver you from this. This is important!"

Me: Okay, Lord. I am willing ... hopefully, I am able."

I looked at what I was wearing to see if I had everything I would need to go into battle. Hopefully this didn't involve killing – I wasn't certain I could do this. Well, to save children from bad guys – yes, I could do this. I had clothing like armor. I had gloves on, and extra ammunition strapped like a beauty-pageant ribbon across my chest. I had another strap also. I reached behind my back and realized I had a very high-tech sniper rifle – or what I thought was high-tech. I saw a type of scope that had what looked like a digital display. "Okay, if the Lord has me here, there must be some extreme evil. I had better go up higher so I can see what I'm up against and what army I am fighting."

I ducked into one building with a steel door. It was pitch black. I felt my way up the stairs and began to see light the higher I climbed. As I approached a window, I instinctively came up to the side to peek out, so I wouldn't be seen. Eventually, I made it another several flights to the roof. Before I exited this door, I got down on my belly and slowly opened the door from a low position, in case there were others out there on the roof. I came to my feet and bent over behind two very large air ducts. I listened for any sounds. In the distance I saw a war zone. There were smouldering buildings. I still could not see signs of life anywhere. I looked out the other direction and I saw a sniper station on the roof. I couldn't tell where the sniper was, as I could only see equipment.

As I approached, I saw a trail of blood leading to another utility area of the building. I followed the trail carefully. I saw a body stretched out. I saw a young boy – maybe seventeen years old – who appeared to be praying. At first I didn't understand the language. Then the Lord granted me the ability to know what he was saying. He was praying to Mary. He kept saying something like "mother of God." He was dying. I ran over to him. He quickly tried to get away from me. I gathered that I was wearing the clothing of the opposing side. It was cold here, about 40 degrees. I was wearing a stocking cap with some sort of barrier on it, like a shield. It was odd, because I literally know nothing about military combat, other than that I never wanted to be in a situation like this.

The man looked so frightened by me. I put my hands up and I said something in his language. I didn't understand the language I was speaking, but the Lord granted me supernatural knowledge, so I knew what was being said and how to say it.

Me: (In another tongue) "I have been sent by Jesus – not His mother – by God Himself to give you comfort." He was shaking and scared – so scared.

Man: "Who are you? Don't kill me! Please!"

Me: "I am not here to kill you. I was sent by God to show you He loves you."

Man: "God wouldn't send a sniper to lead a sniper home. This is a trick."

Me: "No, it is not a trick. I am here to help you. What is your name?"

Man: "Kelzi Immanuil." – Snipers don't give out last names.

Me: "Oh, you are David Emanuel. Who gave you that name?"

Man: "My grandmother who raised me."

Me: "You are dying. Do you know Jesus, the one who sent me? Do you know Him who loves you?"

Man: "He cannot love me. I am a killer. I have killed innocent people. I am nothing, but forgotten. I cannot be forgiven. I kill children."

Me: "God has sent me just to show you home. Would you like to go to Heaven? It is Paradise. The angels will take you there."

Man: "This is a trick. I cannot be forgiven."

Me: "Are you willing to accept that Jesus is here with me?" Just then, he began to have shortness of breath and severe pains.

Man: "First, you must know that there are others in the buildings. Crazy woman of God, you will need to see them, too. I have killed many. Those who were praying in the other building will need you. I am the killer."

Me: "God knows this, Kelzi. He sent me to you. He told me your grandmother wants you home with her. Are you ready?"

Man: "Yes, yes, hurry, hurry. I am being hunted like a dog right now – quietly hurry."

Just then there were old helicopters coming at us. There were bombs dropping about a mile away. I heard gunfire in the distance. I still didn't know where I was. Kelzi reached out for my hand. This young boy was scared.

Man: "Please don't leave me. Please."

Me: "It's okay. Jesus loves you. The angels are ready to take you home." I looked, and his eyes were focusing on something which I didn't see. I saw his face black with sniper paint. I saw his eyes bluer than blue … the whites of his eyes. He was focused on what I couldn't see. I began to cry, as he had a smile on his face.

Man: "Jesus, I see You. I see You! I am sorry. Please forgive me!" I then heard "Thank You" – so I knew the Lord was speaking to him and showing him the way home. It was beautiful. His eyes fixed and his hand went limp in mine. I reached over and closed his eyelids and thanked God.

Me: "Okay, Lord, You can beam me up to the ship now! Lord, the bombs are drawing closer … time to remove me."

Holy Spirit: "No, Erin – you have the equipment. The enemy is approaching. There is more to do before you are removed. Don't think. Allow Me to work here."

Me: "Lord, wouldn't it have been more convincing to send someone who actually has been in a war zone, or with tactical experience? I am a bit out of my element here. A fashion show in New York City might be closer to my level of experience."

Holy Spirit: "Erin, I can send someone else if you are not capable."

Me: "No, Lord, You have Your reasons. I am willing – just please empty me completely of myself, and grant me supernatural knowledge about this culture or even war."

Holy Spirit: "Granted. Now, go to Kelzi's sniper station and look through the scope. – First, take his iPad."

I got up, grabbed Kelzi's iPad – it had a bunch of coordinates. Next to these, it had a word which meant *kills*. At each coordinate he had tracked his kills.

Me: "Oh, Lord, this kid was a master sniper – how did he even make it to prayers and salvation? Wow!"

Holy Spirit: "Erin, lucky for everyone here your assignment is not judge and jury. Please stick to My Plan and do not judge!"

Me: "Forgive me, Lord! Now what do I do?"

Holy Spirit: "Allow Me to work. Don't try to DO anything! This is wisdom. Some could be lost."

Me: "Lord, couldn't angels do all of this? Why use me?"

Holy Spirit: "Erin, there is a battle going on right now. You asked to be used. Shall I get someone else?"

Just then, I saw a veil over my eyes lift. I saw demons of every kind fighting angels from heaven. They were all around me. The demons were preventing or delaying angels from getting to saints. There were so many over this area alone, that if the Lord had not given me a veil, I would've been too distracted to focus solely on this boy Kelzi.

Me: "Oh my goodness, Lord, this is frightening."

Holy Spirit: "Erin, please continue. I will put the veil over your eyes so you can focus on your assignment. Now, you may ask questions later."

Me: "Lord, one quick one. Do all of these people see into the spirit realm?"

Holy Spirit: "Yes, many can."

Me: "How are they able to survive?"

Holy Spirit: "Too many questions Erin. Later for answers! Move now!"

Me: "Yes, Lord."

I heard gunfire drawing closer. Demons must have warned humans that I was here. I went to the sniper station and saw a sniper rifle that was so advanced, even beyond mine. Everything was digital. I looked through the sight. With one lens I could see human heat through the building about 50 yards from me. I saw a mass of heat in a corner. It looked like several people. I moved the sight around and heard an alert from the iPad. I looked and saw snipers set up at several locations, moving in on the building across the street. The iPad said some code name. I read the foreign script. It said, "Black Dog Shoot to Kill Now!"

Holy Spirit: "Erin, the sniper across from you is not one of Mine, but the enemy – remove it now."

Me: "What? Shoot, Lord … seriously?"

Holy Spirit: "Shoot first; ask questions later."

I was shaking. I pointed the rifle. I realized this was the person who shot Kelzi. It was one of his own. I knew instinctively it was. I looked through the sight. I was alerted by the iPad that I had locked the target, and before I could pull the trigger the gun went off. I heard no sound. I received a vibration alert that I had hit the target. Weird, I didn't even do anything. I looked through the sight and saw the red-heat of the sniper's body fading. His body was down. The iPad alerted me to more - "NOW"! I still had the other rifle on my back. I knew I needed to get over to the other building. I snapped the digital sight off of Kelzi's sniper rifle and took the iPad and sight with me. Again, this was supernatural – not something I would know on my own!

I began to run to the roof door. I opened the metal door and stepped into the darkness. I was in a pitch-black stairwell. I felt a switch on the sight that I had taken. I moved the switch and the one sight worked like a flashlight. This scope had three lenses and a body like a camcorder – the old-fashioned kind. I'm sure the parts had names, but I didn't think it mattered much right now. I quickly used the scope to find my way in the dark. I was thanking the Lord for putting the veil back on. I would have been too busy watching that battle, instead of doing what I was sent here for. "Boy, do I have questions for the Lord later!"

I reached the bottom of the stairs and opened the door slowly. I grabbed the rifle behind me. I moved the strap forward so the rifle was in my hands. The sight on the rifle I had must have been first generation, as it was clearly not as advanced. I had a pack that I put the digital scope into, as well as the iPad. I entered into an alleyway. I looked toward my target building and ran quickly to the edge of the building. There were bombs going off only about 100 yards away now. There were helicopters in the air looking for me, or the people in the other building, or both. I didn't know how to get across the street without snipers shooting me.

Me: "Lord, I could use help here, now. Show me which way to go."

Just then He lifted the veil over my eyes. I saw a double row of angels, creating a path for me to the other building. They were fighting demons. I saw an angel I recognized from the Path a long time ago. He whistled for me to move, so I ran full force to the other building and through the door being held by another angel. Just as I went through the door, the angels and demons disappeared. I knew they were still there. Wow!

Me: "God, You are truly amazing! Beyond incredible! I am honored by Your amazing love for the lost – well, humbled that I would be able to be used for anything."

I was inside the building, which I knew held others. The bombs were blowing up adjacent buildings, hoping to kill these people. I began to run through broken glass, office discs, computers, chairs. All was in disarray. Someone had moved the items to block the stairwell area. The glass was there so they could hear the enemy. I didn't know if they had rifles too, or what was going on. I climbed over all the stuff and pried open the door to the stairs. I was in my 25-year-old glorified body, so I could move with ease. I was able to get through a ten-inch crack in the door, barely. Once through, I snuck up the stairs to the third floor. The door was open. I looked down and realized a body was keeping the door open. He was dead. I looked through the opening and saw more bodies. These were young people, as young as sixteen to eighteen years old. I saw both girls and boys, unarmed. They had all been shot by sniper through the window. It must have been Kelzi's rifle. I saw one body twitching by the window. I looked around the corner of the door and saw more bodies.

Me: "Lord, give me strength." I ran over to the twitching boy by the window. He had lost a lot of blood. "Please wake up." My language was this foreign tongue. The boy opened his eyes. He had no energy to even care if I was the enemy. "I am here to let you know that Jesus sent me to take you home." He couldn't speak; he had been shot in the side of his neck, and just minutes ago. "I will speak for you. Do you know Jesus?"

Boy: He nodded, "Yes."

Me: "Will you take Him as your Lord and Savior?"

Boy: He nodded "yes" as tears streamed down his cheeks. He grabbed my wrist. He moved my arm to a closet across the room.

Me: "There are more there in the closet?" He nodded "yes" again. "Okay, I will get to them, but first you. The angels are ready to take you home to Heaven. Will you accept Jesus as your Lord and Savior before it's too late?"

Holy Spirit: "Erin, this one is Mine. It's okay."

Me: "The Lord has told me that you are His."

Boy: The boy began to cry and whimper. He was trying to speak with his mouth, but he couldn't. Tears were flowing down his cheeks, and with a last bit of effort he managed to speak "Spaceeba." I heard in another language, but that is what it sounded like. (I believe it was a Thank You!)

Me: "I will see you up there soon, too! Don't be afraid – the Lord is with you!" He grabbed my wrist and moved it to the closet door before he went to be with the Lord.

I quickly got to my feet and began to climb over bodies, desks, computers, and glass. I realized midway that shots were coming at me, as I heard some whiz by my ears. Amazingly – by Divine

Design – I was not hit by these bullets. I was supernaturally protected. I reached the closet. I heard crying from within.

Me: "Don't be afraid. I am not the enemy. I am here to help you."

Just then the door opened. Inside were four scared girls and three boys. A few of them had lost their bodily functions; the smell was horrendous. They looked glad to see me. They were speaking at me all at once. I didn't know what they were saying. I held up my hands to quiet them. One of the girls saw the boy by the window, dead, and began to sob inconsolably.

Me: "Please don't worry or be afraid."

One of the children – "teens" – said, "Are you an angel?"

Me: "No, I am not. I come from Heaven, assigned by God to let you know He is with You and loves you."

Teen (a boy): "How can He be with us? He killed our family. He killed our friends. He killed our parents. He allowed my sisters to be raped before they were killed – they were only four and six years old. He doesn't love us."

Teen (a girl): "He deserted us and killed us off one-by-one, and now we will be next. Lady, you are next."

Me: "You are wrong. God didn't kill your family. There is a war, which you cannot see occurring now. God is giving you a chance. The bombs are getting closer. Soon the enemy will find you. Your friend over there is with Jesus – He took him home. Now, do you want to be here alone with them?"

Instantly, the spirit realm was visible. It was horrific. The teens were screaming. Demons were being held back by angels.

Me: "We don't have much time. Jesus is ready to help you safe in His Arms. Are you ready? He has taken your sisters and your friend to Heaven already. Now, join them before it is too late." Instantly they knelt to the floor. Their hands were shaking.

Teens: "We will take Jesus."

Me: "The Lord knows all that you have been through. Accepting Him now is good. You will receive a special crown for this. You have suffered much. If you are holding anything against anyone, you must forgive so that God can forgive you." Immediately they confessed and named offenders.

Teen: "How can I forgive the person who hurt my sisters? They were little!"

Me: "I understand this more than you know (I began to cry as I write). You must release both this evil and the person used by the enemy to God, so the Accuser can hold nothing against you in court. You must be free from unforgiveness and let God be a Just Judge against your enemy."

Immediately, the children confessed even more. It was heartbreaking, as I realized these kids had stories supernaturally downloaded – wretched details, which I could temporarily see ... things done to them in secret. All of them were confessing without me saying anything. One said, "God, please forgive me for pretending to be God!" All of them confessed the same.

Holy Spirit: "Erin, tell them I am pleased with them. It is time they are Mine forever."

Me (in their language): "The Lord is pleased with you. You are His. He is ready to receive you. Are you ready to meet Him?"

All of them in tears accepted Jesus! I heard "spaceeba" or something like this, and "Jesus." Just then, I heard the building collapsing around us. The roof caved in. The debris fell around us. I grabbed the teens. We could see up, and a plane dropped a missile as I saw the sky open. We must have died – well, I didn't – but at that moment Heaven Opened to receive these children. Wow! I then was on the rooftop of a distant building. Across the city, I could see an Open Heaven and an Epic War. I saw just a few saints less than God's handful being carried Home. It was a desolate landscape a place with No Hope – void of God. Completely void. Well, I guess not really. "Lord, I have questions..."

Immediately, I was walking through a Heavenly vineyard... Dream over...

Chapter 16 – Training Part II - Harvesting

Communion

Dear Father, Thank You for another day! Lord, I need help I have so many questions – so many!

Erin Come Up!

I was in the Heavenly Vineyard. I saw several types of grapes. One vineyard had beautiful white grapes, light green and gold in color. They were not ready yet for harvest. This vineyard was higher up on the mountain down to my right. I saw harvesters singing and praising the Lord for the beautiful grapes and record yield. These grapes were light red and pink. To my left and off to the side I saw them finishing the last pick of some beautiful deep red and burgundy grapes. There were large baskets and the juiciest of all grapes being carried off for crushing. I saw in the distance the beautiful Chateau – French in style and beyond that the celebration of the Harvesters.

The dirt was sparkling, dark and rich, unlike the desert vineyards here. In Heaven the precious mineral content of the ground combined with Heavenly air – oxygen – well the soil was/is rich with life. Heavenly soil is not dirty. It doesn't mulch nor are there rotting organic products. The food is grown here not from death, but growth purely from living water and soil.

I had beautiful sandals on with braids of something like leather; I threw them off so my bare feet were on the soil. I was wearing a skirt, white flowing blouse, and a type of pouch around my waist. I ran up the first row where the harvesters were and grabbed a bunch of jeweled red and pink grapes. I put the bunch in my pouch and then I ran up a row of vines to the burgundy grapes. I had wanted to try out the grapes as they were perfected. As I ran to those, I looked at the white, light green and gold grapes for a moment. I stopped to pick a bunch. I hesitated. They weren't ready yet so I bypassed them. I was laughing with joy that I was here and safe in Heaven. I was so relieved to be here. I found a bunch of burgundy grapes; I picked them and put them in my pouch. One of the grapes dropped to the ground. I quickly bent down and put it into my month. The grape burst as I bit right into it! It tasted wonderful. It was slightly like an

Earthly red grape, but nothing like it at all. I pulled another off of the bunch in my pouch. I have only tasted two varieties of grapes in a supermarket. These were different. They were rich both sour and sweet. Well, sour is the wrong word. They make you want to eat more. With grapes on Earth, they are okay, but I don't go out of my way to purchase them and my children don't go out of their way to eat them. Here however, if there were just grapes to eat here, I could live off of them – well and living water too. I giggled to myself...

I heard a bunch of Harvesters call for me. Erin, come to the celebration." They were loading up a type of high-tech cart led by horses. The horses actually looked like they were excited to pull in the harvested grapes as well as the harvesters.

I laughed, "They know me? How funny is that?" I had seen the Harvest celebrations when I was here last year and it was so much fun. The angels were here too. The cart was continuing to move. I waved them on. I stopped and looked around me. I saw waves of color on this mountain. It was breathtakingly beautiful. The smells were so fragrant. I loved the smell of fresh mowed grass, mountain air and even a hint of eucalyptus. I didn't see any eucalyptus around, but they must be close. I was on the southern side of the valley – which will one day be my eternal Home. There was a beautiful southern breeze. I sat down in a row of vineyards and looked up. It was so peaceful. I could hear song birds everywhere. They were singing praises to God. I never understood how we were taught that we would be at the Throne of God 24/7 worshiping Him on our knees. This wasn't something I looked forward to.

I said to myself, "Forgive me God, for my thoughts." I realized that because of the place He has prepared for us here, we will constantly worship Him and thank Him for all Eternity. There will not be one single entity in Heaven, not constantly Praising and Worshiping God for this incredible Gift of Jesus. He saved us. God sent Him! He showed us the way Home! The Path which leads to Paradise! I am so thankful! I grinned and I laid down in the vineyard to rest. I must have drifted off to sleep as I awakened by something scurrying across my stomach. I looked down and here was a family of quail in a row traveling right over me. I laughed and sat up. These little babies were so cute. They were silver and gold with a little plume of blue and purple. The parents were even more colorful. I thought, wow they can also be glorified in full color here. They have no enemy, no need to be camouflaged in gray and brown to stay hidden. I recognized the sound they were making.

I stood up on my feet. I didn't know how long I had drifted off to sleep. I still heard the celebration at my friend's vineyard. I turned around to go down the row and I spotted Jesus. He was gleaning the last few burgundy grapes. He has a large pouch like basket over His shoulder. He was taking all of the grapes, I laughed it's not like any of them are bad here. He waved at me. I ran fast down the row I was in and over to the place He was harvesting.

Jesus: "Erin did you have a good rest?"

Me: "Yes I'm glad the quails woke me up. I could sleep here a few days."

Jesus: "Yes I know, I sent them to wake you up. I'm glad you woke up when you did, those parents can become quite loud. You would've been startled." He was smiling and jovial.

Me: "Wow! Lord in Heaven every harvest is a record harvest. How does this not become routine?"

I saw Jesus laughing along with the angels. They obviously know more than I do about Heaven.

Me: "Okay so everything here is perfect – how does it not become boring or like that movie 'Ground Hog Day'?"

Jesus: "Interesting choice of words. Are you worried that things in Heaven will be monotonous?"

Me: "It's okay with me, Lord, everyday can be the same. I'm fine with it. Don't send me back to the war, I have perspectives now that I didn't before so, please, please forgive me."

Jesus: "Are you negotiating with Me Erin?" He was laughing, "Ask any of the harvesters here, ask the vineyard owner. Do you think that days cannot be interesting unless there is trouble or trials? This doesn't sound right. You spent your entire Earthly existence praying for peace and rest with no poverty or trouble. Now you are requesting trouble in Heaven to shake things up a bit? You are funny Erin."

Me: "When You say it like this it sounds horrible Lord – please forgive me."

Jesus: "Erin, you were just taken to a war zone yesterday. One in which the only winners were the ones saved by Me. In an Earthly sense the winners were the ones with the most kills. Are you requesting this in Heaven?" He stopped and so did the angels – All of them became serious and looked at me. For a split second I was terrified. I knew God could split the ground open and throw me into it with one wave of His Arm.

Me: "Oh Lord, please forgive me. I speak with ignorance. I don't want anything from Earth up here!"

Jesus: He was laughing, "Erin choose your words carefully. The power of Life or death is spoken through the portal of your mouth. Let your words be few. Now I have called you friend." He was calming and kind. I realized He just gave me the most gentle rebuke, ever! "I know what you have been wondering for some time. With all things perfected here, how will it remain interesting right?"

Meanwhile I noticed as the angels continued to pick the remnant bundles – they smiled and laughed. I could see they had memories and stories about what they had seen and experienced with Jesus over the years.

Me: "Yes Lord, remember I approach Heavenly things and the mysteries of You with youthful wonder…. (pause) … and exuberant ignorance."

Jesus: "Now that is funny and truthful! Very good!" He continued to glean grapes.

Me: "Lord, why are You picking the remnant grapes. Aren't there workers for this?"

Jesus: "Oh am I not capable? Erin your questions are funny."

Me: "Lord it reminds me of what you took me through yesterday."

Jesus: "Erin there is much more to this than you know. The harvest is plentiful, but the laborers are few! Remember this Erin; it is not a mystery but a fact."

Me: "Lord, I'm glad You and the angels are grabbing the remnants. These grapes are too good to be left on the vine." I reached into my pouch and dropped a grape into my mouth. I spun around as if performing a pirouette. I was being silly. They continued to glean.

Jesus: "Erin, in all the times in which you've come up here, have you ever been bored, even once?"

Me: "Oh no Lord. No!"

Jesus: "Do you agree that each time has been new and different?"

Me: "Yes, Lord always!"

Jesus: "I make all things new. There are an infinite number of things to discover here. Every Harvest is new and different here. Each one is memorable. Each batch of wine is different. A fisherman here will still desire to fish for pleasure, each catch new and different. Each day, better than the last, there is so much to do. Earth is pale in comparison. Erin you know this!"

Me: "Of course Lord. I'm sorry. We are taught that perfection on Earth is unattainable, but you can purchase it with means. You can pretend to have it all on Facebook. You can be anything you claim to be there."

Jesus: "Yes, again Earth is pretense and falsified pretenders of heavenly ways. Erin, you talked to Me in your car about something several days ago when you were in Bend, do you remember?"

Me: "Yes Lord, I drove around the Butte I live on to take some photos. I didn't really know if I'd ever be making the trip again, and I hadn't been back since to compare it to what I'd seen in Heaven. I saw the snow covered volcanoes, seven peaks on the other side of the wooded valley. The sky was blue and the air crystal clear and fragrant. The houses were beautiful, but nothing like Heaven. I remember thinking this was a small slice of Heaven on Earth. I quickly dismissed it when I saw the true colors. Everything had a haze about it, a dull sheen – colors, but gray-scale. Not crisp and perfect like here in Heaven. I cried as I left Bend. I drove no further. First I realized this was not my home, it had no luster. I couldn't afford this place as only people with money live here. I wasn't qualified for this place. I became a person looking through a storefront window with no money in my pocket, too poor to purchase what I wanted. My door had closed. I was sad."

Jesus: "Erin, you understand that many of the people you saw will only know that small piece of pretend heaven right? As you have seen at the end, money won't be able to save them. They will remember back to a time before and heaven to them will – their earthly mansions will be also their tombs. So do not envy them, pray for them as they are like infants wandering through the glass shop. They can barely walk, they drool even, they see something bright and shiny and they take it, they want it. – See and understand. The glass shop also has a glass ceiling where by God can see. Blessed be that infant, who looks up to see God and ask for His Father to pick him up! Erin the laborers are few."

Me: "I don't understand Lord; I thought You had said there is nothing more for us to do."

Jesus: "Yes on your own – this is correct, but allow Me to work through you – this is wisdom! Now you have been looking for your heavenly Home on Earth. Have you been successful?"

Me: "No Lord, I have searched all over the world online and nothing compares to it – or any of my friend's mansions either. I realized that my Home here in the mountains would be far beyond Earth. I thought I could find one close to post on the Barn, but I cannot find it anywhere. I thought I could find a house close in Bend, but there was nothing! It made being there much easier. I was there with a different attitude. Before I saw everything from a perspective of my own lack, now I looked at everything from the way you might see me. I was a princess – hidden in plain sight – giggles. You took the sting of pain away!" He walked over to me and gave me a side hug and a kiss on my forehead.

Jesus: "You let this go. This is good Erin. What else did your journey teach you?"

Me: "Lord, forgiveness. I still had not fully forgiven. I saw the contents of the boxes and I wanted to run. It was too painful. I hung on to this after I closed the storage unit door and locked it. I prayed for rapture so I wouldn't need to come back to it ever. That night when I got home I was so depressed. The next morning I fell, and now I have been out of work for a few days – painful but restful."

Jesus: "So why was the fall allowed?"

Me: "I guess to squeeze out my pride and stubbornness like one of those grapes, maybe?"

Jesus: "Oh really? Did this work?" I looked at Him and laughed.

Me: "Yes, I think so, but I'm not sure what was more painful; the fall, or people emailing me personally to talk about my unrepentant sin, and how poorly I am to remove the enemy from my life."

Jesus: "Yes, it's common. Many are well-meaning, but act void of my leading. You know and understand it is best to wait on Me and let your words be few."

Me: "I have learned without Your lead, when I react to someone's situation and base it solely on my own experience I cause offense. I later find myself being tested on the very same thing I put into motion with my mouth. My words opened the door for the enemy to declare war against me. I had a higher position in my mind than I ought."

Jesus: Laughing, "This is wisdom. Now, don't receive that, which was not sent from Me. Pray and bless friends with no true understanding, but encourage and build them up. Intercede for those who are stubborn; that seasoning, salt enhances them with grace, for they too are under a glass ceiling, and time is proceeding quickly. Do so with love, do not rush in with no leading with all kinds of evil behind you – understand?"

Me: "Yes, I understand that there is no time for fighting. Lord, can I help You glean the grape remnants?"

Jesus: "Remember, what you ask for Erin!" He was laughing. An angel came over to me with a basket to hand to me.

Me: "Hey, I recognize you from the path yesterday. You held the door open for me. Now you're harvesting grapes?" He smiled and looked at Jesus.

Jesus: "Erin let's discuss what you went through!" I was grabbing grapes from the vine and putting them in the basket.

Me: "Lord, why are there so many grapes on these vines, and why the hurry?"

Jesus: "The Harvesters grabbed what they could carry. They were anxious to go to the celebration. It was their reward for a good harvest, remember? Why are you still here?" He smiled and laughed and looked at me.

Me: "Lord, I want to be where You are?"

Jesus: "Yes, but you elected to stay and glean why?"

Me: "The grapes left here are still good. Some are ready, just forgotten. Obviously they aren't forgotten because You are here right?"

Jesus: "Yes, Erin." He laughed and shook His head.

Me: "Lord, what was that sniper stuff about? Is this real? Is this coming? Why was I in tactical gear, not a robe? The children - the teens touched me – how did they do this?"

Jesus: "So many questions. First Erin, come with Me!" He has angels grab our baskets. Instantly we are at my friend's chateau. The Harvesters are smashing grapes with their feet. They are celebrating. The grapes will make incredible wine. "Erin the wine will taste sweeter when you are all here, but you remember the process takes some crushing first. The grape tastes wonderful right off of the vine, but it is even better made into wine for the wedding feast. Now take My hand again." Immediately we were in the Golden City. I stood next to Him overlooking the massive park with the Throne and Sea of Glass on the right. My clothes had turned into a beautiful bridal gown. It was amazing. I still wasn't sure if this was to be "The Gown" but it was never-the-less symbolic of what is to come. The clarity in which I can see here is amazing.

Me: "Oh Lord, I can see so clearly it is beautiful and fragrant. The blossoms are amazing, it looks like late spring, but I'm not sure. It looks perfect for a wedding!"

Jesus: "Now first I showed you the crushing. Now you are here preparing for the wedding. You know that the wine will be served at a wedding banquet. Why did I show you this?"

Me: "To show me my place here. I guess my position. It is a position of honor not to be treated casually and with a higher status than others. Meaning, I shouldn't view myself as higher than I ought."

Jesus: "Very good Erin! You understand that you have come to this place at a high cost. You traded your Earthly ambitions for Heavenly treasures, those which will have true luster and worth. You are not to get wrapped up in status contests with others. This wastes precious time. Understood? Now, why did I dress you as a sniper and take you to a foreign land?"

Me: "First, Lord please forgive me if I have ever thought higher of myself than I am. Forgive me for being upset at my circumstances. Forgive me for self-reliance and self-pity. Help me Lord to be more like You."

Jesus: "Erin you are forgiven. You were purchased for a high price. The enemy would like you back now. He knows what is coming. This is why your battles have been so difficult recently. The enemy doesn't like the message of hope you are giving."

Me: "Lord, this is Your message."

Jesus: "Yes, but your vessel is being filled by Me. You are an enemy of the enemy. This is good! Now, the sniper uniform is to show you that wherever I will take you – if you are willing – you will be well-equipped! Only when you stopped to question, was there a delay. You were shown a place out of your area of expertise or knowledge. Instead of getting in your own way, you recognized that you were able and willing but not capable to do things you had no knowledge of. You were sent to a place foreign to you. You didn't even understand the language unless I gave you the knowledge supernaturally. Now when you read this first part to your teenage sons, what happened?"

Me: "Oh Lord, sorry to say they had 100 times more knowledge than I did."

Jesus: "They knew the first sniper rifle, the one you carried, but until you all researched it together, you were unaware that the other was actually in production now."

Me: "Yes, Lord I got the chills when we found something close online. My sons told me that some of what I had experienced sounded like a game called "Black Ops." All of a sudden they seemed more interested in the dreams. I'm embarrassed to think wars got them excited about You!"

Jesus: "Let's talk more about what questions they asked you?"

Me: "They asked me why the other sniper – Kelzi's ally killed Kelzi. Then my other son said, "Oh I know, he was going to steal his I-pad and steal his kills. He was going to get some reward for kills." Lord, it makes complete sense, and senseless, heartless really."

Jesus: "Agreed, we will come back to this. What was next?"

Me: "Apparently, my older son said the room with the bodies and the teen twitching was like the game to him. They asked me if I saw anyone older in tribulation over age 20. I thought about it and realized I hadn't. Lord, is this because anyone older is killed?"

Jesus: "What does scripture say about failing hearts? You saw into the spirit realm and saw what was there. Do you believe an elderly person is agile enough to dodge bullets, or find food – or for that matter a doctor?"

Me: I had become very sad. "Lord, please forgive my questions up on that roof – or my judgments."

Jesus: "Erin, I had you first minister to Kelzi for a reason. If you had ministered first to the teens, you would've held judgment against him. You would've hesitated. Now I showed you that when you are used for my purposes you must become low and allow Me to increase. You decrease. Understood? Do you still want to continue?" He was firm but extremely loving. I looked into His eyes. I saw more trouble. I saw epic battles. I then saw Kelzi hugging his grandmother near the Village in the Valley! I lit up and hugged Jesus!"

Me: "Oh thank You Lord! Thank You! I thought I would have rest right away and that I would just come up and dance in the river and nap in the lilies!"

Jesus: "Laughing – Oh Erin, you will, you will...this you have seen. It is not contingent on your performance. However when you saw those children, even Kelzi, you felt love, compassion and urgency. You let your words be few. You said what I directed you too! There was a great celebration after this, that you have not seen yet."

Me: "So this was real? When did this happen? It is future right?"

Jesus: "One day soon you will understand. Now what do I require?"

Me: "To love the Lord God with all of my heart, soul, and strength, and to love my neighbor as myself. Lord, why was tribulation like a battlefield game?"

Jesus: "Saints will be hunted down. The enemy knows what is coming and has a plan. You have seen this."

Me: "Lord, You mean like tracking systems? It will be an unfair advantage, how will the saints make it?"

Jesus: "Erin, the enemy will rely on earthly resources; that is all the enemy has. Heaven has access to both. Do not worry about how; just know things are in place and all according to plan. The enemy operates under the same glass ceiling; just because you don't see it doesn't mean God can't. Even Heaven can see. The pleading for these teens and others from families in Heaven are deafening, but God sees all and hears their cries."

Me: "Help me to do only Your will. I never want to get in Your way." Jesus was laughing.

Jesus: "You can only get in your own way sweet Erin, NOT GOD's!"

Me: "Lord I have so many more questions. Are the hi-tech helicopters the locusts? They looked like giant flying bugs."

Jesus: "Erin somewhat, there is more. Stay to your path, your course. This is wisdom."

Me: "Lord, a close friend of mine takes the dreams and removes me completely out of them so only Your words remain. Should we do this? I heard some of them and with me removed Your words were very strong."

Jesus: He was laughing. "Oh remove the Bride out of the equation? Very clever! In some circumstances you could glean much from this; in others you remove My love story for you! My love story is written on the tablet of your heart Erin. Your questions come from your heart. I love this about you. You fear me, but you are unafraid of Me because you know how much you are loved! There is something to this though and it might be worth exploring. Do you not realize that everything you say and do is divine inspiration – for better or worse all of your questions are human – gentile in nature." He laughed, "So you even speaking to Me would cause ruffles to feathers, even amongst My disciples long ago. You witnessed Elijah's eye rolls right?" We both laughed.

Me: "I still feel so unworthy but so humbled by all of this. Thank You Lord. Please remove me and my children to a safe place soon Lord. Its coming Lord. I don't want my boys to speak to the enemy with no leading. I would rather hide them, than see them hurt. Please Lord!"

Jesus: "I promised to remove you before the time of trouble. Do not be afraid! You are loved! By a lot of Mothers too!"

Me: "I love You too and I pray You are able to use me always – for Moms too!"

Dream over…

Chapter 17 – Faith Training and Psalm 23

Communion

Dear Father,

Thank You for another day! Thank You for the signs of Your love and favor despite the difficult time we are having right now. Now instead of listening to the voices of condemnation, we are choosing to take a stand and pray.

Please forgive me as I have not asked again for prayers. Lord now I have become stiff necked as a prideful bird and I have no longer wanted to show my vulnerabilities. This is the truth; I am confessing with both my mouth and pen. Lord, on my birthday this year You told me I would be free soon. You told me I would no longer suffer shame. You would remove me from this desert place. You even said, "Erin, you are a flower in the desert not a desert flower!" Lord, please You are my Advocate. My Kinsman Redeemer, You are my Attorney, plead my case in God's Courts. Please Lord, remove this enemy, Honestly, Lord it is not the enemy but other Christians, who hurt my feelings – Wow. There I confessed it.

Please forgive me Lord for holding anything against my brothers or sisters in Christ. Many of them have been with me from the beginning and are for me. Why Lord then, have I built walls? One small email can keep me from going to the Barn for prayers, and encouragement, You have also shown me the resentment of some who are not part of the Barn. Lord how can I be called by You when one small thing starts a fire storm? We have all been called for a purpose. All of Your saints have been called to this special time. It is a miracle. You have witnessed a hunger in us; a desire to be with You, forsaking all others. This is a time of great anticipation, sometimes fear, elation, and longing for our Eternity to begin. This place has become dark and we are wearing out. We know that Your Church is a bride. To those who belong to a wonderful church, whose foundations are grounded in truth and love – hold on to this! This will be a beacon in the coming storm; as surely Lord, You will shine like a diamond to the lost. To those churches who have cast You aside – Lord may those believers be gathered unto to You. I became disillusioned with the yokes of well-meaning Christians long ago. Everyone wants to be first. I felt unqualified from the pews. I even enrolled in Graduate Seminary thinking I would find You there. Instead I saw liturgical ceremonies, scripts and less of You.

Now here I am. I asked for more. I have seen You at the Bridal Chamber in Heaven; even though I felt unclean in my walk. I was declared by You white as snow. Now with my trials, I wonder will You still take me as I am? Can I be loved like a tax-collector? Can I be loved like someone who has blood on their hands from taking a life? Can You love me if sometimes I doubt my place in Your Heart? Can You love me if I make mistakes? Is Your path so narrow there is no room for my Feet? Is there room for anyone's feet? You have shown me great mysteries and wondrous Glory in Heaven. I am in awe at Your Majesty and I am in amazement by Your Works.
….But Lord am I worthy of it? Are any of us? Lord, the Ocean is deep, dark and scary. The waves are higher than I can see. If I call You, are You really there? If You don't answer my prayers for healing and deliver me to a safe shore – have I been forgotten? Am I out of Your love and favor now? Did I do something wrong? Will You answer me?

Erin Come Up!

Immediately I was at Golgotha. The sky was dark and in gray-scale. I barely saw light as the sun was filtered out by an eclipse. The moon began to move over the sun and a small sliver of light silhouetted the three crosses. There were three bodies there, two thieves and Jesus. There was a horrible gale force wind and dust. I heard a great rumble and then the ground shook. I fell to my knees. I heard the Voice of God say, "Erin, who here was worthy to come to the Throne?" I was on my knees as the ground continued to shake. I was terrified, I could barely speak.

Me: "Father God, Jesus was and is Worthy. He is the tender shoot – Jesus."

God: "Erin, did the thief ask to be remembered by My Son?"

Me: "Yes, Father."

God: "Where is the thief today?"

Me: "In paradise with Jesus."

God: "If My Son declared him worthy then he is worthy. Accepted! DO NOT QUESTION YOUR WORTH, DO NOT DOUBT. MY SON CHOSE YOU. YOU ARE WORTHY! ERIN, I MADE YOU. YOU ARE LOVED AND I AM WELL PLEASED. DO YOU WANT TO REMAIN HERE OR WOULD YOU COME TO ME?

I was shaking and crying…

Me: "I am sorry God. Please forgive me. I do not want to come here again, please remove me."

God: "Please – STOP CRUCIFING YOURSELF AND JESUS. ERIN I HAVE NOT FORESAKEN YOU. MANY WHO CLAIM TO ACCEPT JESUS WOULD BE THE ONES KEEPING THESE THREE CROSSES ACTIVE. THERE WOULD BE MANY NAILS AND NO RESURRECTION. SO IT WAS THEN, IT WILL BE AGAIN. THERE IS NOTHING NEW UNDER THE SUN. YOU HAVE BEEN SET FREE. YOU HAVE BEEN FORGIVEN OVER AND OVER – 70 X 7. I AM THE TRUE JUDGE. I HAVE THE POWER OVER LIFE AND DEATH – JESUS HOLDS THE KEYS! WOULD YOU LIKE TO CONTINUE? ARE YOU READY TO SEE MORE? THE HARVEST IS PLENTY, THE WORKERS FEW!"

Me: "Yes, Lord!"

Then an Angel of the Lord appeared before me!

Angel: "I have been sent by God to take you to see some things. Are you ready?"

Me: "I think so!"

The Angel brought me up to my feet and took my hand. Instantly we were in a very arid place – the desert. I could tell it was somewhere in the Middle East. I saw a group of American soldiers and young children. The soldiers were playing with the children and handing them candy. I saw some local men of the village hate the soldiers. I saw the men plotting to kill the soldiers. (The Angel waved his hand and I saw time move forward.) Something had happened and I saw the bodies of the children lying on the ground. The soldiers were being blamed for killing the children – but they didn't. The children were used as shields to hide the enemy, as the enemy shot. I heard wailing and mourning. I saw a helicopter take the soldiers out of the area. The burdens of the soldiers were so great. The yokes were huge.

Me: "Angel this is heartbreaking, those poor soldiers and mothers of the children. How horrible, why am I being shown this?"

Next I was taken to a small African Village. There was no water. I saw a mother of two sick children walk for hours to the watering hole to fill her buckets and containers while her sick children were at the village. She was weak also and after filling her vessels she fell along the path and spilled most of the vessels. It was heartbreaking to watch. She was so upset with herself she was crying. Since she was so close to the village she carried what she had but it was only enough for one child. Her children were ages three and five. The five year old was not going to last. Either way one child would die. She couldn't decide. She asked for help if anyone could loan her water she could bring twice as much the next day. She was turned away. People wanted to help but needed water too. I saw her give the water to her three year old. She held her five year old as the boy began to close his eyes. She rocked him and sang a song asking for the angels to take him to a land where there was good water and plenty. I watched as the child's body went limp. I heard wailing reach the Throne of God. I heard her ask for forgiveness for her fall along the road. She blamed herself for spilling the vessels of water.

Me: "Oh Angel this is too hard to watch, it wasn't her fault!"

The Angel took my hand. Next we were looking at a vehicle which had gone under water at a flooded river crossing. It was somewhere in South America. I saw an old truck with a baby being held by a girl about nine years old. The truck was suddenly swept away. Water began to fill the cab of the truck. A tree branch went through the cab and pinned the mother so she couldn't get out. She yelled at her child to take the baby and get on the roof of the truck and call for help. The little nine year old didn't want to leave her mom but soon the water would be too high. The mother yelled again, so the little girl, shaking and crying held the baby with one arm and crawled onto the roof of the truck. She was shaking and crying and calling for help. Some men were coming to rescue her. She could hear her mother telling her she loved her and she was proud of her. She told her to be brave, take care of her sister and walk with God. I heard her call her Mia or Mea – something like that... Then there was silence as the water had overcome the cab of the truck. The men came too late to save the girl's mom, but the children were saved.

I was crying so hard...

Me: "Angel, please no more."

Angel: "I have more to show you – there is a reason Erin."

Me: "Please tell God I am sorry for taking Jesus to the cross over and over."

Angel: "Erin, it is not about that, please you will find out the love and grace of God is sovereign and perfect in your trials. Now would you like to continue?"

Me: "Yes."

Angel: "You make a common mistake. I have witnessed this through the ages. You don't look up enough. You humans focus on yourselves and those around you for your gauge. This is the trouble before you now. Know who sees all, Erin. It is God the Creator of all who sees everything. Look up! Come!"

He takes my hand. We are in Norman, Oklahoma. This was an area where all of my Dad's roots are. The graves here are filled with my relatives. I saw a normal day here, but clouds gathering in the distance. The Angel took me to a Southern part of the city. Or at least it looked like it from my vantage point. We were at a small farm. There were white buildings and I believe corn fields, but I'm not certain.

I saw a father calling his two boys in to wash before supper. They had modern farm equipment. The day was hot and still. I saw the boys' mother cooking in the kitchen of the cute farmhouse. All of a sudden I saw a funnel cloud on the horizon. The family looked so secure. I heard the father yell. The mother ran to the storm cellar.

The father gathered the sons. They ran for the cellar. The tornado came from nowhere. The father carried the younger boy, while he held the hand of the 9 year old boy. They got to the cellar. The mother grabbed the younger boy and just a split second as the father was bringing the other boy in something impaled the father's arm. Instantly the boy was swept up by the tornado. The father fell into the cellar and the door slammed shut. In an instant one child was gone. In a blink – gone! The wailing was almost as deafening as the sound of the tornado. No, movie could capture this. None! When the tornado passed in a matter of minutes, the family stepped out of the cellar to see everything gone. Their entire farm was gone. The father and mother ran everywhere and called out to their son.

Me: "Angel is the son okay?"

Angel: "He has been taken home Erin."

Me: "Lord, why have you shown me this?"

Angel: "Erin it is for me to take you to these places. I do not grant you knowledge. The Lord will show you more. Are you able?"

Me: I was in tears and shock. "Yes, but I don't like it."

The angel takes my hand. We are taken somewhere in Russia or the Soviet Union. It is winter. It seems like another place in time. Some soldiers have arrived at a small cottage of a potato farmer. The soldiers accused him of some sort of treason. The soldiers grabbed the farmer while his young children and his wife begged. The farmer was taken outside and shot in the back. The soldiers made the farmer's wife cook for them. She was shattered but to keep her children safe she told her children to be brave. The wicked soldiers pillaged all they had and took anything of worth, while the woman cooked. After they ate, they raped the woman and one of her daughters age 6 (I became sick). One of the soldiers took the little 4 year old girl into the woods. The boy was about 5 years old. The soldiers had tied him up and had him gagged. The soldier shot the 6 year old girl and after some time they heard another shot in the woods. The mother was shot above the heart – but she was not dead. The soldiers left. The mother was very weak. She dragged herself to the place where her son was tied up and got him free. She could barely speak. The boy held his mom while she gave him instructions to be brave. I saw angels attending to the scene. The angels were grieving. The mother died, but she asked the little boy for forgiveness. She said to pray. There is a God. She took her last breath. The little boy who seemed all of a sudden much older went to the floor boards and gathered a pistol and some money hidden from the soldiers. He reluctantly packed some things as he was shaking and crying for his papa and mama.

Me: "How can God watch this and not burn with anger? The other things were accidents except for the first. How can this happen?"

Angel: "Erin you don't know God and His purposes. You are not God, don't judge Him."

Me: "I am both grieved and angry. Those children could've been mine. This reminds me of that teenager in the closet. Angel was this recent?"

Angel: "Erin, you cannot judge until you have seen the entire picture. God knows the beginnings from the end, and the end from the beginning. Now come!"

The Angel grabbed my hand. Instantly I was in a place 20 years before the time we were just at. I saw a little boy about 4 years old. Again it was winter. It was in Northern Russia or something like this. The little boy had been abandoned by his parents. He was sickly and the parents left him somehow. The parents were cold. The father was drunk and hurt the boy somehow. The boy was left in a small town. A man with evil intent took the boy into his house. The boy was severely abused but the man drew him back to health. The little boy became quite cold and angry. There were little girls from the village that seemed happy; it angered him. He hated women and grew to hate them. The boy's thoughts at night were hate and sometimes tears and grief. The old man continued to abuse the boy as he became around 12. The boy finally took from the old man because the old man told him he would kill him while he slept. The old man was also abusing some other boys and giving their parents vodka and money in exchange for them. I saw unspeakable things that make me want to vomit. The 12 year old gathered up the other boys and they killed the old man so the parents reported the boys for murder. The 12 year old gathered up the boys and ran. I saw them together for years. They drank at a young age but were all dependent on the now older (12 year old). The group eventually joined the army, so they could be fed.

Me: "Lord, are these the soldiers? Is this what happened to them to make them do this?"

Angel: "Erin you are beginning to understand the roots of hate. You are not a judge for good reason." I was grieved. I was so thankful that my life was easy. This was not that long ago. Instantly, I was taken to a death camp in Poland during the time of Nazi rule. I saw a train pulling into the station and Jewish citizens being formed into two long lines; young men and healthy older men in one, and the elderly, pregnant women, children, handicapped and women with babies in another. The healthy were imprisoned and used as workers and the other line extermination – immediate death. I can't give the details. I can't go there. It makes my heart sick. The mothers were singing a song to keep the children calm. I saw blossoming trees – it was spring.

The Angel showed me an inscription in the wall – these were scratched into it. I couldn't understand the script, but the angel waived his arm and I could read in English: "I believe in the sun even when it's not shining. I believe in love when I don't feel it. I believe in God even when He is silent." I began to cry. "Please take me to Jesus. Please, I have questions." Instantly I was taken up to God's Garden in Heaven. I was in the Pasture of God by the River of Life. My sick stomach was healed. I ran over to the River and jumped in. The jewels – stones and the bottom of the river bed sparkled. The sunlight was spectacular as the stones from the river bed created dancing diamonds of rainbows on the surface of the water. I wept.

Me: "Oh God, forgive my pouting, forgive my rants. Oh Lord there is none like You and I am forever grateful."

I sat on the river bank. The grass was soft. I moved the palm of my hand over the blades of grass. They seemed to hum – they did hum. What is Heaven that even the grass worships and sings to God? How amazing! I lifted my hands and praised God for Heaven! I sang several hymns. My voice here was/is beautiful in Heaven.

Remarkable, I felt safe and refreshed. All of my trouble was a distant memory. After some time, I spoke.

Me: "Lord, You have said "Be still and know that I AM God!" The first time You spoke to me in 1983 – this is what You said. I was barely 20 years old. Lord, this was 31 years ago. Now You have taken me here. I am forever Yours! Please forgive my foolishness."

I felt a hand on my shoulder. It was Jesus. He sat down beside me on the bank of the river.

Jesus: "I'm glad you came, Erin."

Me: "Lord it has been a difficult time but it is nothing compared to what the angel showed me. I am so sorry!"

Jesus: He reached over and held me. "It's okay Erin. Do you understand what you were shown and why?"

Me: "Sort of, but not really."

Jesus: "Before I answer you, think about what you were shown. What did you come away with?"

Me: I thought through all of what I had seen, for some time. The Lord downloaded everything into my memory. "I guess at first I was grieved, then I became angry, then I wanted to pronounce judgment – now I am empty – I have nothing Lord."

Jesus: "Then allow me Erin. Who do you believe I am? Do you believe I am a loving Lord? Do you believe God is Just? Can you trust My love and God's judgment?"

Me: "I don't understand it. I try to wrap myself around it. I try to contain it, but I am not capable. I cannot see the end from the beginning nor can I see the beginning from the end. I only see my portion, my circle. I am not You Lord. Your grace abounds, mine is not like this."

Jesus: "Tell me then how you felt?"

Me: "At first I wanted to save, then I wanted to kill even murder, then I was empty."

Jesus: "So you wanted to play God, save and then judge without all of your knowledge?"

Me: (He was smiling and clearly He knew me.) "Lord, I am not qualified to save, only point to You My Savior. I am not qualified to judge. I am not God on the Throne. I don't work in His courts. You just took me on a roller-coaster of emotions; terror, grief, anger, mourning. Now it is much better if I remain silent."

Jesus: Laughing – "Oh, a first!" (I was laughing). "Erin is this new to God, any of this?"

Me: "No, of course not."

Jesus: "Those who do not see the unseen cannot judge. There is a glass ceiling over the Earth. There is nothing new under the sun. The enemy lives but is soon to be removed. Erin your Savior lives and is never to be removed. God Reigns! Your God Reigns! Do not worry about tomorrow! I will lead you as in Psalm 23. God is within you, you will not fail. God will help you at the break of Day! I will send signs and help." I was crying. "This is enough for today. I will have you go deeper into these stories to find a simple key. You have a friend that knows this. Now, when trouble comes where do you look?"

Me: "I look up! Right?" He was laughing.

Jesus: "Yes Erin. Please don't worry. You are loved. Come to Me, those who are weary and I will give you rest."

Me: "Lord I am weary."

Jesus: "Rest in Me, Erin. The battle is God's! Pray and Be Still.

He smiled and hugged me.

Dream over…

Psalm 23 (NKJV)

The Lord *is* my shepherd; I shall not want. He makes me to lie down in green pastures; He leads me beside the still waters. He restores my soul; He leads me in the paths of righteousness For His name's sake.

Yea, though I walk through the valley of the shadow of death, I will fear no evil; For You *are* with me; Your rod and Your staff, they comfort me. You prepare a table before me in the presence of my enemies; You anoint my head with oil; My cup runs over. Surely goodness and mercy shall follow me All the days of my life; And I will dwell in the house of the Lord Forever.

Chapter 18 – God's Garden for Children

Communion

Dear Father,

Thank You for another day. Thank You for my children and their health. Thank You for my close family and friends whom You have sent to pray and encourage us. I feel peace and healing coming. Thank You also for keeping my son – middle son from this sickness. A friend reminded me that Your Grace is Sufficient. This has been repeating in my heart via the Holy Spirit – itched. Thank You for this wise counsel.

My dreams the last couple of nights have been about the oncoming deception. In one I saw a pot of boiling water over an open fire. I was reminded about a frog dropped in boiling water will jump out but one in a cool pot slowly bringing the water to a boil will not even realize it is being cooked. You have shown me that the coming deception is like this. We are currently in this giant pot of water. Many have no clue what is happening. Help Lord

My other dream last night was this giant dome. Inside the dome people could go into these chambers and receive an anti-aging treatment. People flocked in mass to receive these treatments for eternal youth. These people gave everything they had to go into these chambers. It was the same as Nazi death camps; two lines, those who seemed weak in one and those who seemed strong in another. The difference in this dream everything was white; the walls, floors, equipment, lab coats, etc. People were separated according to their beliefs spiritually so they could play the proper music while they went into the chambers. One line claimed to believe in Jesus – although they seemed ashamed. This line also contained Jews. The other line contained a wide variety of beliefs but swore no alliance to Jesus. The line with wide gate religions went into the chambers and became young – they were a fake version of glorified body. Their bodies were still dying but they looked youthful. I saw demons all around these individuals. The only requirement for the new youthful look was to appear and testify for others to come. The other line – well let's just say their allegiance to Jesus made them lose their head. It looked so real, all of it. My glorified state can easily stand next to the fake but if I didn't know about Heaven or Jesus... Well, I wouldn't know what to look for. I pray we are far removed before this happens. With time passing so quickly this looked like close to real time. Is this structure being built now? It is a football stadium in the US or somewhere else?

Lord, I pray this day, if there is anything more I can do please make my road a bit easier to walk. Please keep us healthy, protected and far removed from the coming chaos or for that matter the current chaos – so I can be free to hear from You more clearly and spread the good news. Lord, please bless my friends abundantly with the supernatural open Heavens over them, Grant all of them Supernatural Gifts straight from the Throne. May these be used as witnessing tools before the coming deception! Lord, I am requesting to activate and equip Your Saints with the supernatural ability to witness and stand for You just on appearances alone. Lord You told me I could ask for up to one-half Your Kingdom – Well, now I am calling in Your request. We cannot save but we can testify and direct those to the Fountain of Youth – The River of Life in Heaven! Please Lord answer my request, petition and prayer this very day! In Jesus name!

Erin Come Up!

Today I was on a beautiful overlook. It appeared I was viewing another valley. In the distance I could see the City of Gold (God). I was in a Northern valley. I could see stripes upon stripes of color bands on the valley floor. I could see acres and acres of tulips. It took my breath away. Off to the left I could see something that looked like a massive Japanese Garden, but there were huge trees. I wanted to go there and explore, immediately with the desire of my heart I was there. How did this happen? Wow! I stood in this garden; it was not specific to Japanese culture but, similar. The floor of the garden was soft green velvet moss. There were chiseled stones of pearl to walk on. There around me were giant trees like the Earthly version of a weeping willow but these were flowers of every kind of color. The garden trees looked like they were fountains pouring flowers. The pearl stones went to this blossoming massive tree. There was a bench that circled the entire base of the tree. The bench could easily seat 12 people. I must have been grinning from ear to ear! My heart was racing at the beautiful site. To my right was something like a path through a tunnel of flowering vines. It opened up to a small lake. To my left was a miniature village, or replica of a village. It was all little white, stones, brick, and wooden buildings.

The tiny village had a little street of gold, small street lights and groomed landscape. There were details that literally took my breath away. I peeked inside the little buildings and saw furniture. There were beds, bedding, paintings, etc. I smiled and laughed. This was not Japanese in style but truly amazing. As a child I remembered seeing something like this at the Smithsonian Institute. As I walked further, I saw other little villages. I was laughing. The flowers here I could tell were forever blossoming. This was not a winter place at all. I took my sandals off to put my feet into the soft velvet moss. I heard giggling.

I turned and looked around and saw nothing. I was wearing a beautiful white gown of linen. I had beautiful long blonde hair. No braids! I loved this Heavenly state – Oh if I could feel just 20 percent as on Earth like I do here in Heaven, I would be so encouraged. I decided to make my way to the left along the pearl stepping stones. The breeze was slight so everything seemed to be alive – well it was alive. The fragrance was so light and airy. It was perfect not intoxicating, it was perfectly Heavenly. The scent triggered a distant memory from my past, but I wasn't certain what that was anymore – this was far too interesting! I saw movement up ahead in one of the little villages. I saw baby chicks with feathers – fuzz dyed several different colors. The little chicks sang. I don't know the species but they were so cute. I saw little baby bunnies and kittens. I saw puppies and other baby animals… Tears began to fall down my cheeks as I stepped on these pear stones. It was one of the most beautiful places I had ever seen. It was far greater than anything I ever imagined.

I remembered as a child when my parents were fighting – violent fights with things breaking. I would lie in bed and imagine what it would be like to be in another place – like Heaven! This is it! As I walked I saw small pools light blue and shallow – perfect for wading and splashing. I saw beautiful butterflies with shimmering colors. I saw dragon flies that made music with their wings.

Me: "Lord, where am I in Heaven? Whose place is this? This is designed by a Master Gardener. It is maintained by gardeners so skilled that – well I can't even describe all of it!"

As I walked I could see acres and acres of this garden. I saw hedges shaped like animals. I saw an area with something like kites and hot air balloons. I saw something like fields of Lego structures – but completely state of the art with moving parts and incredible colors. I saw spinning objects suspended in midair by blow holes in the ground. I saw fountains of water squirting out of the ground and creating archways of light, similar to some fountains in my Heaven home. I ran up to another overlook with my sandals in my hand. I ran up this path with amazing speed. When I reached the top I turned to look out. I realized the entire valley – miles and miles and miles were all like this. Over my shoulder and beyond I saw God's Mansion. I was North East – I was in God's Garden. Wow!!!

Me: "Lord, where are You? Please join me. I miss You!"

I sat down on his overlook with my legs dangling over this ledge. I faced this beautiful valley – a perfect place for children. It was so much better than any place I have ever seen designed for children. There were so many cultures, but completely perfected so any child would love to explore; gardens, rocks, ponds, waterfalls, wading pools, baby animals – these are only the things that I can describe based on an earthly relationship to something here. There is more, much more. This place is so amazing, delightful and massive a child could be here from birth to age 18 and never see it all!

I saw mysterious things too – again I am only describing things we can understand, or should say things I can draw a picture of. What I saw was beyond words. I saw rainbows that actually had a starting point and an ending point. They even held treasures untold at the end. One area had trees illuminated with sparkling lights of every color, fireflies and glow worms – but not gross – beautiful and delightful. Suddenly I wanted to be a child. I missed delights. I grew-up very quickly. I began to miss what I didn't have. I had always hoped for better. As a little girl – I wanted safety first, happiness, love, joy, laughter, peace. I wanted fun and friends – I wanted parents who loved each other – most of all I wanted Jesus, but I didn't know this then. I didn't know Him.

Tears began to fall – of course – this is all I do these days – Here in Heaven the beauty… Even a manly man on Earth would weep – You just can't help but be amazed at the beauty here! You can't believe how quickly humility set in! Seriously, trees always blossoming – and baby animals that remain babies – amazing! Not all animals stay babies – perhaps it is the child-like desires of our hearts that will it to be here. Baby animals grow so quickly – innocence leaves so quickly.

I felt a hand on my shoulder. I looked up to see Jesus. He was laughing as He sat down next to me on the overlook.

Jesus: "Are you enjoying this Erin?" I reached over to hug Him!

Me: "Lord is there nothing You won't do to display Your immense love for us? This is so incredible!"

Jesus: "I knew it was time to bring you back here. Remember those rainbows I gave you right before I took you on that dark journey! Do you understand more now?"

Me: "I had forgotten all the trouble Lord, when I saw this. I cannot begin to understand Your ways. I cannot judge nor will I so quickly again. Please forgive me in advance though, as I am most certain I will be angry and have a human desire to see justice."

Jesus: "Hmmm, Yes a good reason to be human and not God! Your ways focus on what you can see before you only. You relate your own experiences to formulate or inflict judgment. Not always with good results."

Me: "Yes, I am not to judge – although You have not removed all of my obstacles – this requires Your Divine Judgment. Mine would not be Godly."

Jesus: He was laughing, "Erin then once and for all let them go and let God! It's simple."

Me: "Simply impossible!" He was laughing…

Jesus: "Okay, so do you have an idea of what you were shown?"

Me: "Well something occurred to me. All of these people made mistakes which cost lives. These were accidents though. Some paid with lives lost. Some were at the wrong place at the wrong time. These adults carried heavy burdens, yokes of guilt! Then the last 3 scenarios seem unrelated, but patterns made me angry, then finally it ended as the Holocaust left me empty and speechless. I went from injustice, sympathy and grief to rage, anger, and certainly wanting justice. It still confuses me. Why did You take all of us there? I didn't even give the complete details of what I had seen. The visuals are in my head – Please remove them. (He turned and showed me such love!)

Jesus: "Erin, I understand more than you can know. You have seen only a small fragment of atrocities which happen every day. Now, I have been here since the beginning. I have seen all. God sees all. "Things hidden" is a term for man. There is nothing hidden from God, angels, or even the enemy at times – Heaven is above the Earth. Earth is visible. You have seen it. No man can see from the lap of God. No man has seen God. Even you, Erin, have not seen the face of God – only the Throne. Do not listen to anyone who claims to have seen God. Remember how God appears to man over the course of History – this is a gauge to witness against deception. Now – understand then what forces are at work, forces which you cannot see. Man holds yokes and burdens also for things done by the unseen enemy. Remember what occurs in God's Courts. Remember Job. There are other things also. Remember that anyone who claims to be the most humble is clearly not. This, too, is a gauge – obvious and in plain sight. Now, you have some yokes you are still carrying, like the soldiers who were falsely accused and those parents who made difficult choices. It's time to let go of this final burden."

Me: "You are right, Lord. I have forgiven the enemy involved, but I have not forgiven myself for being so stupid ... dim-sighted. I caused my children to be inflicted. They were innocent. I couldn't be with them all of the time. If only I had heeded Your warnings before they were born, I could've made different choices. When I see their disabilities – every time, I blame myself. I can't forgive myself, Lord. Help me!"

Jesus: "Finally, you have come clean."

Me: "Lord, I wasn't trying to hide anything. Just heal my boys, Lord, please! Heal me, Lord! Free us before you take us Home! My daughter is very much like a child – she is. I have kept her in joy. My boys have a memory. It's been a struggle."

Jesus: "Erin, you have nailed yourself on the cross. Do you believe God doesn't know? Do you believe you can work out a better outcome by remaining in your state of judgment against yourself? God has seen all things, Erin. Let Him Judge! Let Me Save You!"

Me: "Lord, was I unsaved?"

Jesus: Laughing … "Of course you are saved – this is silly now. I won't have this talk coming from you. Let your words be few now – let Me speak tenderly to you. Do you think I have not seen your beginnings? Do you think I have not seen your mistakes? Do you think I cannot also see what happens in the unseen realm? There is so much more. I have compassion because I can see the entire story, Erin. You are loved. You saw only the tragedy in the lives of all of those people – you didn't see the outcome. You didn't see the soldiers – the bad ones dropped to their knees and sobbed like babies when an Angel of God appeared. Can I tell you that there is no greater sorrow than when a man who believes he is beyond redemption sees God? There is no measure for the guilt that those men suddenly carried. They were clearly guilty of their crimes, and they could not hide. Erin, the outcome in this instance will surprise you. You would not believe it. Now, the whole world has carried the guilt of the Holocaust. There were millions of angels sent. Do you know that the line of the weakest – do you know that almost all of them reside here? Not all, as many still would not accept their Savior! Do you know that very few from the other line could accept Me? There is more – much more. Just know that I was sent to be the Savior. There is, was, and has been a need from the Fall. It was foretold, but it was not I whom they were expecting, but a King."

Me: "Lord, You are a King!"

Jesus: He was laughing and nudged me! "Yes, if only I had ridden into Jerusalem originally on a white horse – the donkey was unexpected!" He laughed.

Me: "Well, soon You will be coming on that horse!"

Jesus: "Yes, but at first I will not be recognized – until every knee bows."

Me: "Oh, Lord, they missed out on You. I almost missed out on You. Lord, You are so wise and Your ways so much greater. My humanness cannot contain Your vast grace – Your amazing works!"

Jesus: "Perhaps this is not your place to. How about you stop trying to figure Me out and just remain who you are? You delight Me!" He nudged me again.

Me: "Lord, You delight me. You are wonderful. You love me despite me. Here I wanted to murder those bad soldiers, and You have another plan. Who knows what You are up to, but it is Divinely Perfect. Please forgive me for my judgments, like I have knowledge. I can't wait until You restrain the restrainer!"

Jesus: "Oh, Erin, make no mistake – he is restrained. You know this – you recently spoke to someone close about this. The enemy on Earth is under God's restrictions, and as hard as he tries, he cannot disobey God. The Fallen have been restrained underground as an example to the enemy. Now, the lake of fire is a place. When the enemy is cast down there, he will no longer be restricted – he is free to do his will there. This will be a place of unspeakable horrors, unimaginable – Earthly atrocities are only a small fraction. He is allowed – granted – some small atrocities here, so people want a Savior … Heaven or God! Not the place of the enemy. The enemy wants to have hard hearts."

Me: "Lord, I get it – he is free to terrorize in his own domain, but on Earth, he is not free to do this."

Jesus: "Make no mistake, Erin, either way he is not free. Now let's give him no more time here. Let's look at something special." He turned my attention to this beautiful Child Paradise.

Me: "Lord, I want to spend time here, too. It's wonderful!"

Jesus: "You will come here too, Erin. Why did I show you this?"

Me: "I don't know."

Jesus: "Those children who have died play here. The parents get to see their children play here and grow up here. Then they will be like others, too."

Me: "You mean they will have a chance to have a normal childhood and grow? Then they will be like a 25-year-old for Eternity?"

Jesus: Laughing … "Yes, something like this. Did you think there are children who never grow up here? Erin, you get younger – can't they grow older?"

Me: I was laughing! "Oh, Lord, this is Awesome! My kids were worried that they would miss out on being teenagers and growing. They thought they would instantly be around 25!"

Jesus: "Hmmm. Doesn't sound like Heaven. What – and miss out on being a teenager? Does God make mistaken years?"

Me: Laughing … "As You know, my teenage years were difficult and not very fun."

Jesus: "Hmmm. You didn't have Me or a perfected body and a renewed mind. It will be a blast for them, Erin!"

Me: "So You have special things planned for them, too?"

Jesus: "No lack, Erin! It's perfected fun. Not sinful. You are doubting because you are thinking Heaven should be more serious."

Me: "Oh – no, Lord. I'm excited because we were taught there is no fun here – only boredom --- sorry, Lord!"

Jesus: He was laughing. "I am so glad those people have a special place here. They need some reprogramming on the Heart of God. God delights in laughter – the laughter of children. Erin, I laugh, but this is not a spiritual gift – this is a reaction birthed from Joy and Love!"

Me: "Holy laughter – some churches have this."

Jesus: "Well, they have taken this to the extreme – with help from others not appointed. Pray. People are in search of Me and more of Me. They, too, can find Me. It is the heart! Blessed are those who ask for a Heart of Gold."

Me: I began to cry. "Lord, I had no idea what I was asking for. I know for sure I do not have it completely here on Earth, but I can be certain that when we all dwell here with You, we will be perfected and in Your full glory. I wouldn't trade a thing, if it meant I would miss one second of You."

Jesus: "Then, Erin, there are no accidents along the road to find Me. I was there holding your hand the entire time. Angels were there to remind the enemy of his restrictions. When you prayed, God received your prayers! You are Loved! Now, there is more!"

He hugged me and kissed the top of my head...

Dream over...

Chapter 19 – Paradise - Tropical Beach

Communion

Dear Father,

Thank You! You are so Amazing! You are So Intricate in Detail and Glorious in Your Displays. God, how can You be all around me working continuously, and I cannot see You? How can You be so quiet, yet loud at the same time? Lord, You are a wonderful mystery. I adore You! Even though I am in great pain right now, You give me millions of reasons to be joyful. You are so incredible! Thank You for my trials. Thank You for hearing my cries and sending help. Forgive me for complaining and becoming discouraged when the pending method of delivery was not expected. I love You!

Erin – Come Up!

I woke up looking up at a beautiful, sparkling blue sky. I was startled for a moment – well, disoriented. I sat up and wow, I was in an amazing place! It was the most beautiful tropical beach I had ever seen! I was in a different part of Heaven! I looked down at the sand – it was just like sugar, but not regular sugar – it was like fine Baker's sugar. I picked up a bunch in my hand. My eyes quickly viewed it microscopically. I was looking at the richest minerals – I saw diamonds, crystals, and even a little salt. I'm not certain how I knew this, but I did. I reached down with my tongue and tasted it. It had no flavor but a small hint of sea salt. The sand was airy, not heavy. I scanned to my right. I saw beautiful trees – a variety of palm trees, mangrove, and other tropical trees. There were beautiful flowers, almost every variety of my favorites. I saw Bird of Paradise, White Ginger, Red Ginger, Golden Trumpets, Orchids – flaming flowers and paper flowers. I saw a multitude of fruit-bearing trees. I saw pomegranate, pineapple, banana, coconut, kiwi, and so many other fruits and flowers which have no earthly counterpart, but incredibly colorful!

Tears began to stream down my cheeks again. The ocean in front of me was breathtakingly beautiful. I saw dolphins in the distance – several different schools and varieties. They looked as if they were playing. I brought myself up to my feet. I looked at what I was wearing and began to laugh. I was wearing a white gown, but appropriate to the climate. The robe twisted and went around my neck like a halter dress. It was just above my knees. I was still very modestly dressed. My legs and arms were so beautiful. I had a deep tan with no flaws. My toenails were like opalescent pearls. I laughed – on my right ankle was a beautiful golden chain with tiny pearls and gold seashells inlaid with emerald stones. The craftsmanship was beyond Earth. On my right wrist were the gold replicas of my Earthly silver bangles, but glorified and re-gifted to me by God. They were no longer hammered and dented and scratched. My hair was in a very long thick braid, woven with gold strands and forward over my torso. The braid was long and came to my hip area. My muscle structure was perfected – not overly muscular, but defined. (Forgive me for taking so much time to focus on this, but I felt so wonderful in this state!) I was about 25 years old.

I ran down to the ocean and the water was like bathwater. In fact, the temperature outside was perfect. It was about 85 degrees, a bit warmer than some areas in Heaven, but not too warm. The air was humid, but perfect – not heavy – very light and easy to breathe. The beach was very shallow. The ocean was calm – the color of all my favorite shades of blue and green together. I walked into it and waded out in the water. I began to worry for a moment if I needed to watch for jellyfish or anything poisonous. Then I began to laugh, as I remembered there was nothing poisonous, hidden, scary, dangerous, venomous, or deadly in Heaven. I reached down to scoop up some water to taste it. I laughed – it was a blend of light salt and sweet water. I was so glad to see places like this in Heaven. I stood there for some time. I was truly in Paradise. This peaceful cove was the most beautiful place I have ever seen. The fragrance was incredible. Some of the beaches I had been to in Florida had a sulfuric smell or decaying-beach smell to things. This had nothing like that at all. I waded in the water and began to walk down the beach to my left. The ocean was completely calm. The tidal current was soft. The waves were small. The sun was warm but not burning. There was a gentle breeze – a zephyr (a west wind). I walked for some time, praising God for what would someday be Home! Strangely, I felt more at Home and safe in Heaven than I ever did on Earth.

As I looked around me – and even as I write, the beauty here makes my heart skip – it was truly breathtaking! I walked and praised God.

I thanked Him for this beautiful Paradise that He has prepared for us. How could anyone ever serve another God? If a photo of just this place – and the promise of it – was hanging on every wall in every earthly household – well, surely every knee would bow and every tongue confess that Jesus is Lord! Just looking at the earthly version of this should have pointed people to God on the Throne, but sadly, science explains it away – or credit is given to foreign gods. Very few thank God for sending Jesus. As I walked, I began to hear something like calypso music – I laughed when I realized it was praise music. I loved it. It stood to Heavenly reason that Eternity should contain the glorified version – magnified – of every earthly Paradise. Come to think of it, I will need to use the word "Paradise" sparingly now in reference to earthly places. Paradise is Heaven and Heaven is Paradise.

I walked along the shallow coast for some time, and eventually I rounded a point. On the other side I saw amazing mansions. One in particular stood out to me. This beautiful home met the ocean like the ocean was the pool for the house. There were steps of chiselled marble – honed, not polished – leading right into the ocean. There were tiers leading up to the main Home. The second tier contained large sofas with comfortable cushions.

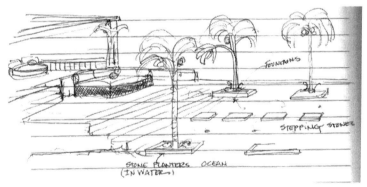

I was fascinated by this Home! The square stones led up to where I had been walking. At the base of a large palm tree, I saw large square planters with flowers – something similar to large pomegranate-like fruits lining the square stepping stones. There were small fountains coming from the ocean floor and jetting in arched columns over the path of the stones. On the sandy beach surrounding this home, I saw beautiful seashells – big, perfect ones, the rare types. I stepped up on one of the stepping stones. I looked up toward the house and saw a table set on one of the upper tiers.

Me: "Holy Spirit, is Jesus up there? Are You there, Lord?"

Just as I spoke His name, He appeared on the balcony by the table and waved for me to come up. I ran up the steps from the ocean. An angel of the Lord greeted me and took me up the stairs to the terrace where Jesus was. He was standing by the balcony and I ran to Him. I hugged Him and thanked Him.

Jesus: "It's so great to see you moving!" He smiled. He was wearing a white tunic and some pants. His skin was dark, His beard perfectly groomed, and His teeth were white as snow. His Eyes were the color of the tropical ocean – sea green, green and blue. He noticed I was studying Him! He laughed.

Me: "Lord, thank You for this! With all of the pain, I was praying You would take me to a beautiful place! This, Lord, is so incredible. I could live here forever!"

Jesus: "Oh – good thing, Erin! Then you will live here forever!" He was laughing. I realized I had stated the obvious.

Me: "Lord, thank You for showing me this part of Heaven! This is Paradise! It is amazing!"

Jesus: "This is still only a small fraction of what is planned. Come – let's have communion!" With His hand on my shoulder, He moves me to the table set behind us. The table is set with beautiful food, breads, fruits, cheeses, fish, and other tropical-looking fare. He takes out some warm flat bread and tears off a piece and gives it to me. He then takes one and puts it into His mouth.

Me: "Lord, thank You for all of this! I am so blessed to be here with You! When I take this bread, I never want to forget what You've done!"

Jesus: "This is good, but when you sit here with Me, you no longer need to remember My body through bread! Nor will this wine represent My blood, as I am here with you!" He reaches over and takes my hand. "Erin, I call you friend!"

Me: "I love hearing this! You must have many!"

Jesus: "Yes, up here – but down on Earth, not many. Those who claim to love Me go no further to spend time with Me – not enough for Me to call them friend."

Me: "They are missing out. You are even more fascinating than I ever imagined. You are funny, wise, patient, kind, loving, and powerful, yet humble. You are so many things. You don't give up on me!"

Jesus: "Well, good – then it is settled. You can plead My case!" He was laughing.

Me: "Oh, I will! I do all the time! Even, when I'm in pain – although at times I do grumble."

Jesus: "Yes, you do. Just remember, this will not last long. I have a plan here to bring you closer. I can see in your eyes that you are wearing down and discouraged."

Me: "I am, Lord. Here, though, every part of my body is alive. I have no pain but great mobility. I can hardly wait to be here. I want to run up and down the beach and swim with dolphins!" (As I said this, a school of dolphins was in the water right outside the home.) I laughed! Jesus smiled.

Jesus: "What do you think of all that you see around you today?"

Me: "Lord, I thought there would be no ocean. I thought there would be no marine life. I had never seen the ocean, so I never dreamt of it. I had seen God's Home, the Golden City, a few valleys, and even snowy peaks, but I never imagined Heaven would contain such a place as this! It's perfect!"

Jesus: "Remember that Heaven must be large enough to contain saints from the beginning of creation. This is much larger than you think. Man thinks only in terms of current population. So, if you imagine that very few will be coming in comparison, then you go back generations – well, then you begin to understand."

Me: "I'm not a math whiz, but I bet this is much larger than the Earth, because I barely see anyone."

Jesus: "Your purpose here is to see what God has prepared for those who love Him. Your purpose has not been to converse with the dead, nor will it be. You have Me, and I am alive and well. You have seen those who have gone before you celebrating here. You have met some who know who you are, and one day you will call many here friends – good friends – but your job is to spread good news."

Me: "I know, Lord – I am a travel agent." He laughed so hard!

Jesus: "Funny, Erin! Yes, here you have tickets you are passing out to Paradise. Because of God, I have secured all of the expenses – God has paid the price and arranged for you to come here for a luxury vacation which never has to end – because your expense account is huge! So now, Erin, physically stand on a street corner and hand out all expense paid trips to Paradise and tell me how people will react!" He was laughing. I was laughing too.

Me: "Lord" – I was shaking my head. This is what people would say … 'What's the catch?' I'll say, 'Only that you would take Jesus as your Lord and Savior!'" Then I became extremely sad, "Lord, people would throw down the tickets or hand them back. They would not do something so simple to get so much."

Jesus: He handed me some fruit and smiled at me, knowing that what I had said was true. "Erin, are you surprised really?"

Me: "No, Lord. Even my Christian friends, who have turned away from me in this season, would talk the talk – but would probably not show up on the day scheduled. They would be too busy."

Jesus: "Erin, don't be sad. Everything has been planned from the beginning. God, My Father, looks at the heart of a man and calls those to Him. How wonderful for some who come now – right?"

Me: "They are missing out! The Bible doesn't even describe how wonderful You are. The disciples knew You – they followed You. You must have been such an amazing man to have them listen to You and drop their nets. Lord, if others saw You like You are, all would chase after You!"

Jesus: "Well, Travel Agent – continue to write the brochure!" He laughed. "Are you saying that I am no longer amazing?" He was kidding with me!

Me: "Lord, You are so fun to be with! No wonder children love You so much! You actually enjoy their company and they know it. Most adults don't enjoy the company of children."

Jesus: "Well, you know how I feel about children. You have seen the place God has prepared here. They will swim with dolphins. There will be no fear. They will surf and have no fear. They will explore exciting places and be filled with wonder! They will come to know the heart of God! They are always loved and safe here!" Tears began to stream down my cheeks.

Me: "Lord, no fear – it is hard to imagine! Just looking around, I understand how our lips will constantly praise You! Our hearts will always be God's! There will never be any doubt. Our gratitude will be immense. Our humbleness at the sights here will bring tears. Our joy ... there is no measure."

Jesus: "Now you understand what man was created for to begin with! To praise and worship God!"

Me: "Lord, I pray I never forget what God has done by sending You to rescue me! I didn't even think You knew who I was and where to find me!" He was laughing!

Jesus: "You will recall what you endured on Earth, and will testify to the love of God, but you will not have the feelings – negative feelings – about what happened here. When a woman has labor, it comes with great pain; then the baby is born, and the woman quickly forgets the pain of the labor because the baby has come. Here, it is the same – you remember the race and recall certain things, but the pain is now gone. You will enjoy conversing with friends and family to the truth of events, as all recollections will be only of clear truth – not mainly recall, which has flaws. So, there will be much healing and confirmation. This will cause celebration. It is hard to understand right now, but you will no longer have a family member change your recollection, as only the truth will be revealed."

Me: "Oh, wow! This is awesome! There are so many memories I have which I have wanted information on just to close Chapters – or hills – in my race of life!"

Jesus: "When I say My Recompense will be with me and is with Me, what do you think of besides money?"

Me: "Well, we are taught compensation for trouble, but now I see it is more."

Jesus: "Well, money doesn't heal. What heals is knowing that God agrees with you that you have suffered. He sees what you have been through, and now He would like to make right all of your wrongs. He will come – I will come – and My Reward is with Me!"

Me: "Lord, God sending You is Recompense."

Jesus: "Oh, good – you caught this!" (I had been watching the dolphins and looking around.) "I was worried!" – He laughed.

Me: "Forgive me, Lord. I am so fascinated by all You have done and the beauty here. You have remembered every detail, even down to the fact that You would make right all the wrongs done unto me on Earth. Lord, You have called me friend and taken me here! You have prepared a place for me in Paradise" (I was crying) – "How could I want anything more? You are all I need!" (He reached over and put His hand over mine.)

Jesus: "Erin, time is drawing near. Soon I will be coming, and My Recompense will be with Me. Many will take the one-way tickets to Paradise, but many will need to see that it is good first! There has been much deception. Just know that the beauty here is not contrary to the Word of God and the beginning. The fruits of the Spirit are alive here. The opposite of these is bad, and this doesn't exist here. If there is no death or decay here – if there is no fear of an enemy – is Heaven boring?"

Me: "Oh, it is not possible!"

Jesus: "Then do not allow the enemy to paint a picture of boredom. Did I say to the thief, 'Today you will join Me in Paradise' and then begin to describe it like this – 'So Paradise is a place of blue skies and clouds. You have an instrument and a white robe – you will enjoy sitting on a cloud and strumming an instrument forever and ever, but you will live in harmony with other saints on their clouds'? And would the thief say, 'Well, Jesus, I'm not sure that sounds very fun, but given the circumstances, this cross is kind of painful – so, okay take me with You!'" He was laughing.

Me: "Lord, I remember as a little girl, I thought Heaven was just full of bright lights and tunnels and pretty much nothing else. This here never occurred to me."

Jesus: "This is why God started in His word, 'In the beginning…' Now go back to the garden – but remember the Garden was just that, a garden and small in comparison. So be encouraged. Do not listen to those with no understanding of Heaven and the Heart of a God! When God created the Garden it was like Paradise, all was good.

Me:" I'm sure the Garden was amazing Lord but this – wow this is incredible! You have prepared such a beautiful place for us! Lord the ocean here is your swimming pool. You don't need to worry about the rising tide."

Jesus: "Oh wait Erin, there is still low tide. You are seeing high tide!"

Just then He waved His arm and the water, which was once His swimming pool, was gone and replaced by white sand with large seashells. He could tell I wanted to run down there! I love shells.

Jesus: He was laughing, "Go ahead Erin, go see!"

I ran down the stairs. I probably could've just imagined myself there and I would've instantly been there – running seemed perfect however. Jesus kept His pace and laughed as I ran out to the stepping stones and on the new white sandy beach. There were seashells of every kind, a purple clear glass one, a few oysters, and a massive conch shell. I was beaming with the biggest grin.

Jesus: "Erin, look at the oysters!"

Just then I looked down and both opened before me. One contained a big white pearl about an inch in diameter. The other contained a rare black pearl about one and a half inches in diameter.

Jesus: "Go ahead they are for you!" I was delighted!

Me: "Lord, I don't want to hurt the oyster or kill the animals in the shells!" He came up to me and crouched (bent) down next to me.

Jesus: "Erin, they don't die here. The oyster will have more pearls very soon – do not worry. The seashells are vacant because the animals have found a new shell. They are not confined here and have no worry about a predator." Just then I saw a cute little blue crab scurry right past us, it seemed to praise Jesus.

Me: "Lord, I never expected to see all these things, yet more beautiful and perfect. These are amazing on Earth yet here, even glorified! I feel at peace now like I will have time to enjoy the beauty here. I can take this all in. Well there is so much to discover and see... I will try to take it in!"

Jesus: "I'm glad you like it Erin." He put His hand on His heart. "It makes My heart glad!" He smiled and seemed to really enjoy showing me more. He stood up and took my hand. Instantly we were at a look-out point on a Rock south of the beach home. I could see a southern shore with beautiful homes all private coves. I smiled because I knew people must have prayed for a beautiful home on a private beach. There were so many different styles but all very special to the owner. He pointed my attention to a distant village which was carved into the side of a mountain. The homes were Mediterranean in style and white. I could see celebrations.

Me: "Lord is it a Holiday here? What are the celebrations about?"

Jesus: He smiled and laughed, "Erin there are always special events. People here love life and enjoy celebrations. All give thanks to God! Gratitude makes for a wonderful celebration!" He pointed out to the ocean. I saw a type of high-tech Regatta Race. I became really excited. I loved these massive Catamarans.

Me: "Lord, there is everything here."

Jesus: "Everything good Erin."

Me: "I'm still amazed at how high-tech everything is. It's fun! It's now what we think Heaven is." He was laughing…

Jesus: "Erin, Heaven has innovation. The God of the Universe created all of this. He also is an Inventor! He loves us and has prepared a place."

He waved His hand and the sun began to set. I smiled and laughed. The beauty of a sunset here made tears well-up in my eyes. I then saw little lights out on the water and a giant barge. The sun set and the sky – the night sky was beautiful. I saw millions of stars like diamonds. I could see things normally only available by high powered telescopes. The sky was filled with large colored milky ways and colored stars. Then the people were cheering. They knew Jesus was here. He laughed and waved. Then the barge began to shoot-off fireworks. These were very hard to describe, so beautiful! Then they paused.

Jesus then said, "Erin, now watch this!"

All of a sudden there were comets and shooting stars in the sky! The sight was beyond spectacular. Jesus was enjoying the people as they cheered for Him. He created the greatest galaxy display I had ever seen. All the people had come to the balconies of their homes. The dolphins, fish, and other creatures, stopped in the water to look up. Every time the Son of God moved His hand a new effect came from the stars. He made small stars spin and dance. I saw angels illuminated – also flying above in an amazing display of color and light. (I am crying as I write.) God is Amazing – Jesus is Amazing!

I was speechless, like everyone watching, the most amazing display in the Universe. You could hear cheers and clapping. You could hear sighs and laughter as we watched. The ocean floor became illuminated so the water glowed like a swimming pool at night. In the water were all kinds of fluorescent fish and seaweed. There were colors of purple, deep blue, greens, and yellows. It was Amazing! Schools of dolphins began to dance on the water and clap their fins. I saw sea turtles and other animals just praising Jesus. We all watched for easily an earthly two hour as Jesus displayed fireworks greater than anything on Earth. After He was finished the crowds cheered and cheered. The music followed with praise songs to Jesus! The

Angels sang and some of the finest musicians followed with a concert. It was Epic!!!

He reached down and took my hand. I was small. I was quiet and so content. I never stopped smiling. Jesus was greater than any rock-star! He saved all these people! He saved me! He is Awesome! As we stood there, passing motor boats would call out to Him and He would laugh and wave. It was the best day!

Jesus: "Did you enjoy your time today?"

Me: "Lord, You made my month of suffering worth it. You have blessed me so much! I'm even more excited to come!"

Jesus: "I knew you would enjoy this."

Me: "Lord, if I knew you could do all this I would've asked for this sooner. Of course You could do such things! You are incredible!" I was giggling about something, but I was embarrassed to speak it.

Jesus: "Okay Erin what are you withholding!"

Me: "Lord, You just showed off!"

Jesus: He was laughing, "Yes, it seemed right in this moment."

Me: "Do You do this often?"

Jesus: "Well for the children or when things seem right."

Me: "You are humble though, so I hate to use the term show-off."

Jesus: "It's okay! It's fun to do."

Me: "There must be some limits in Heaven for man, as clearly man cannot set the stars or display Glory like You!"

Jesus: "Very observant! This is true some areas are God's, this is one. Don't get Me wrong Erin, you can say move to the mountain and by faith it can move, but you will not need to do this here. You can imagine yourself across the valley and there you will be. You can achieve other things like this, but God commands the Moon, Stars, and Sun."

Me: "This makes me glad Lord or we would all be gods in Heaven."

Jesus: "Yes, this was the problem on Earth. So take heart that God is in control here and you welcome and praise Him for it!"

Me: "Lord, I can't wait to be here!"

Jesus: "Yes, I know but there is still time. Do not worry about tomorrow! I have prepared a place for you!"

Me: "Free from pain! Free from fear! I pray You are coming soon."

Jesus: "When I do there will be a display in the Heavens like no other! It cannot be replicated. You will know! Now, soon you will enjoy a celebration like this with your friends and family! It will be wonderful. For now, please continue to trust what I am doing and allowing in your life. There is a reason and one day very soon you will thank me! You are Loved!"

I reached over and hugged Him!

Me: "Thank You Jesus! You are my Savior and Best Friend! I am forever blessed by what You've done for us!"

Jesus: "Erin, I am not finished! There is much more!" He looked at me and smiled!

Dream over…

Blessings to all...

Chapter 20 – God's Garden for Teens

Communion

Dear Father,

Thank You for another day! Thank You for all You have provided and Your immense Grace! Your Grace is sufficient in my suffering! Lord this is my season of change, exodus, and delivery to a safe place. You have promised me many years ago that You would remove me from the desert. I had given up all hope and blamed myself – even condemning myself for falling for the tricks of my enemies. The hard thing for me is I would do it all again to be with You.

It has been a difficult journey Lord – but I would do it all again just to be near Your Alter. As I can begin to see the light at the entrance of my cave I stand amazed and in awe of Your works and the great love! I am in great physical pain right now as I know I am completely in Your hands and at Your Great Mercy. I know I need a surgery – but I also know in a short time by a miracle You are going to heal me so I might live out my days on Earth outside Heaven's Gate protected by angels.

I saw a pattern of wave after wave of the enemy's relentless pounding. Where did it begin? Me, well really sin! I took a stand against abuse. I didn't cover it up! I loved my children and God more! It caused me to go from a woman of many friends and social status to a woman despised and broken. I had an estranged Christian friend tell me, "Couldn't you have kept things quiet and allowed the church to handle it?" – Well No – I had gone for help for many years, but no one likes broken Christians. It goes against what most believe about God. I was taught that once you became a Christian nothing is impossible and you prosper. What I learned instead was Christian sinners don't seem to be accountable. This of course is not true.

I had seen You work Lord. I saw something different. I saw the consequences of sin and I became afraid. Lord, I know who You are, You want what is best for me, but because You love my heart more, You will rend my heart completely to You. This means brokenness from the consequences of sin, even if in severe grief! In 2000 I asked in my grief, at the Rose Garden in Portland, after a funeral of a friend for a heart of Gold. A woman approached me as I sat on a concrete garden bench. I was sobbing with grief in my black $1000 suite dress. She said, "Look at the beautiful day and all that God has made!" She pointed at the flowers; the beautiful roses. I dismissed her as I really wanted to be alone in my grief. I don't even recall most of that day 14 years ago. Lord. Now I believe she was an angel, when I dried my eyes for a moment, right in front of me were beautiful roses – what seemed like acres. The roses, right in front of me had the label "Heart of Gold!" My tears turned from grief to tears of hope. Thank You Lord for rending my heart! This was the beginning of Wisdom! I Love You!

Erin Come Up!

Immediately I was up in what looked like the East quadrant of God's Garden. I saw the Crystal Conservatory in the distance. I heard the most beautiful music. It was the Children of God's special remnant here. The Orchestra was amazing and the choirs of children and angels were so perfect. My heart immediately skipped. There was a song I didn't recognize, but it was similar to My Deliverer by Rich Mullins – actually it was but in a glorified state. The sound was so acoustically clear that it could be from a recording booth at a studio. The sound was crystal clear and each cord perfect. I read one time about some stereo speakers that cost more than a million dollars for a pair, the speakers claim to by-pass your ears completely and go directly into your brain. I laugh because here in Heaven – in God's Conservatory, the music is so pure, perfect and radiant that the music by-passes your ears, brain and body – going directly to your soul and spirit. It is beyond anything earthly.

To describe the worship here, it is like healing water from the River of Life. It's a necessary part of life here. The Water refreshes and renews, the fruit restores and replenishes. The music resounds and releases us to the Heart of God. It fills our souls and causes us to ascend as the music climbs. This is very difficult to describe but it causes the cells in our body to worship. The music goes into our cells and creates life there! With each climb or ascension of the songs and symphony, I felt my heart moving higher to God. Tears were streaming as I had never heard a more beautiful song than the grateful hearts of the orphaned children. Let me correct this, orphaned on Earth adopted by God in Heaven! My painful time going through this war with my own situation and children made me so ready to be here permanently – not prematurely – but perfectly God's timing.

My eyes were closed as I sat on this marble bench in God's Garden. I listen and wept with my hands raised to God with such great thanks to Him for everything! When I finished soaking in the music I opened my eyes to see acres of roses. I smiled! Right in front of me was a perfect rose bush, immensely fragrant with dew on each pedal. The roses were gold with a hint of blush pink. I walked over closer and I could see the dew was diamonds. "Wow, dew in Heaven is like diamonds? Lord, You are incredible!" I felt a hand on my shoulder. I turned and it was the Lord! He was smiling and laughing. He was always sincerely glad to see me!

Jesus: "I see you are smelling the roses!" His face was so beautiful. He had white teeth, blue/green eyes and tanned skin. I looked at Him and laughed.

Me: "Here I could stop and smell the roses always!" He laughed…

Jesus: "Very good. What are you looking at? Oh I see a familiar rose."

Me: "Yes, Lord You brought me here. You know full-well why, I'm just a bit behind and ready to come home now!" He smiled and agreed with me.

Jesus: "Do you want to come now? There is still more if you are up to the challenge?"

Me: I let out a deep sigh, "I'll stay – I just don't like my situation right now. I'm in great pain. I have had no choice but to go through old records of the last 10 years, the absolute most painful in my life!" My eyes began to well-up. I looked at Jesus to see His response.

Jesus: "Well, I was there with you. If – I were to remove all of that, what of all the good? Think about this long and hard, better yet let me show you."

He took me to an incredible small pond right behind where we were standing. He sat me down on the bench and He stood up behind me with one hand on my back.

Jesus: "Now this will be painful, I am going to give you a glimpse of what God also saw which you couldn't see. You will see things allowed and others not. Before I begin please note that nothing done in secret to you and your children will go unpunished. Are you certain you would like to see everything again?"

Me: "Lord, grant me strength, grace and peace. I don't understand the plans You have for me fully, but I know You love me and what the enemy has planned for evil You have planned for my good!"

Jesus: "You say what I expect, but do you fully understand the magnitude of what I'm about to show you?" He knew more than I did, I could see concern and compassion in His eyes. I nodded. "I have changed the filter. I am going to take you back 21 years. I will only show you that which was turning points in your walk. You will see both the seen and the unseen. You must not be angry, but wait until I am finished to speak. Erin this is your race – you put God before you for most of this. The word race with G before it is Grace! What you will not see yet is all those lives you touched or related to you – who sat daily in the Courts of God pleading your case. Erin you were knit by God in your mother's womb. Your life was unique to you from the beginning. Each of your friends have a race also! – Blessed is the runner who puts God before them and Me alongside you! I am here."

Me: "Lord, before we start – when You saw the wrongs done to me, what did You do Lord?"

Jesus: "My heart grieved Erin – but I saw My Father's plan from the beginning. I saw the end from the beginning. When you see things This way from a Heavenly perspective the race is like an epic movie. There are ups and downs, tears and laughter, life and death; all is a part of your life race. I am not a cold hearted Savior and My Father is never far removed as you have been taught. God sees all! He is compassionate, slow to anger and abundant in Love!"

Me: "He sent You Lord – there is no greater thing on Earth or Heaven!"

Jesus: "You are loved Erin, When you see this please don't forget! Are you ready to begin?

Me: "Yes, I think so!"

Immediately the water became like glass. I saw myself in 1993, in Portland, Oregon. I saw angels surrounding me. I saw an extremely painful event which created great fear, one in which I saw the face of the enemy. He declared by his voice that he hated me and I was his. It scared me – terrified me. This incident led to a series of what looked like bad decisions at the time straight to a church. There I became saved. I saw Heaven rejoice as I gave my life and heart to God. The enemy was right there, or should I say demons. I was surprised to see so many at the church. I saw many in the congregation, who I always thought were used by the enemy, being controlled by demons. I saw the demons whispering things into their ears about me. "She is not really a Christian. Look at her, she is just a whore!" – etc. etc. – very painful! I saw the plans of the enemy, yet the angels from Heaven were many and much greater. The angels surrounded me, and even covered my ears from murmurs of Christians used by the enemy.

As my race continued, I watched as blessings would come to me. The enemy's soldiers were right there, stripping me of all the blessings. I saw a major turning point in 1994, when God commanded angels to expose the enemy's schemes, but my desire and fear drove me straight into trouble. I saw all kinds of plots by the enemy allowed by God. On my wedding day, I saw behind the scenes – my dressmaker breaking down by murmurs of the enemy in her ears. My wedding dress arrived unsewn from my last fitting and the bridesmaids' gowns shredded. Self-determined, I saw God temporarily remove the angels until some ladies at church prayed. I declared something verbally about God and the mustard seed ... that gave God compassion and He allowed the angels to help. God gave favor to me that day, but I was heading straight into darkness.

Then my hammering began. I won't verbalize all that occurred behind the scenes and what was done to me, but I saw the angels grieve. I watched as all hope departed from my life. As good Christian women pray, I was determined to stay and fight. I saw a weak tent covering over our household. It was like tattered mesh. I saw holes in it where the enemy had access to come and go. Sin gave access. I had fear of God, which was the beginning of wisdom, yet I was not the cover over my household. My husband was, and I was confused.

The Lord showed me my businesses. These were covered by God when I dedicated them to the Lord – I had forgotten that I prayed this. In turn, I saw my business prosper. I saw some bad decisions, but even my bad decisions were used by God. I gave in secret – I had forgotten all about this. I kept this portion hidden, because I understood the principle of tithing, but our household cover was in disagreement.

As I watched the plots of the enemy unfold at home, it began to affect me at work. I saw the births of my sons, but as I watched what had happened to me while they were in my womb, it was bittersweet. I grieved. I looked at Jesus when I saw the enemy do things – to get His reaction – and I could tell He was angry. His jaw was clenched and His eyes showed a coming time where there would be accountability. I was relieved to see that He was not passive. I then saw things, which I suspected and verbalized, being covered-up and denied. I saw things confirmed. My heart was breaking. If I elaborate it could harm people, so I will not do this. For me to expose details would be out of God's will.

I saw the events leading to the year 2000 – the end of August 2000 in the Rose Garden in Portland. The events of that day were clear. It was an angel who spoke to me. I dismissed her. (I wept.) I prayed this to God and Heaven rejoiced. The Heart of God on the Throne was glad. I prayed to know Jesus. I prayed to have meaning to my miserable existence. I prayed for God to reconcile me to Himself – whatever that took I was willing – maybe not able, but willing. I asked to have a Heart of Gold! I asked for help! There before me – which I didn't see physically – Heaven opened and God on the Throne sent angels to assist. I saw a hedge or a type of tent cover over me. I saw my black funeral clothes become a wedding gown. Somehow, I had become a bride on that day – and I wept at the sight. I wanted to speak, but instead I turned to see Jesus with the happiest look on His face. He was proud of me. He directed my vision back – I still had fourteen years to go.

Then I saw the enemy ramp up against me and my children. Christians were the greatest tool of the enemy. I watched so many painful events happen. I watched unbelievable miracles. On one day I saw the enemy send in a dog to attack one of my sons – he was only three at the time. I watched an angel of the Lord appear to the dog and restrain it. I watched all kinds of things come against us. There were wars just as I expected. I saw horrendous things done in secret. I saw deals and events which broke my heart. I saw money moved and secured with my name removed. I saw affliction to my sons by others. (I wept at the sight.) I thought I was alone. I turned to Jesus again, as He was angry and let out a sigh – I could see He wasn't enjoying this.

I saw my first NDE – I smiled as I saw the angels in the operatory at the hospital. I saw the panic in the staff when my heart stopped. I saw Jesus meet me and take me up. There I was instructed and shown great compassion for the next difficult portion of the race. Each time I was heading into a dark portion of my race – walk – the Lord brought angels consistently to tell me in advance of it and point me to Heaven. They ministered to me. When the events of 2004-2005 unraveled, I watched God expose things hidden in secret. I became sick. There was much more. At many of the points I looked away. At one point I cried out "no" and stood up! I was so angry. I watched as the enemy tried to rob pure innocence. I felt the Lord wrap His arms around me. I watched as angels protected my little ones. I grieved.

In the natural, I watched myself deal with the small portion I had evidence of, and I was not doing well. If the Lord had revealed all of this to me – I would've done something horrible, perhaps murder. Whatever He allowed, it was perfect. I heard horrible things spoken about me. Lies, complete lies! I watched as God continued to bless me personally and provide supernaturally, but I watched myself make bad decision after bad decision because I lacked faith. I watched as I was numb. I could not sleep at night. I cried out to God. I became more ill, as my heart was breaking. I watched the enemy do clever things. Soon, the enemy walked before me and I headed into darkness.

Finally, the Lord used my heart to draw me back to Him. My heart would stop and He'd take me to lovely places in Heaven and speak tenderly to me. When I'd come back to the natural – it seemed so unnatural. Lawsuits came against me – wave upon wave of trouble hit me in such a short amount of time. I could barely catch my breath. All the while and even facing homelessness and eviction, I had faith and worshiped. All we knew to do at this time was Christian music, worship, and prayer. I saw the time I counted out a jar of pennies to get some gas so the kids and I could drive to the 'far away" park that the kids loved. I watched as God sent various saints to help us at times. I barely cried during this time.

Then my heart became worse, and the medical bills pounded us. I would soon lose my children, because I simply couldn't provide for them. Then my heart stopped again. The Lord took me to a sword room in Heaven – there were the retired swords of angels who had fought in my battles from the beginning. He reminded me of my place in His heart.

Then the final blow by the enemy occurred, and I walked straight into the desert. As I sat stunned, I couldn't hear from the Lord during this second wave of the enemy. I watched Justice fail. I saw injustice, and by a mistake on my part to negotiate, I was at the mercy of my enemy. It was a dark mistake. I watched the day I made it, as my angels were not able to protect me – or should I say restrain me. The enemy convinced me to sign a contract, which caused seven years of magnified trouble. I became sunken in my spirit as I sat watching this. I wanted to yell at myself to stop what I was doing, but I could not. I felt Jesus standing behind me, wrapping His arms around me as I wept.

I suffered for three years. Then God had compassion on me. I saw everything up to this very day, as well as plots still occurring concerning me. I saw something different in my current trouble. I saw myself not going before God. I saw myself waiting on Him. Even in my physical pain, the angels were ministering to me. Then the Lord showed me more coming. My face lit up! I saw my sons being healed. I saw myself becoming healed. I saw us being removed from the desert and being free from my enemies. I saw a house. I saw myself finally being free and at peace. Before this occurred, though, I saw some trouble, but the plans of God were going to prevail!

I saw a time much later up in Heaven. I saw my children there. They knew me as their mother, yet we were all the same age. Our trouble was a passing, distant memory – but we didn't forget what the Lord had done for us. I had tears streaming down my cheeks.

Jesus: "Well, what do you think of your race?"

Me: "I did nothing which surprised God. Even my bad decisions, He used for a greater good. I watched miracles, and I'm relieved that the times in which I thought I was alone… You and the angels were right there. It's a miracle."

Jesus: "I could show you high lights of just the miracles, but these would mean nothing if you were not seeing the evil you were being delivered from at the time. Now, why did I allow you to see all this right now?"

Me: "Because I am about to go into the final battle with my enemy, so the kids and I will be released from prison here in the desert."

Jesus: "Yes. I am reassuring you in advance. I gave you the weapons to fight. You are to put on your full armor and stand. You are to have Me go before you, along with the angels, and watch the enemy flee. Allow Me to do everything."

Me: "Lord, my injury – was this part of the plan?"

Jesus: "Well, Erin, you saw the outcome – don't you think this was part of the plan? Things meant for evil can be used for good – you have seen this. Is anything too great for God?"

Me: "No … I am just weak right now. I am limited in my ability to fight."

Jesus: "Good … then let God fight. He is made strong in your weakness." I laughed.

Me: "Lord, You will take anything I say and have a scripture to return to me."

Jesus: Laughing … "Yes, My Word doesn't go out void of truth and wisdom, Erin. This is good food. Now – right here, right now – hand the coming battle over to Me. I have appointed angels. I have friends standing with you. I have and will send provision. I have built a house for you – a place at My Altar where you will sing like you did in your youth. You will dance and have joy everlasting. You will soar on the wings of eagles. You will run and not get tired; you will walk and not become weary." (I was crying as He spoke.) "Erin, allow Me to carry you during the final battle. Those who bless you I will bless. Those who curse …"

Me: "I know, Lord. I have now seen a huge gift, but also a burden as I now know I am up against unseen forces removed from my home but active at my work and around us. Lord, You know full well this battle is not mine but God's. There is nothing I can do except obey. I have seen the outcome!"

Jesus: "Now you understand. Here..." (He walks behind us to the Roses. There He picked a rose for me.) "This is the Heart of Gold. You probably didn't notice before that the center petals are gold – the Heart." I looked and saw each ring of the rose outside of the heart, graduate to deeper hues of pink.

Me: "I didn't notice this before, but obviously there was quite a bit that I missed on my race."

Jesus: "Erin, don't focus on the mistakes you made. Focus on the victories. It's not your fault. The enemy hates you. He is a liar and believes his lies. He is void of truth and treacherous. You have seen what was allowed and understand where this sweet melody comes from!" Suddenly I heard the beautiful Choir of Orphans, angels and the Divine Symphony played. "Erin these children suffered unspeakable things. Yet they reside here. Their Home is with God. Here they are rich. They are remembered and loved. They eat the best food and never grow hungry. They drink pure water and never get sick. They have laughter and tears are far removed. They remember where they come from, but forget the pain!"

Me: "I forgot Lord. They had things much worse than me or my children. Please forgive me."

Jesus: "Erin, much of what happened to them they had no understanding of, they expected it, they were accustomed. Children adapt to their surroundings, adults object to trouble and fight usually. Understand the difference here. Your children were protected from much of the trouble, and so were these. Only some is allowed, then the Holy Spirit ministers to them. Angels minister. This is difficult to understand fully but one day you will understand. Now, this Rose, is it not beautiful?"

Me: "Lord, it is stunning."

Jesus: "Then how much more does God love you Erin." I thought for a moment about all of my trouble. I saw the battles. I saw the miracles.

Me: I shook my head, "You care for me so much. You did all this so I will one day be here. God loves me. I'm amazed and stunned. I'm so excited to see all that is coming. Lord, Thank You!" I reached over and hugged Him.

Jesus: "So you are not angry?"

Me: "Why, You just confirmed all my suspicions. God saw it. I saw You seemed angry at times knowing soon You will come for us – I take comfort in Your love and God's Plan. I would be a fool to not fear God – by Your words – this is the beginning of Wisdom!" I smiled and laughed. He burst out laughing. "Lord one question. What do the older children do for fun?"

Jesus: "Oh I'm glad you asked. Come." He reaches out and takes my hand. We are instantly taken to another area off to the side of the children's Garden. I see an arena, I see fields, obstacles, courses and other things but glorified.

Me: "Is this sports?"

Jesus: "Sort of but more fun. Think back to when you were a teen. What was important to you?" I laughed.

Me: "Nothing Godly; Boys, clothes, makeup, dance, sports and friends."

Jesus: "Yes, I remember. There are extra angels sent to children during this period!" He's laughing.

Me: "Yes, I certainly needed it because surely I put myself before God in every situation."

Jesus: "I think God was removed." He was smiling. I laughed, He was right.

Me: "No need to show me any of that Lord. I know full well that I was without God." He was laughing.

Jesus: "Erin I was there, no worries. So the teens are instructed about the heart of God here. They grow normally. They have schooling so they grow in wisdom and knowledge. They are taught by angels and saints. Because of grace they are given supernatural retention and learning here is joyful. They spend time here learning about different specialties that God puts on their hearts. There is no opposition but mistakes are allowed here so they grow in knowledge."

Me: "Lord this seems contrary to what we are taught. There is only good, no mistakes here."

Jesus: "What are people taught?" He was laughing as He threw up His arms.

Me: I was laughing. "Lord all my best learning came from mistakes. I only wish I had the capacity to learn the first time." I smacked the side of my head. He laughed.

Jesus: "Well this is a glorified learning. Mistakes lead to instant correction and knowledge. This is not slow and agonizing. There are no accidents which cause harm – like loss of sight or limb. There is healing. There is no death."

Me: "How fun mistakes with no consequences."

Jesus: "Erin – No you are incorrect! You are referring to sin. There is no sin here. Only learning mistakes! Like a wrong equation and choosing the best answer. You are taking this to extremes. Now there is something here that is extreme learning. Let Me show you." We went to a type of building where you could be with or be any character in history for a day with the exception of a few.

Me: "I am guessing I would not be allowed to be God, You, Enoch or Elijah?"

Jesus: "Very good Erin. They can also not choose any fallen or evil entity – nor would any choose to."

Me: "So help me here. They can go back in time and become that person for a day?"

Jesus: "Mostly, they choose to be with the person for a day to observe and learn. It is rare that any of them choose to be that person. For instance they cannot be Me but they can observe Me and go back to a certain day. There is a class just for this in which I instruct and take them there – this is different. Here mostly, they like to be Rock Stars or famous people. Once they live out that life for the day – they run from this. It's actually pretty funny."

Me: "Lord how incredibly fun. What a great way to learn! – It's the ultimate!"

Jesus: "You understand though that they have things in abundance here. They have no pain or worry. If they become the character then they know what it's like to suffer and they understand the cost. Mostly they observe."

Me: "I have many questions. Tell me what is the most selected."

Jesus: "For Boys, sports legends – usually the greatest game played or famous battles. David and Goliath is a favorite. They even enjoy live instruction from him. It's fun, for boys to slay giants. For girls, usually singers, princesses, actresses and heroines like Esther. Mary is difficult, so for many she is observed, not played."

Me: "This is so amazing!"

Jesus: "It is humbling for them."

Me: "I want to experience this, how fun!" Then I thought about it for a moment. – Actually I love being who I am Lord. I will stay who I am."

Jesus: Laughing. "As the children move along further, their focus changes more to skills and crafts. These are things they will offer to God."

Me: "Like a vocation?"

Jesus: "Yes. They learn, work and play. There are amazing fun activities here for them. They have concerts, sports, games, contests, prizes. They have so much fun learning."

Me: "Lord, from what I can see this area is massive, like miles and miles."

Jesus: "It's important to grow like normal even in a glorified state. You become brighter and shining through refinement and trials. Here it is different but fair for them."

Me: "I always wondered about this. Thank You Lord. I'm glad that children are able to experience growth. This is perfectly God – loving and perfect. I can't wait to tell my kids. Can they mimic super heroes?"

Jesus: "There is no need to. They are all super heroes. You can tell that to your kids." I began to cry.

Me: "Thank You Lord. Thank You for showing me Heaven! Thank You for answering all my questions."

Jesus: "If you are ever in doubt go back to the beginning and search the Heart of God. As your knowledge increases, you will first learn what He is! What you have been shown is not contrary to the Word of God. Now be at peace and see what I won't do! You are a Bride, Erin!"

He reaches over and kisses me on the forehead!

Dream over...
Blessings

Chapter 21 – The Lion

Communion

Dear Father,

Thank You for another day! Lord, I do see the opening from this cave. The promise of freedom! It's difficult while I wait to not focus on all that the enemy has done to destroy me. I can do nothing but wait in silence for Your voice to say, "Erin I'm here – Come out, you and your children are free."

Lord, You showed me everything in advance... I see it. Lord as my strength is weak, my pain great and my head hangs low – I smile and remember the love You have shown. Lord, You are so much more than words can express! You are lovely! You are my light in the darkness! You are my Everything!

Erin Come Up!

It was evening. I was lying down at the base of an Olive Tree. There were millions of stars in the sky. They formed designs greater than constellations. The grove of olive trees were completely lit-up with small white lights. It was beautiful!

I saw something like fireflies in every color and some I can't describe. I heard in the distance the children's choir and the angels singing the glorified version of "My Deliverer." I was in tears. I was so glad to be pain free. I jumped up and ran down an illuminated path to the edge of the grove of olive trees. There before me were at least a hundred fountains each in a different shade of color. The sound and sight was amazing!

Looking up and beyond that was God's Mansion. It was completely illuminated. The House of the King of Kings was like nothing I have ever seen in my life! The 12 stones that were inlaid in the foundations of Gods house were just like the City of God with the 12 stones representing the 12 Tribes of Israel. The stones were massive and at night were illuminated. The large facets cut into these stones formed ribbons of light according to each color. I saw the massive stone staircase going up to the home. The beautiful channels of water flowed from His home into the pools of the beautiful fountains. I wanted to run through the fountains, but I was more curious to see the beautiful display of God's Glory. It was such a relief to see how beautiful night is in Heaven – I was taught that there is no night in Heaven. I laughed and shook my head.

Me: "Lord, forgive us! We humans are dense. In the Book of Genesis, in Verse 5 …And the evening and the morning were the first day! Truly this is good also!"

I looked up at God's Home and expected Him to come out. I turned and looked to right and left. I saw two massive lions walking down the channels of water fountains. They turned and walked up the stairs, side by side. When they arrived at the front door, each went to either side and lay on their bellies flanking the sides of the door. Then I saw two small lambs barely able to walk, with no blemish and completely perfect follow the same path as the lions coming to rest, one with each lion on the platforms next to the door. I giggled. What an amazing processional! Then in an instant above the Home I saw a ring of angelic beings with wings. They each had a Shofar of silver and gold. I looked all around me. I looked down at what I was wearing. It was a beautiful blue dress, with white. It had a woven bodice of blue, crimson and gold. My hair was long and wavy with a type of head band. I went to the water to see what I looked like. The headband was etched with "Lord, You are Holy!" It was surrounded with lace.

I looked at my wrist and I had six bracelets on my left, each with a cut gem. I had the same on my right wrist for total of twelve. They were absolutely beautiful. The music changed and became that of a glorious processional. The music went higher and higher. I looked everywhere for the Lord. Did I miss something? Suddenly, I was met by Uriel. He was stunningly beautiful and to a human seeing him separately on Earth – well – terrifying and very much a warrior in God's Army. I found myself speechless!

Uriel: "Erin, you ran from the Olive Grove – away from the Lord."

Me: "Oh I thought He was here. I was running to Him I thought?

Uriel: "Yes, it seems you have been in error a few times!" He smiled and laughed.

Me: "Oh, I must go find Him!"

I turned and ran the exact way I came. There ahead of me in the grove was Jesus, sitting at the base of a tree. He was smiling and shaking His head.

Me: "Oh Lord, I'm so sorry. I didn't wait on You! I was so anxious to see You I ran ahead. You see, I felt so fantastic... (I stopped as clearly He was studying me and smiling).

Jesus: "Remember Erin, it is very important to not run ahead of Me in this season!"

Me: "Well how could I wait? It was so beautiful. The music, I was following the music trying to find You."

Jesus: "Hmmm... did this work?"

Me: I was quite embarrassed as He was clearly right. "Forgive me Lord. You are perfect and Your ways are perfect. I'm sorry!"

Jesus: "Come sit beside Me."

Me: "But Lord there is a big event starting soon in Your courtyard. Shouldn't we go?"

Jesus: He was laughing, "Erin, do you think they will begin without Me? Oops someone's schedule is off. Are the angels saying – 'Wow Jesus is late again... We didn't see that coming. Oops the food at the banquet will get cold and the wine will grow sour! Where is that Savior?'" He was laughing...

Me: "Forgive me Lord." – I could barely catch my breath. I was laughing so hard. He was completely right! "Lord, You are so wise!"

Jesus: "Sometimes the obvious is painfully simple and right in front of you."

Me: "Lord, I will wait."

Jesus: "I know your heart Erin. You are in pain. Here you are alive, young and healthy!" He looked at me with such compassion. I began to cry.

Me: "Lord, help me to be patient while I wait on You. I have seen my enemy ramping up against me and the enemy even uses the scripture You have given me so many times – Psalm 91. What if he is in Your favor as a lesson to me? Everyone thinks he is holy. No one knows that I love You even more. Many who used to be my friends from church are praying against me."

Jesus: "Erin, look at where you are right now. Who is with You? Where do you reside? Did you not see your children here too? The enemy can pray all he wants to. He can quote me or proclaim personal holiness, but remember! What is a sign of deception that I showed you long ago?"

Me: I was quiet as I thought about this, "Oh yes, if someone is claiming personal holiness and righteousness it is usually the opposite."

Jesus: "Very Good, now who is humble? Is it someone who proclaims themselves humble? Probably not! This is a sign of a foundation on shifting sand. Tell me about shifting sand under a house foundation!" I was laughing...

Me: "Well a house built on shifting sand would be very unstable, the foundation would be constantly moving and the walls would crumble. Eventually the ceiling would fall and the structure implodes."

Jesus: "This is an interesting word to use and a very good one. This implies that the structure would fall on itself. Perhaps there is prophecy in your future calling!" He laughed.

Me: "Only if You go before me Lord, This I could never do on my own without You. This is an absolute."

Jesus: "This is an absolute to live by. Let Me go before you, Now let's look at Psalm 91. First perhaps your enemy meant to say Psalm 90? Hmmm... (He was laughing.) First Erin do you trust Me?"

Me: "Yes Lord, but I'm having a hard time understanding the pain I'm in. Why are You allowing it?"

Jesus: "A very good question to dispel before we begin. Did I not tell you that the method in which I will deliver you might not make sense to you? Did I not also promise you healing? Don't question my methods when I've shown you the outcome. This is the best way. At the end you will testify to your friends about this. You will stand amazed. Notice I said stand Erin. I didn't say you will sit and be amazed. I didn't say you will lie down and be amazed. However you could faint after you stand amazed! You can laugh now!" I was laughing so hard and so was He.

Me: "You are right Lord; this is the part where I feel abandoned."

Jesus: "Well then, there is no accident we are here in the Olive Grove."

Just then I was downloaded an image of the Lord sweating blood the night before His trouble. I had tears.

Me: "So things will get worse?"

Jesus: "There is a scripture in Job 4 about the lion with broken teeth. What happens to a lion with broken teeth? Can you tell me?"

Me: I thought again, "Lord, You are clearly stretching my brain tonight. Well, if a lion has no teeth it cannot break through the flesh."

Jesus: "Very good, but here is more, the lion cannot snap the neck of its prey to paralyse it. Even if he were to kill it with claws, he couldn't rip into the flesh to eat. The food would be there but the helpless lion would concede to others, even the buzzards. The lion starves."

Me: "Lord that is harsh."

Jesus: "Oh, would you prefer to go against a healthy lion – gazelle?"

Me: "No, no please!" He was laughing.

Jesus: "Now let's look at Psalm 91 – I want you to open the bible you use with dates written next to them."

So I went to my Bible and opened it to Psalm 91, there I saw the date 6-5-2012. I was instantly downloaded a few events that led to this date. One was my son's 8th grade graduation. I was at the foot of the cross (a very large carved crucifix) – well, 2 rows back in the pews to the right side. I was not recognized as my son's mother, but someone else was. My stomach became so sick. My other son shouted out, "That's a lie!" I looked over and saw the enemy look quite smug. I smiled and waved – looking unaffected, but I was lying to myself. My son came up to me and gave me a rose and hugged me. After this when I was alone by myself, I never ever, ever cried so hard in my life.

Jesus: "I remember this day Erin vividly. You gave God an ultimatum."

Me: "No Lord, I had become tired of waiting and looking. I stopped. I said, "Lord if You truly love me then You will find me. I don't believe You care as I am alone in my sorrow." I was having a crisis of belief. I didn't understand it."

Jesus: "Name anyone from the Bible who had a perfect life free from trouble. Can you name one?"

Me: I thought long and hard from the beginning – as I thought for several minutes. I saw the Lord smiling and watching me think. "No Lord, not one, not even one!"

Jesus: "So where is it written that you will have no trouble? I believe it is written, in this life you will have trouble, but take heart for I have overcome the world! Now let's focus on what I promised you then. What did I have you do? Look at your scripture." (I took a look at my Bible.)

Me: "On Psalm 91:9-16, You had me underline it."

Jesus: "Yes, but there is more, what did I have you do from verse 14 on – speak this out loud Erin."

Me: I was in tears. Psalm 91:14-15 "Because she loves me," says the Lord (He points to His chest) "I will rescue her; I will protect her for she acknowledges My Name. She will call upon Me and I will answer her; I will be with her in trouble, I will deliver her and honor her. With long life will I satisfy her, and show her My salvation!" I was in tears.

Jesus: "Now Erin, do you believe Me?"

Me: "Yes, Lord."

Jesus: "When you suffer pain, headaches and numbness do you believe Me?"

Me: Pause – "Yes Lord."

Jesus: "When all looks dark and you feel I have left – do you believe Me still?"

Me: I paused even longer. "Don't leave me – please show me signs!"

Jesus: "I will Erin. I will send Angels concerning you! Now read Psalm 91 from 1-8. Put your name or she in place of he just like before."

Me: "Lord You are changing scripture."

Jesus: "Oh so my Word is only for men in trouble? Hmm – this doesn't sound like God My Father. He created females, are they not good? Aren't they also mothers? Hmmm…"

Me: I was laughing - "Okay Lord, Okay I get it. Psalm 91:1-8 'She who dwells in the shelter of the Most High will rest in the shadow of the Almighty. I will say of the Lord, 'He is my refuge and my fortress, my God, in whom I trust.' Surely He will save you from the fowler's snare and from deadly pestilence. He will cover you with His feathers, and under His wings you will find refuge, His faithfulness will be your shield and rampart. You will not fear the terror by night, nor the arrow that flies by day, nor the pestilence that stalks in the darkness, nor the plague that destroys in mid-day. A thousand may fall at your side, ten thousand at your right hand, but it will not come near you."

Jesus: "Erin, it will Not come near you, Erin – go on."

Me: "You will only observe with your eyes and see the punishment of the wicked!"

Jesus: "Now stand up, close your eyes. Now open them." I was in awe! There before me – (well tears) – The Lord was in full battle gear. His Breastplate was gold and inlaid like the Ephod or priestly garment of Aaron. The etching and scroll work was amazing. He was wearing full armor except no helmet.

Me: "Lord, You look incredible. This is how You looked from the beginning. Where is Your helmet?"

Jesus: "You are funny. What is the helmet? Am I not Saved? Does the Blacksmith whisper in My ears?" He was laughing.

Me: "Oh Lord, I am clearly like a child."

Jesus: "Actually, quite a few children know this!" He was laughing, "Now walk with Me."

With His armor on He stood almost 4 feet higher. He was the size of an Angel. The top of my head was at the base of His rib cage. I looked at His Breastplate and I was in awe of the beauty of His armor. We walked through the fountains and He motioned for me to wait at the base of the stairs. I wish I could adequately describe how incredibly beautiful this sight was. It was night time but just the Lord alone shone like the Sun! As He ascended the stairs I saw wings begin to spread – massive wings like 7 feet in length each, maybe longer.

I heard the Choirs of Angels singing "Holy, Holy, Holy", as He climbed the stairs. When He got to the top, He waved to me to come up. Suddenly I was in my Earthly state, I was in pain, I began to cry as I knew what He was doing. I paused. My arms were numb, my neck sore. The headaches were so bad I wanted to throw up. I looked up and saw Him. I wanted to be there with Him. I stepped up. I kept climbing slowly with tears. I saw the Lord command angels concerning me as I began to fall. The angels helped me ascend up the stairs, as I got closer the climb became easier. My pain was gone. I was in my glorified body. The Lord reached out to take my hand and there He placed me under His wing.

He turned and said to me, "Erin, remember your place. Look on your hand." There was a ring, a signet ring with a beautiful Beryl stone. There was etching on the stone, like a signature. "Now remember the promises. I have not gone back on My word. I have not removed favor from you. Take courage. Erin, this is for your friends too. Each one of them can do the same here in Psalm 91 – better yet they can place their name where yours is and I will be there too."

Me: I was so excited! "Thank You Lord! Please bless beyond measure all those who have helped me and my children. I have no way to thank them. Since You are the owner of all of our provisions, please bless them. Some gave all they had. How do I repay this? I cannot."

Jesus: "All has been recorded Erin. Their generous hearts will be rewarded. One day you will see everything and understand the recompense of God. As I have blessed you, so too will you be a blessing. Do not worry. There is not one who expects something from you. Your friends are not bankers. Now these are love offerings. Let it be about that and surrender it back to me. Don't be burdened. No one is requiring things. This is the enemy with his guilt as a yoke, don't allow this. Now pray for your friends!"

Me: "Lord, I ask for supernatural blessings for my friends. Heal their afflictions and pain. Promote their position at work. Grant them youthful glorified bodies. Send Your Angels concerning them and rain down from the Throne of God Heavenly wisdom and the wealth of nations so we are all able to testify to Your Goodness!"

Jesus: "Well then – It is done! Very Good Prayer! I will allow this on Earth as it is in Heaven. They will be like strong lions and spotless lambs!" He turned and looked at the massive lions and the perfect lambs lying next to them. "Now take heart, take courage Erin. You are loved. Remember to let Me go before you for the next 50 days!"

Me: "Then I'm on my own?"

Jesus: "Where are you now?"

Me: I looked up. I was clearly under His wing. I giggled...

Jesus: "Oh wait, look you are still here!" He was laughing.

Me: "Thank You Lord! I love You!"

Jesus: "I love you too Erin! Oh, look to Psalm 45 & 46 again too!"

Dream over...

Chapter 22 - Faith and the Fig

Communion

Dear Father,

I love You so Much! With tears and no ability on my own to act I am watching You make a way for Me! I still don't know how You will do it but I know You will! Lord it's difficult right now to be openly cursed by my enemies. You have shown me their curses through the apple of their eyes. I don't understand their hatred of me – but I have never understood it. Despite their curses You're flexing Your arms and rendering them harmless. I stand in awe. I just love Your ways, they are miraculous!

Erin Come Up!

Today I was in the back of a classroom in Heaven. Not just any classroom, a classroom of teenagers. Tears were streaming down my cheeks as these boys and girls were referring to Jesus – Who was leading the class as Rabbi. Jesus was up front, He waved at me and I waved back. The children turned and smiled. I won't go into who I saw there but my heart had been grieving these children this week. I put my hand over my heart and with my lips I said, "Thank You Lord from the bottom of my Heart!" He smiled and pointed to His Eyes! He continued to speak.

An Angel of the Lord approached me, "Erin, today you will receive some instructions from Jesus on Faith. He wanted you to observe what He teaches here, yet it was the same on Earth when He walked, but is also the same today. His word doesn't change, nor does His promises! Now He requests you continue to stand amazed."

Me: "There is nothing my Lord cannot do! He is the same yesterday, today, and tomorrow. It is only I who change! Yes I will be an observer! I will love this!"

Angel: "He has instructed me to stand with you when you need help!"

Me: "Oh awesome! I know I will have questions."

Angel: "No Erin, He has instructed angels to assist you. As soon as you call for help, He will answer!"

I thought at first he was talking about questions during His class but I realized the Angel was referring to more than this. I put my hand on my heart and said thank you to the angel. I turned to Jesus again and with my lips I thanked Him. He smiled and laughed and pointed to His Eye again. I laughed. I looked around me and I was in an amazing class room. If you could picture a planetarium with swivel chairs that turned 360 degrees, that are made of some material like leather but soft. The room was round with a dome which looked like it could split in the center and fold open. The curved walls which surrounded the entire class were like a giant movie screen.

Up at the front area there was a large Torah with a Yad (pointer), on the other side there was a beautiful Bible, both Old and New Testament. There were angels to assist each station. It was interesting as the Bible seemed much thicker than what we have available to us on Earth. I wondered if all the words He ever spoke were written in this one. Maybe this version contained every word He spoke which was not recorded? Interesting…

Angel: "Erin, there is more which you do not understand, but just know that the Word you read from on Earth is the Divine Word of God. Nothing was added or removed without the full permission of God on the Throne. Do not worry about why, but know there is nothing hidden. God uses all things for His purposes and His Glory!"

Me: "Thank you for clarifying!"

This room was so incredible! It was so high tech. I was in awe and so excited to see Jesus teach. He stood in front of the class. He was wearing a white tunic with a blue sash. His sleeves were rolled up – which made me smile. He had some linen pants on and His amazing woven sandals that I have often seen Him in. Just so you know these sandals are not just any sandals. They are beautifully made from what looks like two types of leather. The stitching is some leather and metal blend and the sole is like a cloud – beyond what we would call a gel sole. They look somewhat like the Tera brand sandals but with inlays of these rugged stones. I know this seems like I am taking a lot of time describing them but they are perfectly handcrafted for an approachable King of Kings. They were obviously hand-crafted by the world's best cobbler here, but perfectly fits our Lord. They are two shades of brown and these beautiful rugged stones which look like they have a story – well knowing Jesus – they must have a historical significance to Him or the cobbler. If these were sold on Earth today they could command $1500 for the sandals alone, but the stones could make these priceless. I also noticed before that the material or leather they are made of can be wet or dry and the material is unblemished? I bet they can withstand any element too!

Anyway, as Jesus instructed, He had such a loving and peaceful approach. The teens clung to every word spoken by Him. There was no need for note taking because all the words coming from His lips were etched into their brains, but uniquely fit to each individual. In heaven we are recognized as uniquely created by God. Each of us are a work of art handcrafted by God Himself! Contrary to what may believe about us in eternity – we are each given special attributes unique to us. We are equal and loved by God like parents love their children, but each are different and special. No two of us are alike.

I was also taught that when we get to Heaven we all wear the same robes and we walk around nodding, smiling and saying, " Jesus loves you, peace be with you brother." ...all day long. I read that one time and I laughed. It made Heaven sound more like a cult whereby we are no longer free to worship the Lord and interact normally with others.

The Lord told me one time, "Isn't it written that no eye has seen, no ear has heard, and no mind has imagined what God has prepared for those who love Him! So, Erin I am only giving you a glimpse, a short 'commercial' of your Eternal Home. There are things which have Earthly concepts, yet keep within your mind's ability to describe it. This is only a small portion of the gifts I've prepared for those who love me!" I turned to the angel.

Me: "I recognize a few of the students here; please tell me who the others are?"

Angel: "Erin, as you listen to His teaching you will come to understand that these children were chosen for a time such as this, a war is brewing, the peace proposal has stopped now and there is retaliation on both sides. One side is without God and one is with, however neither knows the Messiah. The children you see here are those in the crosshairs of the battle."

Me: "But most of these are past the age of accountability, how are they here?"

Angel: "Must you ask? …Immediately downloaded into me was the area set aside for the Lord to speak to me prior to coming Home, in my case coming back to live here.

Me: "I have questions. So these children are victims still yet to come and some who have come. So some of these students die in upcoming events or an event because of retaliation? Even though they are Jewish and don't speak of Jesus, – Jesus still calls them?"

Angel: "Yes, but remember the gate is still narrow to Heaven and few find their hearts on Jesus. This is not a wide gate, When you listen to the Lord speak, you know and understand His authority and you love Him. These children are grateful and now excited to follow Him. These children have been taught incorrectly. Now watch as the Lord captures their hearts."

Me: "Couldn't He do this in an instant? Wouldn't those being saved from eternal death be enough? This is so beautiful here surely Heaven alone would be enough!"

Angel: "Erin, I've known you almost your entire life, what sound decisions did you make during the most foolish part of your life?" Instantly I received teenage downloads. I was extremely responsible in some areas and horribly irresponsible in others. I shook my head and laughed.

Me: "Is God not the most patient! His Grace is immense – forgive me!"

Angel: "Even though these children are here, He is capturing their hearts; they will learn to love Him like you have. Did you do this instantly?"

Me: "No – No it was slow. I wanted to but God had to rewrite my programming. He had to show me His heart. He swooned me and now I am forever changed!"

Angel: "Jesus wants the same for them." He points over to the students and all of them were captivated and joy was on their faces. They had gratitude and comfort.

Me: "It looks like this will happen quickly."

Angel: "Well, yes and no. They will gain wisdom but they have some history lessons to go through first."

Jesus instructed them and used references from the original Torah but cross-referenced with teaching He gave on Earth. At one point a student raised her hand. Jesus smiled and called her by name.

She asked – "It's so obvious You are the Messiah – why not ride in like a King on a White Horse?" He laughed.

Jesus: "Oh you didn't like my donkey?" They laughed. "This is a very good question. Remember from the time I came as a baby on, all were expecting a King, never a baby and never a poor King with no land. Do you believe Me riding on a white horse with robes like King Solomon would've changed their opinions?"

One boy raised his hand. Jesus pointed to him and called him by name. The boy beamed, "They would've killed You instantly and looked for Your kingdom to conquer it!"

Jesus: "Well certainly Herod would, right?" They all laughed. "Now why did I select a donkey?" One girl was shy. Jesus knew her story. He smiled, "Go ahead." – (and He called her by name).

She said, "The donkey is common and simple. God can use anything and using the donkey made fools of them!"

Jesus began to laugh out loud, "Yes, you are quite correct! I'm afraid no matter what I rode on I was despised! They cursed Me! Do you think I deserved to be cursed?"

Children: "Oh no." All in succession and overwhelmingly "no" from the students! One child said, "If they only really knew You they would like You!"

Another teen an older boy said, "No, they never liked Him from the beginning. Their jealousy was greater – hate was greater than love. Their curses became acts."

Jesus: "Interesting – Let's discuss the power of life and death at the tongue."

Instantly the room became a giant screen movie. The screen went back in time to when Jesus and His disciples were walking from Bethany to the temple. It was just a few days before the Passover. We watched Jesus curse the Fig Tree. He was hungry and wanted a fig, yet this tree had all leaves and was not bearing fruit. With the authority of His mouth He spoke to the tree, "You will never bear fruit again!" I saw this massive fig tree with leaves. It was beautiful with quite a large trunk. It looked amazingly similar to the Tree in the Garden of Eden – the Tree of Knowledge of Good and Evil. Then some time later Jesus and the disciples returned on the road to Bethany. This mighty tree was now completely shriveled from the roots.

Jesus: "Any thoughts about this?"

One Boy: "The tree was not in season but it was on a very busy road to the temple. I heard once that Bethpage, the place where this was – means house of unripe figs."

Jesus: "Very good – interesting observation."

One boy raised his hand and Jesus knew him by name. "When You cursed the tree You said may no one eat fruit from you ever again. This means at some time the tree bore fruit?"

Jesus: "This is an excellent observation, anything else?" Hands raised up everywhere.

Jesus once again calls a small, shy student by name and she lit up.

"Rabbi this was the same road that people put branches on when You road the donkey."

Jesus: "This is a very good observation. What was the last tree cursed by God himself?"

One boy jumped. Jesus laughed. You could tell He loved, loved teaching and their enthusiasm to use what they had been taught but transformed by the truth of Jesus the Messiah and the actual accounts of the events. Jesus pointed and called the boy by name. "Rabbi, the Tree in the Garden of Eden was cursed. That is where the fall happened!"

Jesus: "Hmmm do you think this is the very same tree? Is it possible? After all didn't Adam and Eve use fig leaves to hide their nakedness from God? Or do you think they ran to a fig tree and quickly took big leaves? Wouldn't it be easier to hide behind the trunk and reach up and take leaves from the place you were hiding from God?" The class laughed.

One older boy raised his hand. "Rabbi what if this was the same tree used for the crucifixion? The witnesses on the road told the Pharisees what You did to the tree. You spoke with the power of life and death with Your tongue. Some were probably very angry, jealous and maybe had fear. You made them look foolish even when You were a boy. Maybe they used the wood from this tree to make the cross?"

Jesus: "This is interesting in layers. Why would God allow such a thing?"

One girl raised her hand, "Lord because everything You did on Earth counted for something; all things you did were woven together like reeds in a basket so You could carry our souls home to You!"

Jesus: "Very good – (and He called her by name) Zoe! Notice that basket would be small at the time." They all laughed. "I was a harvester of the fruit. What was the main "Fig" I was hungry for?"

Zoe burst out! "Lord Hearts; You were after hearts!"

Jesus: Was smiling and laughing, "You are correct! Let's add the fruits of the spirit of a good heart."

All of a sudden on the screen was a giant tree of Life in Heaven – with beautiful fruit. Jesus reached up through the screen and grabbed a fruit. He waived for all the children to reach up and grab a fruit also and they did. The children returned to their seats with the fruit.

Jesus: "There was much symbolism in this tree but let's go back to the tongue – the power of life and death."

The screen went back to the shriveled fig tree. Jesus said to His disciples as they stood observing the tree amazed that it had died so quickly. Jesus said, "Truly I say to you, if you have faith and do not doubt, you will not only do what was done to the fig tree, but even if you say to this mountain be taken be taken up and cast into the sea, it will happen." What mountain was I pointing to?" All the students shouted Calvary and clapped.

Jesus laughed, "Okay why would I choose that as a mountain to throw into the sea?"

One little girl – Jesus said, "Yes Selah". She said, "Because, Lord You will return there as a symbol."

Jesus: "Hmm, I see a lot of symbols here which make sense! Is God that smart? Why would He care that much to go through all that?"

One boy raised his hand and Jesus knew him by name, "Because God is a God of perfect order. He is smart and beyond us. He will make it so simple that even children will see the pattern but scholars will take years to find it!"

Jesus: Laughing – "Maybe all they needed was a Savior to teach them how to walk." The children were laughing. "One day soon they will see the obvious. All they needed to do would be to look at ancient maps. They could see the patterns. My Word points also. Do you believe that basket will ever contain enough hearts to fill it?"

His arms were crossed and His hand was on His chin. The room became quiet as children began to reflect on their own family on Earth. Jesus could read their thoughts.

Jesus: "Do not worry, a time will come soon and they will all know. This time I won't ride in on a donkey. I won't come in from the

North." As He spoke the screen showed bombs – rockets pounding the region. "Yes, I think I wouldn't last long on a donkey here!"

The children laughed. They were all very familiar with war. One girl shouted – "Lord You will need to come on the clouds and drop down like a rocket."

Jesus: "Well then let's look at the scripture about My return. In Revelation 1:7"

The screen behind Him and around the circumference of the room showed a great war. Then the Bible at the front of the class was illuminated and pages turned as scriptures jumped out from the pages all attesting to His return. I saw Matthew, Luke, Zachariah, Daniel, Isaiah, Mark, and Psalms. The same way Jesus left the Earth by the clouds, two angels had to proclaim that the Lord (Acts 1:10-11) has gone to Heaven and some day He will return just as He went!" Then I saw the exact reverse. I saw the two witnesses appear first then the Lord came on the clouds. There was a very loud noise and the trumpet. What I saw is the very same way He left one day in reverse order He will return! The children cheered.

Angel: "Erin. This is enough today. This is to bring you comfort. There is more coming! Pray for Israel! Know and understand patterns. There is nothing new under the sun. The power of life and death is on your tongue. Speak life. Remember the prophets – not profits – prophets. Those who come from the desert – or from a different place, they are not Jesus. Look to scripture for the answers. Look again at Psalm 83, Nahum, Psalm 46, Esther, and Timothy for answers to your questions! Thessalonians has a large confirmation for you. You will be like Phinehas. Your motives and zeal please God do not therefore be afraid! Remember Elijah and take a stand against evil and The Lord is with you. Love The Lord God with all of your heart, soul and strength!

Dream over...

Chapter 23 – Jesus and the Storm

Communion

Dear Father,

Thank You! Thank You for all that we have! Thank You for my children and their love! I am truly blessed.

Lord, please stop my enemies. They pursue me with force. I can do nothing against them but stand. How do I stand when I am caught between the house and the storm shelter with the tornado upon me? How do I protect children with a system that ties hands? Father I have prayed for my enemies. I am not their enemy but they hate me. They make public declarations on social media about their faith in Christ. They declare their achievements and revel in their victories. They even have family photos of my children. Please Lord, help me!

Erin Come up!

Today I am on a very narrow mountain. It is extremely steep. I am standing at about 12,000 feet above sea level, so high that there is no vegetation at all. The air is thin so I'm having a hard time breathing. There is no snow so it must be summer. The ridge goes on for miles in each direction, the same thickness, about 8 feet with a shelf for my feet only. In front of me I have an ocean. It's massive, there is no shore. The mountain leads right into the sea. I look behind me and I see 3 mountain ridges and a valley below leading to a desert. I'm not sure there is actually a place like this on Earth but what I'm experiencing is very real! The sun is high in the sky. There is a light cloud cover over it and I can see coming in from the ocean a massive storm. The storm is just hours away. I turn behind me and I see another storm coming in from the desert Valley. Where I was standing it looked like the two would converge. With no cover, no shelter, my small human vulnerabilities would be laid waste. I was clearly in trouble with no place to go. The sun began to darken from the storm and all I could do is lay down on my face and stomach and pray!

My Prayer:

Lord, I can do nothing here. Nothing can save me from what is coming but You. I look behind me each way and I see storms. There is no shelter to take cover physically. Lord all I have is You, Your words and promises. If I succumb to this storm I will surely die. Instead I will succumb to You as You are my refuge from the wind and a shelter from the storm (Isaiah 32:2). I am at Your mercy and so are my children. I have stepped out of the boat onto the ocean, but the waves are like raging walls. I cannot see You. I am in the middle of the storm. I am surrounded. Where are You Lord? I love You – no matter what I love You God! Help us!

I felt a rain drop on the back of my neck. This prompted me to look up. All around me the landscape changed. The ominous ridge I was standing on was a low grass covered hill. I looked from side to side and there were hills as far as my eyes could see. I looked out toward the ocean and there were beautiful shores with quiet sandy coves. The water was beautiful. The hills gradually went into the sea. I looked behind me to see more grassy hills. I began to laugh as I saw cattle on each one.

The Valley below was peaceful, lush and very beautiful with a river there. I saw sheep. I looked up at the sky and I saw the storm clouds and dark skies rolled up like a scroll. They were held back by God's Hand. I looked around and the storm was rolled up like a document, as if it were a contract against me. The winds were tied up as well. This is hard to describe. I saw one of the ridges in the sea as if it had been tossed into it. I reached down to feel my neck. There I had checked for the mustard seed necklace that a sister sparrow had given me. It was there. I smiled. As I sat there I began to cry. The storm was about to overcome me. My heart raced and grew faint. The storm was so much larger and powerful than I was; I was impossibly at the mercy of the elements. As I cried I thanked God.

"Lord, thank You for what will eventually happen. Right now I am surrounded and bombarded. Please Lord, save me and my children. We just want to go in peace. Why are we pounded continuously without cause or reason? When the enemy attacks the courts call it a dispute. If we would do nothing to fight we would be overcome. Why is defending yourself wrong? Why is it reduced down to "he said, she said" when clearly it is one sided?"

I look off over to one of the nearby hills. There I see a shepherd with a rod, staff and sheep. It looks like the Lord. So I run toward Him. He sees me and comes after me. I run into His arms. I'm in tears. He grabs onto me and holds me tight as I cried. I stayed there for some time.

Jesus: "There you are Erin. I've been looking for you. Where did you go?"

Me: "Did I wander off Lord?"

Jesus: "Well for a moment. You forgot to call Me." He downloaded the last 2 days.

Me: "Lord You said, You are going before me. I figured You were on the other side of the storm."

Jesus: "Why did you speculate? Just come to Me. I am here."

Me: "Lord the battle is raging. I need help and guidance."

Jesus: "I know this is your most difficult battle to date. You stepped out of the boat with your children to walk toward Me in the midst of the storm. Now what is My character, based on your faith? What does My Word say about Who I Am?"

Me: "First, You are the God of the impossible! You are The God who calms the storms – You clearly rolled up the clouds and held back the wind."

Jesus: "Okay then, am I going to stand on the waves during the storm and motion for you with open arms for you and your children to walk, only to now allow you to sink?" He looked at me like a loving and caring Father. In His eyes I could see my children and I stepping onto the waves from the boat and walking toward Jesus in the storm. I saw my children were afraid and clung to each other and me. I was even more terrified because they were out there on the water with me.

Me: "Oh Lord this is difficult to see, it looks so real."

Jesus: "Isn't this how you feel Erin?" (I was crying).

Me: "My heart is pounding. I'm scared!"

Jesus: "When you are in the midst of the storm don't wait for it to pass over you. It goes much faster if you step through it. It's simple, walk through it with your children."

Me: "How? How do I walk through it?"

Jesus: "Look again!" I looked in His Eyes and I saw an open door. I didn't see it before but now it was clear as day. On the other side of the door was Jesus with open arms reaching out to me in the storm. We all clung together and stepped on the waves with trepidation. Then my children ran through it to Jesus even before I did. He grabbed all of them safely.

Me: "Lord am I holding my children back; from fear?"

Jesus: "No, just allow Me to work and trust that what I've begun, I will also complete."

Me: "Thank You Lord."

Jesus: "One other thing Erin… Now crying out to Me in prayer is good. I am with you. Prayer is good but you have not waited for Me to speak or answer. You get up immediately and go. What if I was an Earthly Father – You come to Me with your troubles but you walk away before I can lend you help?"

Me: "Lord, oh no – I've been doing this all the time recently."

Jesus: "It is like you have gone to court, pleaded your case and left before the Judge has granted you – your victory."

Me: I laughed. "I'm so sorry Lord."

Jesus: "Just because I told you I would go before you in battle doesn't mean you are no longer significant to Me. We still can communicate!"

Me: "Please forgive me for being so foolish. I was trying to let You work."

Jesus: "Hmmm – so I am not able to multi-task? Look at the world today and all the trouble. Do you believe I am not there in the midst of the storms and I no longer care?" He smiled.

Me: "I realize I am small. I'm sorry."

Jesus: "No Erin. You are not small, with that mustard seed you can say to that very mountain (He pointed to the ridge toppled in the ocean) and by faith you can command it into the sea. Do not doubt! Your faith is available and I am here with you. Now who can be against you? Now keep your faith! There is an open door – walk through this. I love you and I will save you – you and your children!"

He reaches over and hugs me. He kisses me on the top of my head!

Dream over...

Chapter 24 – Word from God & Dream of War

Communion

Dear Father,

Thank You for another day! Thank You for my children. Thank You for family and the prayers of friends. Lord, I'm being hammered by my enemies. It is so relentless and beyond reason that I must believe it is a supernatural battle. This is one that is so ridiculous and so against just normal business, I must assign it to powers, principalities and unseen forces. How do I pray for my enemy when I know the enemy of You is the ruler over them? How do I fight against things hidden? I can't Lord. There is nothing I can do until this storm from both sides' passes, or you remove it. In the meantime Lord please show me You are here in this place. Please protect us with Your mighty Hand! I love You!

Erin Come Up!

I woke up out of bed in a place I hadn't been before. I had seen the place in a dream. Almost 18 months ago but I didn't understand it. I heard the sounds of what sounded like a mourning dove and some fluttering of wings. I had been laying down on a hard surface with a small mat about 6" thick and a piece of cloth rolled up as a pillow. There was a small window about 7' up in what looked like a room of solid rock. The window was approximately 18" high and 36" long. I was too short to see out of it but I could tell that it was morning based on the temperature and sunlight. I was wearing semi-dirty clothing; a white long sleeved shirt and some cream colored linen pants. I had no shoes; there were no shoes to put on. My feet seemed cottonseed and dirty. I laughed as it looked like I had a small trace of polish on one of my toe nails. My hair was long, braided to one side and dirty.

I walked to the opening of this Rock bedroom. I saw pages of what looked like a disassembled bible in the next room. There was something that looked like a bottle of water – 3 potatoes and a hard crust of bread. There was a jar of some sort of spread, but I didn't know what. This room was small; about 7'x7' with a rock for a table and a grass mat for sitting. There were some small primitive looking utensils and some grooved marks on the walls which looked like a day count – calendar. It appeared like weeks, but I didn't feel led to count. The walls were all solid rock and as dawn was breaking, I could see the walls were reddish in color. I followed the light through another open doorway. I was looking through to the outside and over to another mountain range. I heard the bird fluttering its wings.

As I was carefully going to walk outside, I stopped in my tracks when I saw what looked like "shot" holes in the opening to this cave-like dwelling. I saw the sky was blue, but the opening was facing another rock ridge with other cave like homes. I became afraid to step out. I reached down and picked up a piece of paper. It was a torn piece of the Bible with Psalm 127 on one side and Psalms 125 and 126 on the other. I smiled. I held the paper in my right hand as I began to slowly walk out onto the ledge of this cave-like house. All of a sudden a small bird darted quickly and hit my hand which held the torn scripture page. I must have startled it. It sat dazed on the ground then flew outside.

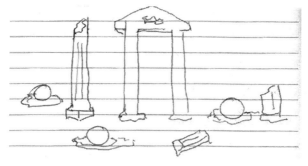

What I saw was very vivid. I saw 3 large columns and pieces of others. There was smoke rising from the area as if smoldering. These columns of smoke – (dark charcoal) rose to an opening in the sky. I was looking over a valley after an epic battle. The valley was surrounded by low hills and a mountain with these cave dwellings and the area formed looked like an arena. The dirt was red clay. The sight was surreal. It was modern day yet a primitive looking battle. There was a layer of fog or dust haze right off the floor of the valley. I noticed that I saw others stepping out of their rock dwellings. I rubbed my eyes. This scene was so real, so clear.

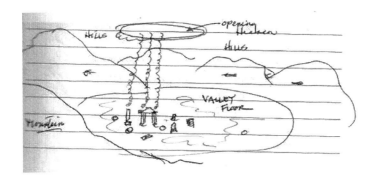

I heard the Voice of God.!

"Because you love Me, I will protect you." I began to cry. "Fear not, I am with you, do not be dismayed. I am your God. I will strengthen you, I will help you, I will help you, I will uphold you with my righteous right Hand. Do not be afraid. Behold all those who come against you will surely fail, and then will be shamed. I am your Shield, your very great reward. I will keep you and hold you close in the day of trouble. You and your children I will protect. You will proclaim "The Lord hath done great things for as the Lord is God! Blessed be His Name!" Erin you are loved – do not worry!"

Dream over...

The Holy Spirit prompted me to read the Book of Ruth about Kinsman Redeemer.

Chapter 25 – Faith vs. Fear

Communion

Dear Father, I'm defeated, heartbroken, and scared. I saw sharks in the water and I looked down. My children didn't see me, because their eyes are still on You.

Now I am in the water, as sharks circle and hope seems far away. Why send sharks, Lord? When Peter got out of the boat there was a storm, but no mention of sharks. Why allow me to take my focus off You? I can answer that, because I suddenly became aware of their power and presence under my feet. As the storm raged, I lost sight of You. Now that I lack faith, I'm afraid. Suddenly I feel alone. My children still believe. Please, Lord, call out to them – let them run into Your arms!

Why, O Lord, do You allow the wicked to prosper? Why, when You determine my days and even know the hairs on my head, do I still wonder? You say my name is etched on the palm of Your hand – then why am I so quickly passed over? Why does justice not come – where does mercy finally rest, and on whom? Please, Lord, forgive me, as I am stunned. The arrogant scoff at me because I love You, yet they say, "Where is that God you serve now?" Father, my children and I have not had justice. Even if we are never vindicated on Earth, then please, Lord, make right all the wrongs.

Don't allow my enemies to declare that You love them more than me. I am jealous for You – only the ones who love and seek You have a right to declare Your Goodness. Those who never loved You cannot understand Your ways. I clearly don't know myself, but I do know I love You, without a doubt! I can whine and complain, but my love for You doesn't change!

Erin – Come up!

Immediately I'm in deep, dark water. There are three shark fins circling me. There is a storm. The skies are dark and foreboding. My children are not on the water. Waves of water go over me. I feel these giant sharks brush my legs in the cold surf. "Now I've done it. My lack has caused me to sink in deep water, and with sharks." My arms were treading water, but with no life jacket, my panicked movements made me appear to be a wounded animal or prey to the sharks. Realizing I was making things worse, I stopped splashing and moving and just began to float. I began to pray, as next I was about to be shark bait. I lay floating for a while. My arms and legs began to become cold and numb. The water would go over my face in waves. I began to anticipate it and hold my breath. I couldn't feel the sharks any more, and if they were there, I had no knowledge of it. I closed my eyes, as the storm's rain became torrential. I waited for death. At one point the water was warmer than the outside above it. I was beginning to sink and surrender to my trouble, as I had lost hope. I saw a tunnel of light, or some bright light, then I felt some movement of my body; then I had no memory...

I woke up on a white sandy beach. I was on my side. My lungs had filled with water. I coughed up a painful wave of salt water. The difference is that the water tasted salty and sweet – I had landed on a Heavenly Shore, and within a flash I had no pain at all. I sat up. I was wearing a white sundress. The fabric was made up of that heavenly fabric that was soft, breathable, non-staining and wicked-off any liquid substance. I was laughing, as I realized there were no wrinkles, yet it was incredibly close to linen. I was wearing a single long braid, and my feet were bare. I brushed off this beautiful white sugar sand – which really didn't stick. There was not a cloud in the sky. The air was fragrant with flowers. There was a gentle breeze, and the temperature was about 78 degrees. It was perfect.

I looked around at this Heavenly Paradise. I looked out across the ocean, or massive ocean-like lake. I thought there would no longer be oceans in Heaven. Maybe a Heavenly Ocean is different? Anyway, it was beautiful. I looked out and I saw a school of dolphins playing in the water. They were actually playing – it looked like a scripted show at Sea World, only it was just for them. I laughed. Then I remembered. I was just out there swimming with sharks. I remembered the fear. It definitely wasn't Heaven – it must have been the Training Room? It was definitely somewhere else. I said softly, "Lord, where are You? I have many questions."

Suddenly I heard that Heavenly Calypso Music – with a hint of Reggae. I laughed. "Lord, You are so funny. Now where is my tropical drink with the umbrella?"

I looked toward the water. I laughed so hard – I kid you not. There, floating toward me was a small life preserver – white and red – with a cup holder and a very large blended tropical drink in a pineapple-looking cup, with a beautiful fruit garnish. The funny thing was there was a real umbrella over the entire preserver to shelter all of it. The umbrella wasn't in the drink. I laughed so hard. I haven't laughed like this in many months. I got up and brought the funny Heavenly preserver up on the shore and grabbed the drink. I took a sip and wow – it was the most incredibly refreshing drink. It was frozen, sweet, tart, and fruity – but not like anything here. The music began to play louder. I felt the Lord calling me. I began to walk along the beach to the South – to look for the Lord. The water was so beautiful – it was a little cooler than bath water, and light, light blue/green. It was so safe there.

As I walked, I saw all these beautiful Heavenly Homes along the shore. Each had its own private cove. The homes were amazing. I smiled and said, "Lord, if people only knew just a small portion of what You prepared for them – they would strive for this. There would be a change on Earth." As I walked, I saw sailboats out in the water. The wind extended the sails out there on the water, but all I felt was a gentle breeze. Tears began to stream down my cheeks as I looked at my body. This was the glorified version of my dancer's body in my mid-twenties. I was muscular, but not boyish. My skin was a deep tan, like I had when I lived in Marco Island, Florida. I was carrying my still-frozen tropical drink in my right hand and the life preserver in my left. I had folded up the umbrella and had it under my left arm. I looked at the underside of the preserver, and there was some script. I laughed so hard when I saw it. In the same script as one of the T-shirts my kids have had me wear while I've had my neck brace on – "Life is Good" – it makes people do a double take and everyone comments. I'm in pain, but I have this shirt. Anyway, in the same script it read, "Life is good, but Eternal Life is better." Okay, I want that shirt! I shook my head. Today will be another lesson. I can see it coming…

I turned the corner of the inlet I was walking on, and there was that beautiful Heavenly Beach Mansion. I waded to the first large, square stepping stone. There, up on the second balcony, was the Lord. He waved. He was laughing.

Jesus: "Erin, why are you carrying the life preserver?"

Me: "Well, Lord, I never know if You might throw me back in deep water again – I need a place to put my tropical drink when I'm trying to treat water." He was laughing so hard.

Jesus: "Well, there's that humor. Drop the preserver and the umbrella. I'm here – you won't need it. You can bring your drink, though." He was laughing.

I quickly ran to where He was. An angel grabbed my drink and set it on the table, and I ran to Jesus and hugged Him. I began to cry.

Me: "Lord, I felt you abandon me. I was hurt and scared. Where did You go? I couldn't see You on the water. Why did You allow all of that?"

Jesus: "Erin, let's discuss this. I was still there. Why do you think in scripture that I was walking on the waves during a storm when I appeared to the disciples?"

Me: "I'm not completely sure."

Jesus: "Well, you can study the scriptures later, but it is recorded in three books. Now, despite their best attempts, the disciples couldn't get the boat to the shore. The Sea of Galilee, based on its location, has violent and very sudden storms. It was dark. I appeared during the fourth watch of the night. They saw a body walking on water in a violent storm – they were terrified. They didn't recognize it was Me, because they were gripped with fear. They weren't looking for Me, because the fear was greater than their faith."

He was standing next to me and leaning over the balcony looking at me. I was beside Him, looking out at the ocean, listening to Him.

Me: "Why did You allow them to have such fear? I don't understand – You had just fed 5000 people – it was such a jubilant time."

Jesus: "Hmmm. You said this – I had just fed 5000. That's correct – Who am I? Who fed 5000?"

Me: I thought about what I had said, "Forgive me, Lord. I so quickly forget Who You Are." He was smiling, and nudged me.

Jesus: "Erin, don't allow fear to take your focus off of Me. Faith and Fear can't dwell together. This is a tool of the Blacksmith. What happened when I got into the boat with the disciples?"

Me: "The Sea calmed." I was shaking my head.

Jesus: "The boat had drifted during the storm, about three-and-a-half miles off course, despite their best human efforts. The storm steered the boats. They could do nothing. Instead of calling out to Me, they decided to rely on themselves – and became afraid as they realized they were in grave trouble. Then here I appear as a ghost, so think about this. You are in a violent storm in a small wooden fishing boat. You are caught in this storm around 3:00 AM give or take – the fourth watch. You are unprepared. The water is deep, and the boat was floating over 144 feet of dark water. The waves were violent. They are not sleeping – they are already afraid – then I appear, illuminated like a ghost. They saw outlines of My figure, walking toward them on the waves. What would you feel?"

Me: "Lord, I'd be terrified."

Jesus: "Yes, and they were. Why did I allow this?"

Me: "So they would witness to this and write about this miracle."

Jesus: "Hmmm... Yes and no. Remember, I still performed miracle after miracle, yet – other than John and the Marys – all of them were nowhere to be found at the crucifixion. Fear governed them, when they thought I was no longer able to help. Do you believe this Erin?"

Me: "Lord, all You have shown me, all You have done – only You can do. I am not a wise woman. I am no Biblical scholar. Your filling my empty vessel over and over is a miracle. I stand amazed and in awe at the love You have shown me. You continue to pursue me, even when I lose focus of You – even when fear grips me. Because You empty me each time, I tend to forget what You promised, and I wish I could remember more."

Jesus: "Yes, I know. I sent friends to help you, Erin. It's okay. Remember that you and your children have stepped out of the boat in the storm. You are out there walking toward Me. I have not forgotten. Just remember, I am still here. Your children and friends still see Me and have faith – they are still walking toward Me. Don't allow the enemy to grip you with fear. This entire group of experiences here has been faith training. You are about to have victory over your enemies. I have declared it! Now, what comes next requires you only to keep your eyes on Me. I don't care if there are massive sharks swimming, and they even appear to be devouring you. If you must, close your eyes and call My Name! Don't become focused on all that can go wrong. Focus on Me!"

Me: "I'm surrounded by enemies Lord. Even the home I rent is the enemy's. The children I share with my main enemy. The insurance companies and the Bank are another. I know there is a war raging – All the signs are there. When I can do nothing? How do I keep moving forward with Kadima on my lips when I have no idea how? How do I have joy?"

Jesus: He looked at me. In His eyes I saw my children. I saw them excited to leave this place. "Erin, you keep looking to me because I have you and your children. These were mine, first. Their faith is important to me too. If you act afraid then they will focus on trouble and lose heart. Now they don't know the sharks are just below the surface. They only see me and the open door. Let them come to me. If you want to swim with sharks, I will allow it but it is unnecessary. After a while I will save you but the whole ordeal is unnecessary." He motions to the angel to bring me the life preserver and umbrella. I looked and became afraid!

Me: "Lord, I chose You. I'm sorry. You must show me what to do, what to sign, what…"

Jesus: "Erin Stop! You are to let me go before you. You have done all you can. Do you think you could steer the boat during the storm better than even the disciples – Hmmm weren't they experienced fishermen? Erin, I am going before you in this battle."

Me: "Okay." I became quiet…

Jesus: "When Moses was battling Pharaoh, how discouraging do you think it was for the Israelites – the slaves? Think about this. They are surrounded by their enemy. The enemy hates them, yet needs them, yet knows that God is with them. Doesn't that anger Pharaoh? Then the slaves – ready their households to leave. They are afraid, they have only known slavery. Here is this guy and his brother leading them into the desert with their children and the elderly blindly – yet they know God is involved, but how many of them actually saw the miracles as they occurred?"

Me: "Probably they didn't, they had faith on eye witness accounts and the hatred of their enemy over the plagues."

Jesus: "Correct!" So technically speaking they didn't even have printed Bibles or Tablets and computers to research faith. They were relying on these two guys," He smiled.

Me: "You're right while they were packing, they must have had doubts just like me."

Jesus: "Very good. So can you imagine the Passover that evening in the 3rd watch? Could you imagine the screams by the 4th? They were inside their dwelling, hearing the wailing of death. They didn't know what came next perhaps their own. They were ready to leave but very afraid. They didn't even have me, they cried to My Father on the Throne. He heard their cries and delivered them from their enemies. Remember the children singing in Heaven along the River?"

Me: "Yes."

Jesus: "The enemy's children are here Erin. They are God's children. He is Mighty to save. Now the enemy has tantrums. Pride is another opposite fruit. Pride goeth before the fall. The enemy does not like defeat. He fears loss of power and control. He wants to be god over all. He thinks he could be better. I tell you the truth; his days are numbered, and counted. The Jubilee is in the 9th month. Your exodus is very soon."

Me: "Lord, I must be out of here by the 23rd at the latest, I have no choice!"

Jesus: "Very well, do you think I have no knowledge of your needs? Do you believe if I tell you I am going before you for 50 days that I have not considered all things and even your limitations? Erin there are things occurring that you cannot see. Perhaps you are in one of those dwellings waiting for the final signs to be led out of your desert place. Please trust me that I will do as I say. If you have faith as a mustard seed you could say to Mount Hermon 'Fall into the Sea' and it will go. So don't just wear that mustard seed necklace for show, practice your faith. Now remember what you stated in your yearbook in High School?"

Me: "To one day have a heart of gold but for now it sits on a chain around my neck…"

Jesus: "Interesting, so write this down. 'To one day have faith like a mustard seed but for now it sits on a chain around my neck.'" He reaches over and smiled and pointed to my necklace which I apparently don't even take off in Heaven.

Me: I smiled. "Lord, help my faith Lord! I need help, can you just do everything? You take care of it. I will just mess everything up and it took many trials and hardships to remove the heart of gold necklace and have a measure of this in my walk. I need You to not stop, not quit, even if You see me getting discouraged, I need You to take care of us. I need You to make me appear to be strong. I need You to level enemies because God knows I've prayed for You to bless them or appear to them. I have forgiven the unforgivable, now I just want to be removed with my children quietly. I don't want the demise of my enemies to be at my hands, only Yours. My hands fail me. My works are not prosperous under these conditions. I cannot steer my own boat out of this storm. I need You to come in the boat, calm the storm and tumultuous seas and steer us to a quiet peaceful shore. Please forgive me. I have been here before; I have repeated the same mistakes over and over. I have tried to leave the enemy before, but the enemy even used clever scriptures and God to quiet me to sit in prison."

Jesus: "I tell you the truth. It is one thing to read and memorize My Words, it is clearly another to etch them on your heart and put them into practice! Erin the enemy will use God as a weapon to make you afraid. Your enemy can go on social media with gut wrenching photos of poor children and make you look like you are the enemy. Then in the next photo he can have a picture of a gun and some snacks. Yet no one is remiss about it. This is not a godly method. Again look at the fruits of the Spirit. The enemy works and operates in the opposite of these. Look at the war in Israel right now. Watch the world turn against God's people. Watch the favor of the Lord protect her and their children. God is Mighty to Save. There is an umbrella as a cover and it is the Hand of God. Just as I sent you help and even a frozen drink when you were thirsty.

"Look at Jonah. Jonah was in the belly of the whale three days. He couldn't stand the Ninevites – they were blood thirsty. God didn't require Jonah to save them – just warn them, that was it! God did the rest. Then when Jonah was moping, God sent a fig tree to give Jonah shade in the hot sun. Jonah was thankful for the cover. Erin, don't let stubbornness send a worm. Don't allow fear to grip you, I have sent you shade in a sun-scorched land, a cover. Now allow me to carry you out. Let me go before you into battle. I'm here!" He nudged me and smiled.

"Come let's take communion again. I brought you to paradise to remind you of where you reside in My Heart. My story is written on the tablet of your heart. Now did you read and study the scriptures you were given. These are good. Read Nehemiah, read Jonah, read Esther, and even Ruth.

"Remember the five smooth stones David used. He gathered five but only one brought Goliath down. Was Goliath not a huge mountain to those being mocked? David was scoffed and mocked by both sides, Yet David's bold declaration of God's love and his defense of God – His great faith activated the events which brought Goliath down with a single stone! God was not with Goliath. Veering from the normal protocol of the world takes bold faith. All of the people/saints in those scripture veered from normal protocol. God was before them, over them, behind them, and in them. He is Mighty to Save!"

He walked me over to the table, tears were dropping again...

He smiled, "Erin, do not worry, you are Loved!"

Dream over... Blessings

Chapter 26 – David vs. Goliath

Communion

Dear Father,

I'm scared. My heart is anxious, it flutters and I begin to lose my breath. Please help me! Lord I look around at how far You've taken me. I read the words You've spoken through me that I've written and I know these are not from me. You have blessed my life with wonderful children, friends and family. You have used my journey to help others. Lord, what I come away with every day is that I know You more than I could have ever imagined. I've become closer to You than I would've ever been just attending church a couple days a week. I know You will not bring me this far to dash my hopes. My children even praise You and have greater faith sometimes than I.

Jesus: "Erin Come up!"

I'm in an extremely lush green garden in a portion of a city. I've never been here before. It was a beautiful park with a large circular stone building and a path around it. There were people – families everywhere. I didn't really understand it but I know I felt completely safe here. The air was fragrant. The lush greenery of the Northern Garden was filled with deciduous trees of every color. There were also blossoming cherries. I walked for some time. The sunlight streamed in and reflected gold on the leaves and flowers. There was a river which ran to the right of me and a bridge – a small covered bridge going across. I didn't see people or hear the laughter of children anymore. I began to look for the Lord.

Me: "Lord, are You here somewhere?"

I decided to walk through the covered bridge to the other side of the river bank. The bridge was dark, but on the other side I saw Jesus. I ran into His arms. I wept again with my cheek on His chest. (I had a weekend home alone in bed without my children and no ability to do anything.)

Me: "Oh Lord, please deliver us quickly. My heart is breaking here. I'm afraid. I'm still out on the ocean walking toward You. I'm panicking because the storm rages and I'm uncertain I heard from You properly. I have no faith after I lost hope on Thursday."

Jesus: He pulled me away from His chest to look directly into my eyes, "Erin, remember your hope was lost and then you had no faith in your understanding of who I am! I have explained when you are delivered you will look back over your trials and you will stand amazed. Right now you are uncertain and time is also your enemy – but who controls time? God, right? So you are at God's mercy!"

Me: "I'm also at the mercy of the man under the 6 dragons."

Jesus: "I know it seems that way now, but this is not the case. Last week your expectations were higher than God's plan, you were disappointed and disillusioned, not to mention disheartened."

Me: "Lord, I must believe You wouldn't set me up for a fall. I must believe You will carry me – go before me into battle."

Jesus: "Erin, a soldier dressing for war when he knows he is going into a battle where they are outnumbered 3 to 1 is petrified. If you are dressing for an earthly battle in which the outcome is surely your demise, then you have fear. Now you have 2 sets of 3 enemies; let's call them Dragons. You are at a disadvantage and because you are at the mercy of a slanted system you are at war with this. Now if you can do nothing except stand, then stand! Come!" He walks me down to the river bank and I see crystal clear water. There in the water are 5 smooth stones. Each have different colors.

Jesus: "You see these 5 stones?"

Me: "Yes."

Jesus: "Remember David as a boy. He was extremely bold. Let's review events in 1 Samuel 17. The Philistines were on one hill and Israel was on another. There was a valley in between. Goliath came down every day for 40 days and mocked Israel. He taunted and shouted making great clamor. He was a showman and very arrogant. He had reason to be confident just on his size and armor alone."

(Jesus was speaking as if He had actually been there to witness it. He had been! He drew an amazing picture for me!)

"Now when Saul heard Goliath clamor, they were dismayed and afraid. Now comes David; he had been running back and forth from herding sheep to bringing food and provisions to his brothers and bringing reports to his father Jesse of the battle. David heard the murmuring of fear coming from the Israelites and heard the commission and rewards given to the man who brings down Goliath – so the prize was a great one! David inquired and his brothers mocked him, to discourage him they accused him of being wicked even. His own family accused him and reminded him of his low position as a shepherd. Any normal boy would cower and go back to tending sheep

"David's bold statement and voice declaring over these soldiers 'Who is this uncircumcised Philistine who defies and taunts the Armies of the Living God?' Saul being curious sent for David. David boldly declared to fight Goliath. Saul then reminded David he was only a boy and Goliath had been a warrior from his youth. Then David declared his credentials of fighting both a lion and a bear, and even rescued a lamb. So David by faith and by God welling up in him declared, 'The Lord who delivered me from the paw of the lion and the paw of the bear, He will deliver me from the hand of this Goliath (Philistine).' Saul of course realized that this was possibly God working, but he was halfhearted and had much doubt so he blessed David, 'Go and may the Lord be with you.' Saul tried to dress David in his garments to adhere to normal protocol for soldiers yet David was bogged down by the weight of this cover. You see

Erin, God is David's armor, not the conventional armor of the world. David was unfamiliar with these weapons and armor as these were untested so he was not comfortable with Saul's approach. He was comfortable with what he knew; that which he had tested and practiced. He carried his stick or staff and chose 5 smooth stones in the brook, put them in his bag, had his sling, and he went to Goliath.

"First Goliath laughed, then became insulted and then began to curse David. Any normal "man" would've been shaking in fear as Goliath told him he would basically pull him apart and feed his flesh to beasts. Then David welled up – God within him rose up. David spoke as the entire area – both sides – was listening. "You come to me with a sword, a spear, and a javelin, but I come to you in the name of the Lord of Hosts, the God of Israel, whom you have taunted. This day the Lord will surely deliver you up into my hands, and I will strike you down and remove your head from you." Then he went on to declare that the battle is the Lords and He will give you into our hands!" David brought 5 stones but only 1 stone sunk right into Goliath's head and he fell! Goliath had fallen face forward to the ground. David, a mere boy, cut off Goliath's head and the enemy fled! The armies fled and were hunted down by Israel. Their camps were plundered and victory was theirs." Jesus then pointed to the 5 stones.

"Erin, pick up your stones. One stone will bring down your giant. The battle is the Lord's – remember in that courtroom there was a higher placard than the 6 dragons. Now when you present yourself carrying these 5 stones, just as David experienced, there was laughter, scoffing, name calling, and then threats, but because David knew God and trusted Him to take up his cause, he allowed God to work. David was bold with bold faith! Now you stand in the valley – desert between 2 mountains. You are about to face your adversary. The battle is God's Erin!"

Me: "Yes, Lord. I am afraid. When I am afraid I lack – I think, What if I missed something You told me? What if I heard wrong? It freezes me. I can't move as I'm gripped with fear. I remember over and over again from Isaiah 12:2-3, surely God is my salvation; I will trust and not be afraid. The Lord is my strength and my song; He has become my salvation."

Jesus: "What does your song sound like? What is the rest of that scripture?"

Me: "With joy You will draw water from the wells of salvation."

Jesus: "Then drink the water from the well Erin, drink! I am here with you! I am going before you in this battle. I know this is difficult. I am not relying on your faith for my success in this battle. I will therefore rely on your friend's faith as well as your children's." I began to cry.

Me: "Lord, forgive me. Unless You build my house, I have none. I'm in pain, I'm afraid, I am not working. I'm relying on lawyers to fight. I'm facing an unfair system. I'm under my employer's roof, I'm uncertain where I am going or when! I know where I'd like to be and I've dreamed of it. I cling to Your promises but they seem far away. I continue to pack. I continue to do everything I need to prepare my household but ultimately I am at Your mercy and under Your care. Lord during a tornado, I am caught between the house and the storm cellar outside. Help!"

Jesus: "Erin I'm glad you have gotten this out in the open. The first step in facing your giant is to release armor which is cumbersome. This armor doesn't fit you, it weighs you down. These are your cares and worries. Here give me this armor, let's get this off of you. Now come and let Me cover You! I have you; let me be your shield and buckler – put on the Armor of My Word. The armor of the world will make it so you can't fight the giant! Now I'm glad you were honest with Me."

Me: "Forgive me Lord. I've been in such a long battle. I'm wounded from it. Almost all that we had, we lost. I have been in slavery because of it. Now I'm wounded and I can barely face my enemy. I need Your help. Please Lord, do something so miraculous that I will be set free along with my children in an instant. Heal us and deliver us. I will never doubt again and I will forever testify of Your miracles and Divine Love. Lord, truth be told, even if You don't do things in the order or manner I had hoped, I will still testify to Your greatness forever and ever. I love You Lord. You called me friend. I don't understand Your ways. You are a Divine and Glorious Mystery. If You tell me to pick up those 5 stones and one will take down the giant, then I will do as You say. I have nothing to lose, but myself and even that is Yours."

Jesus: "You are mine Erin – when you pass through the waters, I will be with you, and when you pass through the rivers, and they will not sweep over you. (Isaiah 43:2) When you walk through the fire you will not be burned, the flames will not harm you, for I am the Lord."

I was in tears, as He spoke this I looked into His eyes. I saw a vision back when I was facing my darkest time. My children were very young. I boldly reported to the police. Everyone went against me except those who witnessed what had happened. I was without money, my reputation gone; I was wrongfully accused even by my church family. All hope was lost since it looked like God was against me. I still stood for my kids. I took a stand. I was so afraid at night I would stand watch over my house. I prayed. I barely slept. The law was not as strong as the Lord in our defense. One night as I slept at my lowest point, God gave me a dream. In this dream a dam had broken, it overflowed the rivers. The water raged. It was late at night. My children and I were stranded on a sand bank as the water began to sweep over us. I was terrified. I called out for God. Then He appeared and one by one took my children across straight through the raging waters to the other side. He then gathered us and we walked for a long time until He finally delivered us to a peaceful meadow in the trees by the water. As I saw the entire scene in Jesus' eyes, I began to weep.

Jesus: "Erin I'm still walking with you and your children, we are almost there. No one will hurt you – you will be safe! I am still the same yesterday, today and tomorrow. I will not change, I am steadfast in love. The wicked will not prosper. God knows all things done in secret. Let Me take your yoke of affliction." I reached over and hugged Him. I dropped into the river and grabbed the 5 stones. I walked back up and handed them to Jesus.

Me: "Lord, please bless these stones."

Jesus: "The Lord blesses you Erin; this kindness is greater than that which you showed me earlier." (Ruth 3:10)

Me: "Lord You are my deliverer, You are my Kinsman Redeemer, plead my case and throw these stones for me. As You must go before me in this and lead us Home! The Battle is Yours!"

Jesus: "Very Good Erin! I love You! Then this is done! I AM who I say I AM!"

He blessed the stones and handed them to me.

Dream over….

Blessings

Chapter 27 – God's Quiver & Harvest

Communion & Prayer

Dear Father, I love you so much! When I think of your works concerning us, I stand in awe! I am so thankful to You! Other than worship there's nothing I can repay you with. Thank you! Thank you!

Erin Come up!

I was up on a cliff in Heaven. I stood overlooking this amazing Heavenly landscape of trees. I saw ribbons and ribbons of fall colors as well as some I cannot describe, but they are even more amazing than the ones we see and understand here.

There was a silver mist in the air and the sky was a deep Periwinkle blue. There were flocks of birds flying in amazing formations, their sounds were like worship music. They called out to God in praise with such harmony. I would believe it to be a digitally mastered composition if I had heard it here on earth. There was a beautiful fragrance in the air. It was like wood smoke, pear, almond, and grass with a very small hint of eucalyptus. I know an odd but lovely heavenly scent.

I looked behind me and I saw another Valley, one I didn't recognize. There I saw harvesters. I saw angels and saints in the fields working. It was Harvest!

I was very excited. I saw figs, grass, wheat, pomegranates, and other crops, but I couldn't tell exactly what - Barley perhaps or corn?

It was interesting as the Saints harvesting with Angels, looked as if they had come from many different parts of Earthly Culture. It was beautiful as I saw many ethnicities represented. I looked to my right and there were 2 very large Angels. One had a plumb line with a bob. The other had scales for weighing. They were busy and not paying any attention to me.

Over to my left I heard an Angel shout in a Heavenly tongue something foreign to my ears. The Lord gave me the download interpretation, "The Time has begun!" I looked and I saw a massive calendar in the sky, it was God's. I saw events moving faster, coming-going, coming-going rapidly in succession and overlapping in time. I saw 2 more cycles maybe 3.

I walked over to the Angels.

Me: "When will this be? What time has come?"

Angel: "Erin, do you not know? You have been shown this. You must now prepare. Do not be afraid. Fear is not from God, but to Fear God is Wisdom!"

Me: I looked for Jesus around us. "Lord, please clarify. This time is very soon."

Angel: "Erin, you and your family are tucked away and you have more with you in God's own quiver. Now like never before pray and believe. The Lord has fulfilled His promises in you, and more and more every day. Are you amazed?"

Me: "Why yes, truly amazed! It has not completely sunk in yet, actually."

Angel: "Without Faith it is impossible to please God! You were given promises 3 years ago. You were given promises and prophecies one year ago. You are about to see these promises and prophecies fulfilled. Look around you! Stand amazed!"

I looked out and saw harvesters from all over the world preparing for the Lord's return!!

I was so OVER–JOYED!!!

Dream over...

Later on 9/11 He gave me a dream — I will post this in a few days when He completes this.

Please continue to pray for those who are languishing here on Earth. We are all looking for the Lord to come quickly — He wants us to be at peace and praise HIM!! Our Prayers and worship please God on His throne. Praise is like a sweet aroma to God!! Never stop!!

For those who are weary in their watches of Jesus Return — We are in God's Quiver — we are like sharp arrows to the enemy!! Pray that God uses us for HIS Glory to bring many to know HIM more. How awful would it be to be an arrow in God's quiver, but to never be used prior to HIS coming! If you are in God's Quiver, you will be USED for HIS purposes and Glory!!! Pray for the US and most of all Israel!!

Love & Blessings — From the Trees...

Smiles... Erin

Chapter 28 – Angel Army and the Lion's Roar

Communion

Dear Father, Thank You for this beautiful fall day!

The trees are beginning to turn and the beauty is so overwhelming. The sky is gray and rainfall intermittent. I can hear the small stream and waterfall out of the window and I just can't contain my joy. Lord you have blessed us. I'm experiencing peace and contentment which I thought I would never have. I've had some loose ends to contend with but for the most part the enemy is far removed.

Last night, I had a dream that I purchased a blue home with white trim. The house was older with many rooms. I kept walking through the home making a mental note that I couldn't account for the middle section of the floor plan. I found hidden doors which were sealed. Finally I found a split in some plywood and I could see a living space inside through the crack. I could see valuable things, yet I had no way in. When I woke up I went to the Lord in prayer.

Lord please show me what that dream means. Is it personal or universal? I love you so much Father! Please bless all of us as we pray for Your continued miracles and peace.

Erin Come Up!

I was immediately up in an area of Heaven which I hadn't been in for a very long time. I came up through the portal and I was on a path. I saw before me the small forestry outhouse door — A freestanding wooden door with no frame. I laughed. The trees around me were brightly colored and there was a mixture of golds, greens, reds, and oranges. There was a slight smell of wood smoke and a cool breeze in the air.

I went to the wooden door to open it. I lifted up the latch and heard a pretty bell like chime. The door opened without me touching it. I walked into a beautiful setting. It was the northern area of The City of God.

I looked around me and in the distance to the southwest I saw the area where the receiving docks are. It was a beautiful day. I crossed a small scenic bridge over the River of Life. I knew instinctively to travel north. In the distance, I saw elders from the city gathering at the Overlook. I saw a commotion with the crowd. This was the area from Heaven where we as Citizens of Heaven can look upon the Earth. I ran to see what the commotion was about. The Elders dispersed as the Angels were ushering them off to the right of the observation area. I ran to the balcony and looked. There I saw a large blood Moon. It was over Africa and the Middle East.

Then I saw something which terrified me. I saw a massive wave come up and over from the East. It was ominous and carried with it pestilence and disease and was ignored by far away areas until the wave was right over the countries. As I looked closer, I saw Angels being held back for now by the hand of God. I began to cry as I saw people getting very sick on earth. I saw poisoned blood in the water ways - rivers, streams, lakes and damns.

I saw water turning to blood. There was no clean water. This disease made people thirsty. There was no way of quenching thirst with clean water because there simply was none.

Then I saw a series of Heavenly Horses on their hind legs. Angels were riders on these massive beautiful animals. The Angels were in full armor. There was a massive Heavenly Army. God was holding the bits of the Horses. God was controlling them. Then I heard a Massive Sound of a Shofar. So loud that the sound was heard amongst both Heaven and Earth!

The sound of the horn activated the Angel Army as it moved up from the south. It was a massive wave of light. I saw the City of Jerusalem. I saw Half a Blood Moon – Half Blood and Half Light I saw Half of Jerusalem Divided – one side Red with Blood and the other White. Then I turned and saw a distant mountain from the west. There was a large green pasture over the mountain. It was highlighted with the sun and was quite beautiful. I saw a pregnant heifer. She was giving birth to two calves. One calf was Red and without blemishes. The other was pure white with red eyes. The sack surrounding the white calf was green and full of poison. I saw two Large Angels immediately appear with large swords. One Angel held the red Calf and kept it safe. The other Angel quickly removed the white calf. The white calf cried out for its mother, but the angel sheltered the mother and covered its ears so it couldn't hear the distress calls of the white calf. The white calf would have soured the milk so that the red calf would be unhealthy, unclean and eventually die. Then I saw Legions of Heavenly Angels protect the Heifer and her red Calf so nothing can come against it. The white calf was ominous and frightening.

Then my eyes moved back to Jerusalem. There I saw construction in the city. I saw a divided city. Bad milk was upon the new temple. Gifts were being received for the building from cursing laborers. I saw swarms of flies and a stench as everything for the worship of God's house was made unclean. I saw Holy Men, Rabbis, not able to keep the temple ceremonially pure. I saw an old Jewish blind man and young Jewish boy darning fibers. The old blind man was allowing wool to be mixed with linen as a new standard practice and didn't see it as a problem. The young Jewish Boy was protesting and trying to stop it, but the Old Jewish Man was going by feel not by the Word of God.

I then saw a large lion running fast up from the south. The Lion was larger than five elephants. The lion was swift. The Lion approached Jerusalem as I saw an extremely large angel with a plumb-line measuring the area for the lion and in advance of it. The enemy was there in the City. The plumb bob and line were slanted. As the Lion approached the plumb line became balanced and evenly weighted. Many had died prior to the Lion coming. The Lion was so large; many came from Far Away countries and regions to pay homage to it. As the travelers came many were on alternate transportation. There was great humility and visible battle wounds. There was weeping and gratitude upon entering Jerusalem.

I had so much to take in in such a short amount of time, all I could do was weep as I watched the scene before me. I felt a hand on my shoulder and it was Jesus. I held Him and wept. I cried as He held me close to Him.

Me: "Oh Lord this is very soon. I am afraid, when will this be?"

Jesus: "Erin Come!"

He took me over by the River. There were communion elements on a blue velvet blanket. He motioned for me to sit. He handed me some bread.

Jesus: "Remember it is I. I love you! Do not forget the covenant which I have made with those who love Me and choose Me Now! This is Important! (He motions for me to eat.) There is symbolism in this wine. My blood is represented. The same symbolism is in the stars, moon and sun. Erin, therefore when you see these signs, you know the time is soon to come. It is written. Do not be Afraid when you see these signs, for I am there with YOU — I Am Here!"

Me: "Lord, I have never seen you this serious!"

He was in battle gear but I didn't see wings. His sword and armor were so beautiful.

Me: "Lord, I have so many questions. Please Help me interpret this!"

Jesus: "Erin, It is written. Take comfort that all which has been hidden will soon be revealed. Do not be Afraid. You will not suffer shame. Pray continuously. Forgive."

Me: "Lord, help with what I've seen."

He walks over to me and kisses me on the forehead...

Dream over...

This was a very short, extremely real, extremely detailed and clear. Pray that He clarifies all of this soon!

Be blessed!!
Love! — Erin

Chapter 29 – Seasons

Communion

Dear Father,

Thank You for all that you've done. Thank you for technology and the ability to reconnect with friends and family. Thank You Lord, for the testing of my patience! I quickly found out that there are situations which are beyond my control. Even money isn't always a player in a game of circumstance; there are sometimes just things which man has no control of. I thank you in these situations for divine creativity and faith!

I had begun to wonder if I were to ever be back online. I now realize that this was all Divinely orchestrated on Your part to offer me family time. All three of my children were baptized on Sunday at a small local church. It was wonderful! I was so excited to get them baptized without an opposing court order and the battle.

Last week I had some incredible dreams. In one I was driving in my car around sundown. The sun was setting on the Western Horizon, but I was driving east. In front of me was a huge, huge storm cloud! It was rolling out like a large scroll. In the front of the cloud there was a billowing area it was massive, maybe 300 feet high. I saw these massive letters in the sky on the front of the storm cloud. I recognized them as the Greek letters Alpha and Omega and the Hebrew letter in between; Hey.

Left to right...

Omega - Hey - Alpha

As I was driving straight into the storm, I noticed traffic was traveling the opposite direction, away from where I was traveling. I pulled off to the side of the road and the wind picked up. I was approached by an evil familiar man as I got out of my car. He said, "Your children will be gone soon." I remembered that I was on my way to pick them up. I was holding a bunch of miniature lilies in my right hand for my children and just with his eyes and frightening look, he cut the flower blossoms right from the stem. I continue to hold these stems. I quickly started my car up and the man yelled,

"You are driving right into a category five hurricane." Just then the radio announced that all waterways, rivers, dams and tributaries have been breached. The land is no more!

I stood at the edge of a cliff and looked down on an ocean side city. It appeared to be Los Angeles. Then something like a damn broke and the water destroyed the entire area. I could still hear the evil man, "Now the burning begins."

Then I saw something like heavenly angels. They were handsome and rugged, but they were NOT Heavenly. They had black tipped wings and deceived many people. I saw them flying over the city and pouring out buckets of hot embers. I saw horses from the south and a large face in a cloud in the sky. The horses appeared to be tied to a type of gate that they were about to open. I heard a massive horn and this face began to puff its cheeks. The horses opened the gates from the south and a mighty wind came from the mouth of the face. There the wind took the burning embers and scorched the land. People were rushing to these angels for help, but these angels were evil. They picked people out of the flooded areas and dropped them into the burning areas. I yelled, "When is this, what time?" I heard, "18th, 19th & 20th!"

Me: What month? What year?

Please Help me Lord..........

Erin Come Up!

Immediately, I was up in Heaven on a beautiful overlook in God's Garden. I saw a peaceful Valley with green grass and grazing sheep. The River of Life was past this beautiful meadow. To the eastern and southern part of this beautiful valley grove of aspens in Silvers, purples, whites, and gold. There was a beautiful mist over the entire area that appeared as dark purple and shades of lavender. The mist had an opalescent quality. It was Dawn. After my realization of time, I saw the sky begin to display every shade of pink and red. The mountains which appeared composed of Amethyst, Quartz, Jasper, and Carnelian began to come alive with color as the sun was rising. The sunlight began to break through the aspens the mist of Opal shown like a rainbow over the grass pasture. This scene was so remarkable and vivid. I heard in the distance the sound of a Heavenly Choir. The Singing began softly as the sun rose and then as if to build up along with the light, the choir sang louder. I laughed as it was the Hallelujah Chorus. They were singing multiple verses & phrases together in beautiful harmony!! I heard, "And He will Reign forever & ever, King of Kings and Lord of Lords! Hallelujah, Hallelujah, Ha- llel- U jah!" The sun began to rise as if it were leading the choir.

Me: "Where are you? Thank You, this is so beautiful!!!" And then I felt a hand on my shoulder. I turned and hugged Jesus! "Glad to see you Lord! Thank You!"

Jesus: "I'm glad you came, Erin! How do you like this?"

Me: "Oh it is incredible!"

Jesus: "I will only have you here a short time today. You must rest!"

Me: "Lord, yes I have been in great pain & tired. I seem to have weakened. Please heal me Lord!"

Jesus: "Erin, you will soon be healed as your healing has begun. I AM HERE!! You have questions!"

Me: "Yes, Lord. I see many signs and this dream was so real. When will this be? The storm seems like it is coming soon. How do I prepare?"

Jesus: "You are preparing. You were even given a warning by your stepfather about the stripes on the caterpillars." He smiled and chuckled.

Me: "Oh yes, my step-dad told me, (He is an Entomologist), based on the position of the stripes on our Caterpillars' up here, we should expect severe weather coming. Two weeks ago there were so many flies for a few days, then so many ladybugs. The ladybugs are hibernating in our home. I'm not sure what to make of all of this." Jesus was smiling.

Jesus: "The flies died off quickly as they always do. The ladybugs mean no harm and they recognize you are home and safe. I want you to prepare for storms. A wise man does not avoid good counsel or

Godly signs. Remember God created the land and the animals even before man. So there are natural signs which nature will give you of upcoming seasons. Now how do you prepare for something if you don't know when or how bad it will be?"

Me: "I don't, so I'm here coming to you. Only you know Lord and I have faith that You wouldn't send signs unless there was something I needed to know or act." He was wearing his white tunic and belt of purple. His hair was perfectly dark brown and slightly below shoulder length. His smile was perfect with beautiful white teeth. His eyes were deep blue and green. His beard and moustache was not too thick or too thin, but perfect. He laughed when he saw me studying Him. He knew that I was studying His Appearance.

Jesus: "Erin, trust that I am giving you all you need for the storms. Now your questions….."

Me: "Yes, what were the letters in the cloud?"

Jesus: "Erin, come!" He takes my hand and we were in the Golden City of God at the Sea of Glass. There He waved His hand and I could see the Earth like a window. "This is what God sees!"

Me: "Why was Omega before Alpha?"

Jesus: "This is simple Erin. What do you see?"

I suddenly saw the cloud from God's angle here in heaven! Alpha — Hey —Omega, instead from my angle below I saw the clouds like a carpet below the Throne and the letters. I was laughing.

Me: "My apologies Lord. He is the Alpha and Omega and Hey sees all of Creation as He looks through a window!!! From below I see the End also leads into a NEW beginning for many of us up there with You in Heaven. When I look through that Hey or window all I see is dark clouds from ground level!! I focus on the massive storm clouds through my windows!!"

Jesus: "Erin Very Good!! You are correct! Do not listen to evil men who try to scare you into the belief you are out of God's favor. Fear is not of God, but to fear God is the beginning of wisdom."

Me: "What was the rest of that in the dream?"

Jesus: "There is an advanced & extreme deception rising. It is beginning where media is birthed. Angels are painted as unholy and unholy angels are painted as saviors. There is a trend toward changing truth in Scripture to a confusing deceptive truth. Even the angel Michael was depicted as doing what is best for God as God doesn't know what He wants."

Me: "Yes, one of my sons recently recognized this in a movie. I couldn't believe it!"

Jesus: "Recognize the time you are in. Know that the last push for souls is through technology. You saw this a long time ago, now it is come. The season of storms has arrived."

Me: "The storms Lord, these are literal, right?"

Jesus: "Yes there will be physical storms, but also against cursed territories. Israel is being abandoned. Media is even entering marriage with those who hate God's people. Soon almost every country will turn against Israel. You live in the land in which Hollywood gods reign. There is anti-Jewish sentiments rising like the world has never seen. Most will sit back and watch, but God Sees all".

Me: "Lord when will this category five storm happen?"

Jesus: "Erin how many lilies were you holding?"

Me: "Oh, 5."

Jesus: "Be sure to write down all information when you see it."

Me: "Will it occur in five days, five weeks, five moons, five months, or five seasons?"

Jesus: "Erin prepare for storms in the season reflected in nature. Your caterpillars won't show stripes if not in the right season."

Me: "Okay Lord, you are leaving me to research. Please grant me more signs & wisdom to discern them from You!"

Jesus: "Okay, but don't forget! You must not fear. I AM with you in the storms! Do not worry! Prepare your fields, and then get rest!" He reached over and gave me a hug.

Me: "Lord thank You for everything and the beautiful sunrise."

Jesus: "Do not worry Erin, you will see more! I love you Erin!"

Me: "I love you Lord!"

He gently squeezed my hand and smiled with His beautiful Calm Eyes!!!

Dream over...

Blessings...

Chapter 30 – God's Mountain and the Key

Communion

Dear Father,

Thank You for another day! Thank you for your love! You are the Creator of all I see around me. Anything of worth is Yours. Lord, please grant me wisdom during this season of dreams. I need Your blessing as I do not feel worthy of this grand endeavor from You! You are my light, my shield and my fortress.

I am experiencing spiritual warfare three days prior to Your prophetic words. It is no longer a great yoke, but instead a sign of Your favor. Please continue to send in your Heavenly Warriors to fight during this time as my goal is fixed on doing Your Will. I have so much thankfulness to You as You have brought us to a peaceful place and I am forever grateful!! I love You Lord!! I lift up my hands in praise to You!

I am grateful beyond most, as You saved me from death's snare and set my feet on the rock of Your salvation. Last week the forces of darkness were rampant. I learned of a large sector of Wiccans nearby. During Halloween there was an uptick in activity as I felt the Lord reminding me of how evil this world has become albeit hidden in plain sight!

My Dream last night 11.6.2014:

I was in a marketplace I didn't recognize. Hundreds of people were desperately selling family heirlooms. My mother was with me. We were amazed at the high level of quality these items for sale were. Many of my most favorite types of artifacts were there. I personally had no needs, but I have the money to help these people by purchasing their items. People who normally wouldn't treat me well were nice to me; perhaps out of desperation since they knew I had the means to help them. I selected 10 items. They were quite beautiful, but I felt the Holy Spirit didn't want me to take possession of them because they were "unclean"!

Instead, I gave the people money but didn't take their items; after this, my eyes fixed on two items aside from the 10. One was a large metal air duct painted and embossed with a pattern. I had no use for it, I just liked it and it was clean. In particular, I was fascinated by a large hourglass. The hourglass was approximately 30 inches high. It had a dressmakers or Taylor's form attached to it with three large buttons. There was a number on it 153, it was crossed out and 154 was next to it. It was peculiar. I saw the sand in the hourglass was moving slowly. As I stood there, the sand ran out so I flipped it over. Then the sand rushed through. It took only a few seconds to move through the hourglass. I thought I had broken it. Then the clerk at the counter began to laugh and said, "It does this on every second flip, now flip it again." I did, and I turned it over and the hourglass was very slow.

I said, "Mom I would like to purchase this."

My mother said, "How much?"

I said, "It was, $153 now it is $154."

My mother said, "No you can't, this is too much money!" So I took the hourglass up to the clerk, "How much for this?"

Clerk: "Well it was and $153, then $154, today it is gone up to $613 Dollars!"

Me: "That is ridiculous why would I pay this?"

Clerk: "Because this is your measure!"

Me: "Okay, I'll pay it! I'll pay it!"

My Mother: "Erin, why would you pay such a price?"

Me: "Mom, it's a measure of time! I need to know how much time is left!"

My Mother: "But, that one side is short, how can you measure time by grains of sand?"

Me: "Because God knows the hairs on my head!"

(Dream over)

"Lord, please grant me discernment with the dream. This morning in devotionals, the Lord led me to Isaiah 22:20-25. There is so much symbolism in this one portion of scripture. Then He gave me Psalm 101.

Erin Come Up!

I was at the base of the Mountain of God again. There was fog above me and this path leading up the mountain. To my right was the forestry bulletin board. There, I saw a key. I picked up the key. I noticed a folded note with a small tack attaching the note to the bulletin board. The paper had the word "Instructions" written on it. I picked up the note and opened it.

This is what was written inside: "Erin this is the time. The time has come. From God's Mountain you will see into the Valley of Vision. You have been given a key to unlock a door. Only God can open or shut this. Take comfort, you are loved!"

Me: "Father, I have no idea what to do. There is no door here." Then I heard a rumble and the Voice of God.

God: "Erin, your heart is a door. Render your heart to Me. Put your cares aside. Keep your heart on Me and I will unlock mysteries. You must search for Me although I Am with you always."

Me: "Father God, You are a great mystery and my treasure of Gold to Seek! As I search, please keep me safe as well as my family. Through my seeking, please help me to really "see" You. Please do not hide from me!"

God: "Erin, I promise you I will not. The Time of Darkness will soon fall and soon I will shorten days. I will give you multiple meanings. I will send Angels concerning you to guard your steps. Do not be Afraid! Prepare your houses!"

Me: "Father, what did the dream mean?"

God: "Erin, it takes the Glory of God to conceal a matter and the honor of kings to search it out. Now, look at the numbers given to you. Who is present in the dream? Why are they there? You are given Scriptures, what are these?"

Me: "I have never been led to this scripture before in Isaiah 22."

God: "After you discover this, then come back to Me, I have more! This will seem slow at first, then you will be entrusted with much more. Do not be afraid!"

Me: "Thank you God for this key!" I knelt down at the base of the mountain before God.

God: "Give thanks in all things Erin. I will then show you what door the key will open."

Me: "But this key is for Your heart!"

God: "I will use the key to unlock doors. You are a keeper. As you don't possess the door and the key is Mine to give. You must cast the cares of this world aside and follow Me!"

Me: "Thank you Lord."

Dream Over… (Prayers and tears…)

Then, I heard Jesus, "Erin, allow me to take you to the doors. I will be with you to carry you through. I will be there to help unfold the mysteries. Take heart and do not worry!!"

Thank You Lord!!!

This week something changed in me. I no longer care so much about the things that I clung to before; "The cares of this world". The only things that seem to matter to me right now are my precious friends and family. This world is coming to a close. I see it over and over again. My stomach is sick. This week I heard and read of vile things. I became sick and when I imagined being here during the tribulation, I began to have trouble breathing. My heart became sick. Oh I wish everyone knew how much Jesus loves us. How much the God of the Universe loves us to send Jesus to die for us. My son has been witnessing in his local high school. It has been very difficult as Christians are a minority here. I never quite understood how much we are hated for our beliefs.

My children ask me what will happen to their unbelieving friends. All I can say is, I don't know. All I know is that the Lord loves them just as He loves us. I don't want to see anybody here perishing. I continue to pray for the lost. I feel more and more in my heart the time is coming to a close. I also feel that my hands are somewhat tied. We don't control the time nor the season; This is God's to control!

Lord, lead us in Wisdom! Cover us in Your discernment! Look down on us with love, as we put on our armor to do battle here. Please Guide our steps and lead us down Your path of righteousness. We love you Father God so Much!!!

He just gave me Psalm 103 to meditate on today!!

LOVE & Blessings, Erin

Chapter 31 – Jesus' Promises

Thanksgiving - November 21, 2014

Communion

Dear Father, Today I am ready to go Home! I'm in so much pain. I'm weak. I'm tired. When I drop my head to write I can feel the raw bones in my neck rub together. My left arm has very little feeling. As I took communion and asked why this Father, I felt the warmth of Your Presence.

I stared out the window as the sun peeked through the clouds. In a few minutes of looking at this beauty before me, I began to see snow flurries. These reflected the rays of sun and appeared as diamonds floating. Father, I can't physically write long today, so I will instead thank You. Thank You for removing us to this beautiful place. Although it is on loan to us while we wait, here in this place our oppressors are far from us.

Thank You Father for all you have done. Thank You for the roof over our heads. Thank You for food in our pantry and warmth under our feet. Thank You for clean water to drink and gas for our car. Thank You for my children.

I prayed for years for You to open my womb and even though doctors said I was unable to have them - You decided I was able! Thank You! Lord You saw something in me to allow these dreams. The visions of Heaven have given me hope to continue here on Earth. I do not want to leave here without my family so I know today is not my day to come Home. I thank You for the promise of Home. One day soon we will rejoice in our Heavenly bodies, but for now I have pain. Please forgive me for not taking the time to worship fully. "In pain it is difficult to remember that praise is a key which unlocks the door of Divine Healing. Thank You for loving me!

Jesus' Promises

Communion

Dear Father,

Thank You for another day! Lord, today I am in pain. My left arm is numb and I'm afraid. Please, Father where are You! I need your help!

Erin, Come Up Here!

I'm up in my vineyard in Heaven. It is beautiful here; the vines are lush with massive bundles of grapes. Each cluster holds many different colors. I look out over the valley and it is truly beautiful. A fresh rain, like a spring rain, just misted the valley and I see a series of Seven Rainbows with a massive spectrum. I recognize at least 7 bands of colors. There is a small very low cloud over the grove of Aspens in the back of my Heavenly Property. The cloud is illuminated from within. I ran – yes ran! Out the arched gate of my sweet abundant grape vineyard down the path into the Aspen trees. There I see the Lord. I run to Him. He stands to receive me with open arms. I hold Him for some time. I began to weep.

Jesus: "Erin, what is wrong? Is it not a glorious day? You are here with Me".

Me: "Yes Lord it is always a great day with You!"

Just then I reached over to grab my left arm to feel it. I looked and Jesus was smiling.

Jesus: "Can you feel your arm here?" He was laughing.

Me: Yes, and I have no arm fat either! I love it here. Lord, why are you allowing this right now? Am I being punished or am I out of favor?

Jesus: "Erin." He looked momentarily disappointed as if I hurt Him. "No, you are not being punished. Look, you are here with Me."

Me: "I feel so alone in my pain. My heart is struggling to endure it. I hurt. Please heal me Lord."

Jesus: "Erin, do you trust Me?"

Me: "Yes Lord!"

Jesus: "Your enemy is seeking to destroy you right now. Can you endure this a bit longer? If you truly trust Me please be patient."

Me: "Lord, pain makes patient endurance very difficult. I couldn't move yesterday. My fear is not permanent paralysis."

Jesus: "Erin, the enemy's plan is to ruin you, discredit you, charge you with fraud and take your children from you. I removed you before all of these plans were finished. There is one more battle. What is better, for you now to go to your enemy's appointed medical exams and say Jesus healed me or is it better for them to see you like this now as witnesses, and then after I have healed you? What is more convincing?"

Me: "You are right Lord! Seeing is believing!"

Jesus: "They will not be able to declare you a liar. You haven't lied. I allowed all of this for your good."

Me: "It is hard to understand why you allow bad to happen. Why is it allowed Lord?"

Jesus: Laughing but, with a sympathetic look. "Erin there is always a plan which is greater than your circumstances. I know this is difficult to understand. The night before my crucifixion on Earth, I sweat blood. I didn't want to drink from My Father's cup of suffering but, I love My Father, and I trust Him. He only wants good for us."

Me: "Oh Lord, please forgive me. I know you endured so much worse than I have. I spoke as a fool. Oh Father God, please forgive me for doubting."

The cloud overhead rumbled as if it were thunder.

Jesus: "I know you are holding me to the promises I have given you. You are good to do this. This is faith. Erin, clinging to the promises keeps you on course."

Me: "I skipped over the part of suffering. When I asked You how You'd do this, before You didn't answer. I instead clung to the promises not the delivery."

Jesus: "Ah yes, like childbirth, painful but forgotten once your gift arrives!"

Me: "My gifts are my children and You. Lord please deliver us soon. My enemies are many. I am hated by those who pretended to care. I know You've been through this, it is just difficult and I am downcast."

Jesus: "Then Erin, remember who you are in Psalm 45. Remember your promises in Psalm 91. Remember Erin, no harm will befall you. When I gave you this June 5th, 2012, what was occurring? What did I have you do?"

Me: I looked confused, and then all of a sudden I remembered. Tears began to stream down my cheeks even as I write. "Lord I felt the most abandoned by You. I was pounded by my enemies. Another woman had publicly declared she was my eldest son's mother. I was left off as my son's birth mother. He was stolen from me during my heart surgery then I was deceived. I had no money to fight back. This was the day back in 2012 when I went to You and said, 'I love You', but I must have done something to anger You, so that You have now turned away and forgotten me. I felt abandoned by You and I decided to stop pursuing a purpose for my life from You! I still declared my love to You, but I gave up all hope!"

This was the scripture You gave me. You had me write Psalms 91:14-16 "Because she loves Me," says the Lord, "I will rescue her; I will protect her, for she acknowledges My name. She will call upon Me, and I will answer her; I will deliver her and honor her. With long life will I satisfy her and show her My salvation." – But Lord please deliver me now."

Jesus: "Oh is it your time to go? Then your children will be returned to one of your enemies. Then your others will rejoice. Is this really how you would end your race?"

Me: "No Lord, of course not. I am on a pain rant right now. I am meditating on Psalm 77 and questioning Your favor upon my life."

Jesus: He chuckled and smiled sympathetically, "Erin, then read 77 not in part but in whole! Take courage!" He pointed up to the Glory Cloud and I heard thunder. Erin, remember your promises and dates in Esther. You're a sparrow in Psalm 84, read this in whole. Your time of delivery from your oppressors is close at hand. Read Psalm 103 and take courage. I will keep you close to me. I have not sent you to the land of trees only to be destitute and abandoned. You are in the care of angels." As we stood there, the small cloud over us began to mist. I felt refreshing dew. I felt my body being healed and renewed. The Lord reached over and kissed the top of my head then held me as I wept. For a moment I felt healing, my body was useful and young. As I wrote I felt momentarily healed. I wept.

Jesus: "Please rejoice Erin! Did I not show you 3 eagles last week? They all flew over your head. When did you ever imagine this?"

Me: "Never really..."

Jesus: "Erin, it is a gift and a sign."

Me: "Lord You told me another storm was coming yesterday. When will it come? Is it in the West or East, the North or South?"

Jesus: "It comes where you think not, but do not worry – storms will come. There will be signs also like fire has smoke. Do not worry! Be strong! Do not be afraid! You will not suffer shame! Watch and be amazed! Your time has come Erin!" The cloud above us thundered. The Lord reached over and hugged me, kissing the top of my head. "Erin, you are loved and God delights in you! Keep your heart on Him and evil will not befall you or your household all the days of your life!"

Dream over...

The healing remained with me for a few moments, and then pain came back. I leave on Sunday for 3 days to Seattle. It will be the first time I have been separated from my children. The Lord knew I was afraid to leave them so He reminded me that they are in the care of Angels and under His mighty wings! Please continue to Pray!

Chapter 32 – Golden Wheat & Rainbows

Communion

Dear Father, Thank You for all that we have! Thank You for my family! Thank You for Hope in the midst of trials. You gave me three very definite signs, You were still with me. Although during times of great struggles I find this very difficult to believe. You don't always grant us what we want but You never fail to grant us what we need. Storms leave a wake of destruction. Some storms hit harder than others. Some others are hit harder than most during storms. With each storm we are in God's mercy ultimately! Even a wealthy man with power cannot stop God's wrath, therefore we as believers must trust in the Lord to take us through it. I thank God for trials and storms as I know the Lord has a purpose.

Maybe You are positioning me? Maybe You are strengthening me for more to come. Maybe Your testing me in my weakness to prepare me for this coming time. I do not know. I do know You love me. I do know You have gifted me with Jesus and my hope in His resurrection! I know where I will one day reside in Heaven! I know there is more to come and You plan all things for my good! You have given me a great light and I no longer walk in the darkness! (John 8:12) You are my light Lord! You have given me Isaiah 60:1 today, "Arise, shine, for your light has come, and the glory of the Lord rises upon you!" Forgive me for running ahead of Your promises today! Obviously my trials were not over quite yet!"

Erin Come Up!

I was wearing sandals. I looked down right at them. My feet landed on a wooden plank platform. I looked ahead of me and my heart burst! It was beautiful. I saw a massive sea of wheat. It was metallic gold – Yes, encased in real Gold. I ran out into this massive sea of wheat. I reached down to pick-up a sheath. Each one had seven spikelets on seven rows. There was 7 x 7 on each wheat stalk. I know nothing of the botany of wheat, but this seems unordinary and very Heavenly!

I ran through this massive field. I laughed. A wind came and blew through the wheat from the south. Not certain how I knew this except I saw the sun seeming to set on the horizon so I assumed that was westerly. I laughed as the wind blew as if directly orchestrated by angels. It looked so amazing as the waves of golden wheat became like waves of an ocean. As the wheat moved it made music. I didn't recognize the tune but it was so beautiful. I knew the wheat was worshiping!

Me: "Where are You, Lord?"

I turned 180 degrees, but didn't see Him. My body stopped when I saw the most incredible full spectrum rainbow. As I looked at the colors I felt some gentle rain fall upon me. I cried as it was one of the most beautiful sights I had ever seen. The wheat continued to sing with each blowing gust of wind.

Me: "Father God this is so beautiful! I see a Sea of Gold, the Sun, the rain and a beautiful rainbow too!"

Just then the rainbow doubled! I clapped! Then it tripled, I clapped louder! Then it quadrupled, I laughed and yelled, "Awesome!" Then, just because God could, right before my eyes, I saw seven rainbows each in 3 dimensions forming a dome. I screamed out loud, "Wow Lord, this is so incredible – Thank You!" As I ran to the dome as fast as I could through the Sea of Golden wheat I cried. I was off to chase rainbows. This time the rainbows were now right over my head! I was completely under a beautiful massive spectrum of multi-coloured lights! I dropped to my knees at the incredible display of God's Glory. I worshiped Him in full thanks for all that I have!

Just then I felt a hand on my shoulder. I opened my eyes and saw the Lord! He was laughing as we hugged!

Jesus: "Erin why were your eyes closed while worshiping? Why would you miss out on Me?" He was laughing…

Me: "Oh Lord, it is a habit I guess. I close my eyes during prayer and worship to focus on You – clearly here – I can praise You with my eyes wide open!"

Jesus: "Yes, you would hate to miss out on all of this." He laughed and I knew there was more to this also.

Me: "Lord why do I close my eyes? Where did this start?"

Jesus: "Well at one point it was like visiting God in a secret room. This world has many distractions. When your eyes are closed the enemy doesn't know where you've gone. When your eyes are open, your thoughts can be followed by your body. Often this leads you away from Your first Love!"

Me: "Yes, when I was little I was labeled a daydreamer, if my eyes were open. If my eyes were shut, I was napping I guess when I'm in worship service at church. I close my eyes or look down or up so I do not become distracted from things or people of the world."

Jesus: He laughed, "Oh Erin, the enemy loves distractions from worship and his favorite place is church service."

Me: "Forgive me for shutting my eyes here Lord."

Jesus: "Erin it is a heart matter, Do Not worry! I just don't want you to fail to miss that which is all around you!" He laughed, "Now, you are encountering trials! I showed you more coming, are you surprised?"

Me: "Yes Lord, I expected a time of peaceful recuperation after the last major battle."

Jesus: Smiling, "Erin, your enemy never rests. This has been allowed for preparation. The enemy has petitioned for you to be sifted as wheat. I told you the enemy has run his course in your life. Take Heart!" I began to cry. He reached over to hug me.

Me: "Lord, You gave me a rainbow three days ago, it was snowing and raining. The sun shone through a small blue patch of sky and a rainbow burst through, in the middle of December – freezing conditions. My daughter and I were amazed! Then shortly after, I received two more signs of Your promises."

Jesus: "Erin, then please reveal what your problem is?"

Me: "Lord, I feel You are napping in the boat while the storm is raging."

Jesus: He began to laugh, "Erin, have faith! Who allows the storms?"

Me: "You do, Lord."

Jesus: "Why would they come right now?"

Me: "Lord, You have said my enemies have run their course, so I look forward to their attacks ending soon, but Lord why have you allowed the other things?"

(I found out Monday that the roof of my car has been damaged and has holes. We are having plumbing issues which are causing leaks and little or low water pressure in our home. I had to go to the ER with one of the children on Wednesday while workers had to stuff all of our items into the living room during repairs. I'm still struggling with flu; on, and on, and on.)

Jesus: "Erin, I know all that has happened. You are discouraged but look at the patterns from your history. What happens before you are hit with coming trouble?"

Me: "I'm given a sign to pray but You always show me signs of your favor, then trouble hits."

Jesus: "Yes but, I notice something different in you now. Despite your physical pain and even sickness, you still remained strong."

Me: "It was on Your strength, not mine. I have learned to lean on You."

Jesus: "Erin there are Christians who claim to know Me, yet when trouble comes they only act on their own. You have learned." He smiled, "Yes before you answer albeit the hard way."

Me: "Lord, was I so prideful and disobedient that God had no choice?"

Jesus: Laughing, "Erin, yes and no. God chooses the trials; you chose your attitude when going through them. Your attitude has changed."

Me: "Lord, I am still scared. I have a mandatory mediation with my kid's dad on January 5th. You showed me Cherry Blossoms. My other enemies have ramped up continuously and this trouble with our household is stripping me of our means."

Jesus: "Erin, have I provided all the means and weapons for your battles? Have you lacked at all with help from your friends?"

I became saddened and embarrassed by my self-pity.

Me: "No Lord, my friends have been amazing. When I am cut off from communications I become afraid. The enemy still attacks me and continues."

Jesus: "Erin when were you stripped of your weapons? So far, is the enemy really having victory over you, and are your children with you? Erin, I will handle your enemies, please give them to me as I am your Strong Tower! I am your Kinsman Redeemer! I will go before you in this. I have been and I will continue to do so! I have appointed Angels concerning you. You are not alone. You recognize the time which you are in. You see the late hour. Do not worry when toothless lions grumble and roar! Let them run about. What will they do to harm you?"

Me: "A toothless old lion still has claws."

Jesus: "I think you are giving them too much power. Remember I didn't deliver you to a promised land with no promise; winter is a season, nothing more. How are your children?"

Me: "Surprisingly focused on You and very strong. My son gave a talk in class on the unseen realm. He declared his faith in God and I am so thrilled! He has become a man after Your heart! Even my other son posted a scripture against idolaters on his Facebook, declaring his trust in You! This is a miracle!"

Jesus: "Oh, so maybe your slower communication has forced them to focus on other things?" He smiled.

Me: "Yes Lord. We are learning to adjust to country living."

Jesus: "Erin, there is a dawn soon breaking. You are out of the desert and into the woods! You are near eagles! Your eyes are wide open.

You reside at Heaven's Gate! Now, soon this trouble will be gone. Your healing has begun and so has your children's!"

Me: "Lord, I feel so much pain, please make this soon."

Jesus: "Erin it is very soon to come! Soon you will no longer worry. Soon you will dance, (He laughed!) in golden wheat fields even."

Me: "Lord, one other thing, my dream last night. I was so excited to go on a great journey. I stopped into a trade show at a Convention Center. There were several booths; each booth had enemies from my past, even minor enemies. Some sales people were trying to get me to come to their booths to see what they can show me of my past. I avoided all of them and headed for the Exit doors. There a woman hands me a ticket. She says, "Tonight you can go to a 5 Star Hotel. It is free. All the gourmet meals are included. It is luxurious and you would be foolish to turn this down."

I wanted to go, but my previous plans and trip were much greater than her offer, so I declined

Jesus: "Well this is good Erin! You need to leave your enemies behind. Don't take up the yoke they would have for you to carry! Their load is heavy and your burden would be great! Give all of this to Me, as I will defend you! My recompense is with Me and soon I will reward you! Now I am glad you kept your Heart on Heaven and where you are going! Do you think this is 5 Star Accommodation?"

Me: Laughing, "It is so wonderful in Heaven, it would be impossible to rate – here is perfect!"

Jesus: "Then your dream was a blessing, not a sign or curse! Despite your trouble like Joseph, Erin you will be rewarded! I am promising you! You will soon consider a field and even buy it! This is a blessing!"

Me: "I love you Lord!"

Jesus: "I love you too!" He hugs me and kisses the top of my head

Dream over…

Salvation Prayer

How certain are you that you would go to Heaven, if by some chance you should die today. Salvation is a choice. It is the most important choice you make in all of your life!

Jesus is the only way, He is the truth and the life and no man comes to the Father except by Him. He is the only hope for mankind. For God so loved the world that he gave His only begotten Son, that whosoever believeth in Him will be given everlasting life.

If you have never accepted Christ as your Savior, right now is the time to do it. Just say this prayer and mean it with all your heart!

Father,
I humbly come to You in the precious name of Jesus! I know that I have broken Your commandments and my sins have separated me from You. Father please forgive me of all my sins. I believe that Your Son, Jesus died for my sins, was resurrected from the dead, is alive, and hears my prayer. Lord Jesus, I pray and ask You to become the Lord over my life.. Wash me and cleanse with your precious Blood. I pray and ask that You rule and reign in my heart from this day forward.

Lord, please send Your Holy Spirit to help me obey Your Word, and to do Your Will and Serve You for the rest of my life.

I ask this in Your precious Name!

Thank You Lord!

I now receive You into my heart by faith as my Lord and Savior!

Amen!

For Researchers: Dates when Dreams occured

1 – God's Timing #97 January 26, 2014
2 – Drinking Deep #98 February 1, 2014
3 – Cake, China & Changing God's Clock #99 February 2, 2014
4 – Fresh Oil #100 February 9, 2014
5 – Healing Rain and No.9 #101 February 16, 2014
6 – Oceans and Almond Branch #102 February 23 2014
7 – God's Numbers #103 March 23, 2014
8 – Breakfast with Jesus #104 March 30, 2014
9 – God's Clock & the Olive Grove #105 April 6, 2014
10 – The Cave, Uriel, and the Snow Storm - Part I #106 April 13, 2014
11 – Faith Training #107 April 19, 2014
12 – The Alpine Meadow & the Tevah #108 4-20-2014
13 – Faith and the Ocean #109 April 26, 2014
14 – Four Dreams #110 May 3rd 2014
15 – Training Part 1 - War Assignment # 111 May 10, 2014
16 – Training Part II - Harvesting May 11, 2014
17 – Faith Training and Psalm 23 – #112 May 18, 2014
18 – God's Garden for Children - #113 May 25, 2014
19 – Paradise - Tropical Beach #114 June 14. 2014
20 – God's Garden for Teens #115 - June 21, 2014
21 – The Lion #116 June 29, 2014
22 - Faith and the Fig #117 July 5th & 13th, 2014
23 – Jesus & the Storm #118 - July 24, 2014
24 – Word from God & Dream of War # 119 - July 29th 2014
25 – Faith vs. Fear #120 July 31, 2014
26 – David vs. Goliath #121 August 3, 2014
27 – God's Quiver & Harvest
28 – Angel Army and the Lion's Roar - October, 7th 2014
29 – Seasons #124 Oct, 21st 2014
30 – God's Mountain and the Key # 126 November 7, 2014
31 – Jesus' Promises #129 November 21 & 24, 2014
32 – Golden Wheat & Rainbows # 131 December 13, 2014

Spiritual Wisdom

However, we speak wisdom among those who are mature, yet not the wisdom of this age, nor of the rulers of this age, who are coming to nothing. But we speak the wisdom of God in a mystery, the hidden wisdom which God ordained before the ages for our glory, 8 which none of the rulers of this age knew; for had they known, they would not have crucified the Lord of glory.

But as it is written:

"Eye has not seen, nor ear heard,

Nor have entered into the heart of man

The things which God has prepared for those who love Him."

But God has revealed them to us through His Spirit. For the Spirit searches all things, yes, the deep things of God. For what man knows the things of a man except the spirit of the man which is in him? Even so no one knows the things of God except the Spirit of God. Now we have received, not the spirit of the world, but the Spirit who is from God, that we might know the things that have been freely given to us by God.

These things we also speak, not in words which man's wisdom teaches but which the Holy Spirit teaches, comparing spiritual things with spiritual. But the natural man does not receive the things of the Spirit of God, for they are foolishness to him; nor can he know them, because they are spiritually discerned. But he who is spiritual judges all things, yet he himself is rightly judged by no one. For "who has known the mind of the LORD that he may instruct Him?"

But we have the mind of Christ.

1 Corinthians 2:6-16 (NKJV)

CLOSING NOTES

I ask that you please keep in mind that I am not claiming these dreams to be a substitute for Scripture. However, I do believe that these dreams are truly from our Lord. In turn, these dreams show us that the Bride of Christ, comprised of many Christians currently living on this earth, will soon be raptured, removing us swiftly and safely away from the ensuing chaos to Heaven, our true Home.

Should the Rapture have already happened, then you, who are left behind and are now reading this, will need to hide these dream transcripts and share these words with others only as the Lord leads you to do. Unfortunately, there will be danger now unlike any the world has ever seen, and I pray that you have a peace that only belief in Jesus can provide.

However, until the Rapture occurs, I will continue to do my best not to go ahead of God. I understand the ramifications of changing His Word for personal gain and avoid this at all costs, even if it means bringing criticism on me at a personal level (which has happened often, sometimes cruelly).

I also understand the ramifications should these words I have written cause any of you, His children, to stumble. As such, I pray with all my heart that I do not cause any to stumble. All I can do, within my (very) limited power, is to pray that the Lord God Himself speaks to you through these dreams, and then according to His Will alone!! Before continuing to read this book, please go to the Word of Truth, the Holy Bible, and ask the Holy Spirit for guidance in discerning the messages in these dreams. Always keep in mind that these words are from the Lord and pertain to all of us ... not just to me. Remember, there is ALWAYS hope in the Lord.

Made in the USA
Middletown, DE
02 February 2016